DATE DUE

STOCKTON
Township Public Library
Stockton, IL

Books may be drawn for two weeks and renewed once.
A fine of five cents a library day shall be paid for each
book kept overtime.

Borrower's card must be presented whenever a book
is taken. If card is lost a new one will be given for
payment of 50 cents.

Each borrower must pay for damage to books.

KEEP YOUR CARD IN THIS POCKET

DEMCO

TALL ANIMAL TALES

Amazing True Stories from the Star of TV's Animal Hospital

Rolf Harris

with Mark Leigh

and Mike Lepine

Thorndike Press
Waterville, Maine USA

This Large Print edition is published by Thorndike Press, USA.

Published in 2001 in the U.S. by arrangement with Peake Associates.

U.S. Softcover ISBN 0–7862–3518–7 (General Series Edition)

The text of this Large Print edition is unabridged.
Other aspects of the book may vary from the original edition.

Set in 16 pt. New Times Roman.

Printed in Great Britain on acid-free paper.

Library of Congress Cataloging-in-Publication Data

Harris, Rolf.
    Tall animal tales : amazing true stories from the star of TV's
Animal Hospital / Rolf Harris ; with Mark Leigh and Mike Lepine.
      p.   cm.
  ISBN 0–7862–3518–7 (lg. print : sc : alk. paper)
  1. Animals—Anecdotes. 2. Large type books. I. Leigh, Mark.
II. Lepine, Mike.
QL791 .H25 2001
590—dc21   2001034747

ACKNOWLEDGEMENTS

The authors would like to thank the following people for their invaluable assistance (and patience):

Dom Franklin, Dennis and Mary Hatton, Gage Hatton-Lepine, Philippa Hatton-Lepine, Edith and Philip Leigh, Debbie, Polly and Barney Leigh, Eileen and Harold Lepine, Juliana Lessa, Judy Martin and Lindsay Symons.

While every attempt has been made to verify the facts in this book, no liability is accepted for any incorrect assumptions, names, events, dates or places. In these cases the publishers apologise for any oversights and any corrections will be made in future editions.

CONTENTS

CHAPTER ONE

ANIMALS 1, MAN 0

Postman Colin Summerfield isn't scared of any dogs on his round in High Wycombe, Buckinghamshire. It's a cat called Snoopy that terrifies him. He's been attacked by the black and white cat on numerous occasions. Once he was chased up the garden path with Snoopy clinging to his trouser leg. Once she leapt at him after hiding behind a tree, and the time he thought he'd delivered the letters safely, she was waiting inside the house and clawed him as he pushed the post through the letter box.

Now, with the full support of his Royal Mail bosses, Colin refuses to deliver letters to Snoopy's owner, Pamela Perham. Instead, she has to collect them from a neighbour. This will continue until Snoopy ceases being a menace, and although she's a bit fed up with the situation, Pamela does sympathise with the postman's plight.

She said, 'I once saw Snoopy stalk across the lawn and hide in my front garden as the postman strolled up the drive. Then she pounced. I can't understand it. She is just a family cat who has never done anything before. Perhaps she doesn't like it because the mail blocks up her cat flap.'

Her daughter-in-law Liz Perham also witnessed one of the attacks. She saw Mr Summerfield running across the grass being chased by Snoopy and yelling, 'Get off! Get off!' She added, 'He was scared of the cat. I don't think it's pathetic—I think she really hurts him.'

A spokesman for the Royal Mail said it was the first time he had heard of the post not being delivered because of a cat attack, but added that their first priority is to safeguard their employees.

When it comes to investing in the stock market, it doesn't pay to monkey around. Well, unless you're Carolina, a chimpanzee at Krakow Zoo in Poland.

Up against a local stockbroker, Carolina used quite an unorthodox method of choosing her investments—by picking oranges each with the name of a company listed on the Warsaw Stock Exchange written on it in felt pen. Some oranges were picked at random. Others were studied more carefully. But over a three-month period in 1996, the chimp outperformed her rivals, achieving more than a ten per cent return on investment.

I wouldn't have believed this story myself, but I've seen it in two different sources, and it's actually credited to the Russian newspaper *Vecernaya Moskva*.

A holiday company had been asked to arrange a wild bear hunt for a wealthy American tourist. They duly bought a performing bear from a circus and released it in Moscow's Perdelkino Forest. As the hunter set out in search of his prey, the bear startled a postman on a bicycle who was taking a short cut through the woods. He fell off his bike in surprise and then ran off, though not before seeing the bear run up to his bike, pick it up and pedal off (remember, it was a circus bear). The American tourist never did find his prey and sued the holiday company for fraud.

How's this for bad luck? An angler was fishing from the banks of the Rio Negro in the Amazon when he was suddenly attacked by killer bees after his line got tangled in a tree. To escape from the huge swarm he jumped into the river—and was eaten by piranha fish.

Did you know . . .
Clive James and Sylvester Stallone
have both shared the same unusual
job—cleaning out lion cages!

Two very stupid neighbours, known only as Pete and Dave (their surnames were withheld in an attempt to save them any embarrassment), decided to get rid of a large bees' nest between their houses. Rather than call in a pest-control officer to move the nest to a safe place, they decided to take the matter into their own hands—by using a Second World War grenade.

Placing the grenade beneath the hive, they pulled the pin and ran—but not far enough. The resulting explosion shattered sixteen windows and peppered the men with tiny fragments of shrapnel. The only thing that wasn't damaged were the bees, who attacked the men as they tried to climb into their cars to get to the hospital.

One of the would-be exterminators then discovered that he was violently allergic to the venom in the bee stings and spent fourteen days in intensive care.

Everyone loves koalas—except the Australian Ministry for Tourism! In 1983, John Brown, Australia's then Federal Minister for Tourism, launched a scathing attack on the koala. He said that koalas stank, scratched, piddled on people and were riddled with fleas. His comments made headlines, but it turned out that the koalas had some influential friends.

Newspaper editors, opposition politicians and even the Prime Minister rushed to defend the little marsupials. The papers even published pictures of royalty cuddling the koalas, pointing out that they hadn't been scratched or piddled on in the process.

Eighteen months later, a very apologetic John Brown tried to make amends with the koala community when he opened the new koala compound at Healesville Sanctuary near Melbourne. In his speech, he made a full and frank apology for insulting the koala and then, to demonstrate his new-found love for the bear, gave a koala named Narrumpi a cuddle in front of the cameras. It took one look at him and bit him on the stomach.

Kelly Kyle was home alone at her father's house in Pennsylvania when she noticed a deer in the back garden. Just as she was going to take a closer look another one smashed through a plate-glass window in the lounge and was joined by four of its friends. All five deer then proceeded to stampede from room to room, gouging holes in the walls with their antlers and knocking her father's prized ornaments and trophies flying before leaving the way they'd come in. Kelly hoped her father would believe what had happened. He was out at the time—deer-hunting.

5

In 1995, police in Wisconsin raided a breeding kennels which they suspected also dealt in drugs. There were a lot of nerves before the raid, because the kennels specialised in breeding malamutes, which are large and quite wolf-like. Taken by surprise, the kennel owners were completely compliant and helped the officers in every way they could. They even chained up all the dogs for safety, except for a bitch who had just had a litter of puppies and was considered particularly docile. She didn't seem interested in the police officers, preferring instead to dig under an old unused outbuilding while the police set about their task. However, an extensive search of the property failed to uncover any drugs at all. The police were forced to make a grudging apology to the owners and were about to leave when the malamute reappeared from under the building, wandered up to them—and dropped a package at their feet containing a pound of uncut opium.

The Elephant Hills golf course in Zimbabwe is renowned among the golfing fraternity for the many hazards a player might come across. I'm not talking about bunkers, sand traps or lakes—but the various wild animals from the banks of the Zambesi that use the greens and fairways for grazing. After one tournament in 1977, Sam Torrance of Scotland told officials that it was one of the hardest courses he had ever played. He complained, 'I encountered baboons at one hole, warthogs at another and heard a rhino only a short way away in the rough.'

He was lucky, though. British golfer Noel Hunt found himself having to take a shot from a shallow pond, just yards from where a crocodile was sleeping. He took off his shoes and socks and waded into the pond, while his partner Warren Humphries watched his rear, 'armed' with his trusty eight-iron. Hunt recalls that this was one of the fastest shots of his career.

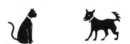

Mr and Mrs Diehl of Quakertown, Pennsylvania, needed a new mattress, so they went to their local department store and, after trying many out, chose the one which seemed the most comfortable. The trouble was, although it had been perfect in the store, the Diehls couldn't get a good night's sleep. Mr Diehl accused his wife of wriggling around in the night, while Mrs Diehl claimed she did no such thing—it was *he* who was doing all the wriggling.

This went on night after night, and in the end they had a close look at the mattress and nearly collapsed with fright. Living in it was a twenty-six-inch snake!

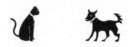

It was a good thing that Michael O'Farrell decided to take his young golden retriever Jessie Woo with him when he went to a local recycling bin with some old clothes for the Salvation Army. As he dropped the clothes into the bin, near his home in Tiverton, Devon, he also dropped his torch inside. Michael climbed over the edge of the skip to see if he could find it, overbalanced and fell in! Once inside, he found he was stuck, with no way of getting out. After four hours of shouting for help he was still there. Luckily, Jessie Woo had stayed with him all the time and attracted the attention of passing police officers, who called the fire brigade to cut Michael free. 'Once I got out I saw the funny side, but it wasn't much fun being stuck in there,' he said later. 'Jessie Woo is the best dog in the world!'

Amateur owl breeder Neil Simmons was almost overcome with excitement when he thought he had a wild tawny owl roosting at the end of his garden in Stokeinteignhead, Devon. He made the appropriate calls, but the owl didn't answer. Then, unknown to Neil, another amateur ornithologist, Fred Cornes, moved in next door to him. One night, Fred heard Neil making the owl call, believed it was a real wild tawny owl—and made the appropriate call back. For twelve months, the two neighbours would hoot at each other every night, each believing the other to be a real owl, and diligently logging their encounters in their bird-spotting notebooks. It was only when their wives got talking to each other that they discovered what was really happening!

A brilliant French lawyer got a pack of delinquent rats off the hook in 1521. The rats were charged with destroying a field full of barley and ordered to appear in court. When they failed to turn up, the lawyer, Bartholomew Chassenee, claimed that they had been intimidated by 'evilly disposed cats' recruited by the prosecution! If his clients were to appear before the judge, he argued, the court must guarantee them a safe passage to the building with no fear of being attacked by cats. The prosecutor failed to guarantee the rats' safety—and the case collapsed.

Although he came from an aristocratic background, the English MP Sir Giles Mompesson couldn't resist the lure of more money. He misused his power as a Royal Commissioner to extort money from tavern owners and manufacturers of silver and gold thread—and was caught. In 1621, the courts found him guilty and imposed one of the strangest sentences of all time on him. He was fined £10,000 and banished from England for life—but before that he was made to walk along the Strand with his face pressed into a horse's bottom!

Police in India were helped in solving a murder case by Poona, a cat who belonged to the victim, Peggy Pease.

Peggy and her husband ran a small animal hospital in India and Peggy continued the work after her husband died. Now in her seventies, she decided she was getting on a bit and scaled the operation down, just choosing to look after stray animals, including several cats, one of which was Poona. Helping her were her cook and two servants—a middle-aged man and a young boy.

One day a friend came to visit her but was

surprised to find no one at home—not even the staff. This was odd since Peggy was frail and hardly left the house. The visitor called the police, who were also unable to locate the four missing people. The only living things they found in the house were four cats locked in a small cupboard. All had nearly suffocated, and in fact only Poona survived the ordeal.

Poona used to visit the police station every day, trying to attract the attention of one of the detectives assigned to the case. Her persistence paid off. Acting on a hunch, the detective took Poona back to her old home and gave her an item of Peggy's clothing to sniff, just like a sniffer dog. After a few moments Poona walked out of the door to a patch of vegetation, then stopped. Hidden in nearby bushes was a bloodstained mallet.

Then Poona walked towards a flower bed and began scratching at the earth. Police were called to begin digging and there they found the bodies of Peggy Pease and her cook.

The other two servants were still unaccounted for, but then one of them, the middle-aged man, was seen locally and taken in for interrogation. He explained that he'd been missing from the house because Mrs Pease had given him permission to visit his sick brother. Although his fingerprints matched those on the mallet, he said this was because he'd used it to do odd jobs around the house and garden.

There was no evidence to link him to the two murders, but just before the detective was going to let him go, he decided to bring in Poona to see her reaction.

As soon as she entered the room Poona flew into a rage. She leapt straight at the man's face, clawing him viciously, and had to be restrained.

The detective explained to the suspect how Poona had located the murder weapon and the bodies. Knowing that Poona hadn't witnessed the murders, the superstitious servant immediately assumed the cat must have supernatural powers—and admitted to the crime.

He had been dismissed for stealing and was so angry that he decided to kill his employer and get rid of any possible witnesses (he'd thrown the other servant's body in the river).

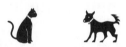

During the Falklands War in 1982, a group from the 148 Commando Forward Observation Battery were landed on a remote beach under cover of darkness. They were there to observe Argentinian troop movements, and soon after digging themselves in they heard Spanish-sounding voices from behind a nearby ridge. The soldiers kept calm and remained motionless all night, hardly daring to breathe, listening to the chattering conversations going on just yards ahead.

After a night with their nerves on edge, dawn came. And with the light they saw their enemy—a large group of penguins.

Did you know . . .
hang-gliders are banned from
national parks in Ethiopia because
herds of antelopes apparently
mistake them for giant vultures and
stampede in panic.

Adam Zebrak was attending an auction in Sussex when a wasp flew down his shirt. Adam panicked, and started flailing his arms around in all directions, desperately trying to swat the wasp before it stung him. When he sat down again, he discovered that he had successfully bid for an antique cigarette lighter and now owed the auction house £500!

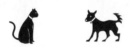

Alerted by strange bulges and frenzied wriggling in an airline passenger's trousers, customs officials at Miami airport stopped the man and uncovered a hoard of rare animals. The smuggler, a Barbadian pet-shop owner named Rodney Carrington, had put on two pairs of trousers and then dropped no fewer than fifty-five four-inch-long rare red-footed turtles between the two pairs! He pleaded sheer insanity . . .

Tiger the mongrel dog was the mascot of a British Army outpost in southern Sudan in the 1920s. He was called Tiger because of the black stripes over his olive-coloured coat, and certainly not because he was fierce. He was more of a camp clown than anything else. Tiger evidently believed that he was in charge of the base, because he liked to supervise the mounting of the guard, inspect the drills and parades and check that the sentries were at their posts. He also believed he was the camp bugler. Each morning at reveille, he would stand next to the official, human bugler, throw back his head and howl in accompaniment. His job done, he would then allow himself an idle scratch and a roll on the dusty parade ground before trotting over to the kitchens to see what was for breakfast.

Tiger followed the same routine, day in, day out, until a new base commander took over. Annoyed by Tiger's unique version of reveille, he hurled a boot at the unfortunate dog and told him in colourful military language to be quiet. The boot struck Tiger. He yelped, stared at the commander in disbelief and then hobbled off.

Days went by, and there was no sign of him. Everyone on the base was upset and the

14

commander very quickly regretted his actions. Then, several days later, as the bugler strode on to the parade ground to sound reveille, there was Tiger—with a new girlfriend, a local wild dog, trotting at his heels. Both dogs sat down next to the bugler, and as reveille sounded they flung up their heads in unison and howled in accompaniment. That was it. In mid-reveille, the bugler collapsed, helpless with laughter, the dogs got a thunderous round of applause and no one ever tried to stop Tiger sounding reveille again.

President Clinton's dog unwittingly caused an international incident in 1997. News that Clinton had called his new dog Buddy went down like a lead balloon with one Sheikh Badi Rsheid al-Yahya Bani Sakhr, the mayor of Basilia in Jordan. Badi is pronounced 'Buddy' in Arabic, and the mayor started getting called 'Clinton's Dog' by political rivals and even by his constituents. Dogs are considered unclean vermin in Islam, which only added insult to injury for the mayor, who ended up afraid to leave his house. He tried suing the American president for £5 million for psychological stress and loss of earnings, but the courts only saw the funny side of the story.

In what could have been a scene straight out of *The Birds*, Don Weston from Gloucester has been repeatedly attacked by a ferocious seagull which dives down at him, pecking him and covering him with droppings. But it's not just an isolated incident: the attacks last for two months each year.

The bird in question appears every June and conducts a hate campaign against car-park manager Don until the end of July, when it disappears. It quite happily ignores all the other customers at the car park and singles Don out for the special treatment.

'It just goes crazy,' Mr Weston told a national newspaper. 'There must be four or five hundred people who walk in and out of this car park every day and the bird takes no notice, but as soon as it sees me it starts attacking! It goes crazy. It swoops down and dive-bombs me and the only thing I can do is run away.' He once tried to trick it by wearing a disguise but the gull saw right through this and bombed him with droppings.

Mr Weston is mystified as to why he's the bird's target, and can only think it might have something to do with an incident a year before the attacks started when he found a young gull that had fallen out of its nest and put it on top of his shed to recuperate, out of sight of any neighbourhood cats.

The bird flew off later that day and Don never saw it again. He thinks the gull that attacks him is the same bird. 'It must be the same gull coming back year after year because its evil squawk is so distinctive. It sounds like a banshee wailing—I've had nightmares about it.'

Whether the bird is angry at Don for separating it from its mother is anyone's guess. Even the Royal Society for the Protection of Birds can't shed any light on the gull's behaviour. What they do know, however, is that as gulls can live for up to twenty-five years, Mr Weston has quite a lot of trouble ahead of him!

Clarence Anderson made one major error of judgement when he held up a convenience store in Portland, Oregon. In his haste to get away he forgot to take his dog, which he had tied up outside the shop.

All police had to do was check the dog's tags and then drive to Anderson's home, where they promptly arrested him.

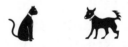

The US Forest Service had to close a campsite in South Dakota's Little Spearfish Canyon officially when it was discovered that porcupines had been crawling under campers' vehicles and gnawing on the brake lines in order to drink the brake fluid, to which they'd become addicted. A spokesman for the Forest Service, Galen Roesler, stated that, 'Obviously, if people get into their car in the morning and start down the canyon and suddenly discover they don't have brakes, well, that can be a real hazard.'

Tom Murphy of Pittsburgh was glad when he finally sold two of his prize racing pigeons to owners in Amarillo and Austin in Texas. The new owners weren't so pleased, however. Four weeks later both birds flew the 1,500 miles back to Tom!

Did you know ...
crickets hear through their knees
and cicadas through their stomachs,
while snakes pick up sound waves
with their tongues.

Do you believe in ghosts? The Bambrick family of Old Hill in the West Midlands didn't—until a number of strange and terrifying things started to happen in their quiet semi-detached home in early 1999. Terrible piercing shrieks seemed to come out of nowhere. Then there was the moaning and the hissing and—worst of all—the sound of sharp phantom claws scratching away at the walls. In desperation, John and Jackie Bambrick called in a priest to exorcise the ghost—but to no avail. The haunting continued and became so terrifying that the family soon fled the house and refused to go back. Intrigued by the strange goings-on, a neighbour decided to investigate. Realising that the haunting seemed to be concentrated on the living room, he removed the gas fire— and discovered a very large irate ginger tom which had been stuck up the chimney for some five days. The cat was none the worse for the ordeal, and the family quickly moved back in again.

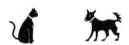

You expect political parties to indulge in a few 'dirty tricks' before an election, but the Jarkland Mukti Morcha party in India could not believe the lengths their opponents went to just before an important election in the state of Bihar.

Activists in the social democratic Janata Dal party had gone round capturing wild parrots, and indoctrinating them by continuously repeating their party slogans. The birds were then released back into the wild, where they campaigned on behalf of the Janata Dal candidates, outraging their opponents.

The biggest sporting bet in history was a wager on a race—between a man and a horse! In 1877, a prospector at the Copper Queen Mine in Arizona became convinced that he was the fastest man alive. He challenged all comers to a hundred-yard dash and beat them again and again. Eventually, he got so cocky that he boasted he could even outrun a horse, running a hundred yards to a post, turning and running the hundred yards back to the starting point. In fact, he was so sure of himself, he was prepared to bet his entire stake in the mine on it.

The day of the race came and, surprisingly, the miner actually managed to outrun the horse and its rider over the first hundred yards, but was no match for them on the way back. He lost the race and the bet—his stake in the mine that would later go on to be valued at $20 million!

Incidentally, the miner wasn't as crazy as he might have sounded. In 1936, Olympic gold medallist Jesse Owens beat a thoroughbred racehorse named McCaw over a hundred-yard course in Havana, Cuba. More recently, decathlete Daley Thompson raced a greyhound around Wimbledon dog track at a fund-raising event. He covered the 290 metres in thirty seconds but finished second. After getting his breath back, Daley's first comment was, 'One more leg and I would've beaten him.'

A seagull scored the vital goal in a junior football match between Stalybridge Celtic Colts and Hollingworth Juniors in Greater Manchester in 1999. Thirteen-year-old Colts striker Danny Worthington had let loose with a thunderous volley that looked set to soar over the crossbar—until the gull swooped down and headed it straight into the back of the net! 3–1 to the Colts! Understandably there was some controversy over the goal, but experienced referee Damien Whelan allowed it to stand. 'If the ball does not go out of the pitch area, it can't be disallowed,' he explained to the bemused players. His decision was later upheld by the Football Association. Spokesman Steve Double said, 'To the best of my knowledge a seagull has never scored a goal in football before. The referee was right. Whether the ball hits the referee, a dog or any other animal, even a seagull, if it goes into the net it is a goal. Our commiserations to the losing team—and the seagull.'

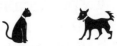

A successful long-distance runner knows how to pace himself. So, when British athlete Chris Stewart saw a local runner come rocketing past him at breakneck speed during a fifteen-mile road race in Kenya, he just laughed to himself. After all, his opponent would soon tire. Chris decided he was happy maintaining the same slow, steady pace—until he glanced over his shoulder and realised that the other runner had actually been fleeing a rhinoceros that was now bearing straight down on him.

Even the most ardent golf enthusiast was stumped: can you play a ball stuck in a sheep's bottom, or is it officially 'lost'? Peter Croke was playing golf at the Southerndown Golf Club near Porthcawl in Wales when he hit a wild shot on the seventeenth fairway. The ball came squarely to rest—in the back end of an unfortunate sheep. The sheep had been grazing peacefully but—understandably worried about this new turn of events—it sprinted off on to the green with the ball still wedged. Eventually the ball did get shaken loose, thirty yards nearer the *right* hole, making it a simple putt for Peter. The rule books were dutifully consulted, and, although there was nothing specifically covering these particular circumstances, it was decided that he could play the ball from where it fell.

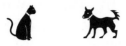

Willie B was a 450-pound gorilla who loved to watch the television just outside his cage at the Atlanta Zoo. However one day, like all of us, one of the adverts made him see red. The advert featured American Tourister luggage. In the commercial, a similar gorilla got hold of one of their suitcases, but no matter how hard it tried, it couldn't even put a dent in it.

Well, American Tourister hadn't banked on Willie B. He saw the commercial as an affront to primate pride and his own masculinity. In a recreation of the commercial staged by a local TV station in 1981, Willie was given a similar suitcase to try out. And try it out he did!

He threw it around his cage, slid it across the floor, jumped on it, and smashed it against the bars. You name it and Willie B did it to the poor unfortunate suitcase. After a short while he'd proved the commercial wrong. The suitcase was in two parts: he'd broken the hinges and ripped the leather-like cover off the hard casing. He then took one of the halves to his drinking fountain and filled it with water, from which he proceeded to drink in celebration of simian over suitcase!

Postmen are used to being nipped by dogs, but

those working in the town of Viborg in Denmark were given advice by a top dog psychologist. His advice to postmen, when threatened by an angry dog, was to 'keep a straight face, crouch low and make chewing noises for twenty seconds'.

Did you know . . .
an ostrich's eye is larger than
its brain.

During the Idaho Gold Rush of the mid-nineteenth century, one prospector's dog was out trying to dig its way into a gopher burrow when it excavated a gold nugget. This turned out to be part of a huge gold mine—of which the dog was given a share by its grateful owner.

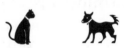

In 1984 PC Michael Parker chased and arrested two suspected burglars in north London. The arrest was easier than he'd imagined—the crooks took one look at the police Alsatian that accompanied him and were only too willing to give themselves up.

Only when they were handcuffed did PC Parker reveal that the dog with him *wasn't* his police dog. It was just a stray that had happened to follow him down the street when he started chasing the suspects. The burglars were not amused.

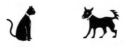

When a deadly king cobra was spotted waiting to strike in the long grass beside an electricity sub-station in Tilehurst, Berkshire, the man who'd seen it rang the RSPCA and then stayed on the spot to warn people to keep well away. The RSPCA meanwhile called the Ark Animal Sanctuary in nearby Caversham, who despatched Bob Andrews to tackle the reptile. Kitted out with a net, box and goggles to protect his eyes in case the cobra spat venom at him, he cautiously made his way, inch by inch, towards the cobra while a crowd of onlookers watched fascinated—only to discover that it was a rusty old exhaust pipe.

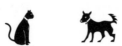

It was a real test of faith. The Reverend Stephen Grey was giving a service in St Michael's Church, Bamford, when a ferret shot up his cassock! The vicar bravely carried on with his sermon until the ferret reappeared and was caught by one of his parishioners. 'I was trained to carry on regardless,' he says, 'but I must admit the prayers speeded up a bit towards the end!'

An unnamed girl in Lahore, Pakistan, was about to elope with her boyfriend. To put her parents off her trail, she dressed a monkey in her nightclothes and left it in her bed.

On discovering the monkey, her parents' first thoughts were not that this was a monkey in their daughter's bed—but that their daughter had been transformed into the animal by some form of black magic.

They tried all sorts of rituals to transform the monkey back into their daughter—without any luck. Then a neighbour, in passing, happened to mention that he had seen the couple run away two days earlier.

CHAPTER TWO

ANIMALS AT WORK

The Staffordshire police force don't seem that lucky with their police dogs. Take the story of Barney, a four-year-old German shepherd.

Barney was alert, intelligent and fierce—a perfect combination for a police dog. There was just one thing that let him down: he was scared of the dark.

Barney had worked with the Staffordshire police force since 1996, during which time he was involved in many daring raids, helping to capture criminals including burglars and drug dealers. But it was on a raid in 1999 that his phobia was noticed. Police had been alerted to a suspected intruder in a golf-course clubhouse at Cannock Chase. PC John Taylor and Barney went to investigate, but Barney refused to go in until the light was turned on. It's not known what caused Barney's condition. PC Taylor said, 'All dogs go through a thirteen-week course which involves training in the dark, and there were no apparent problems with Barney. When we discovered his problem we took him on a special training mission. Again, he wouldn't go in until we switched on a light.'

Barney is now permanently off duty and is leaving the police to become someone's family pet.

Did you know . . .
polar bears can outrun reindeer.

How's this for an odd request. The Brazilian Environmental Protection Institute announced that it would seek a ban against animals appearing in TV commercials for beer in which 'chimpanzees drink and drive with bikini-clad women'. They added, 'Driving a car while drinking beer is not a monkey's natural habitat.'

Well, it's hard to argue with that.

One of the greatest British actors of all time passed away in October 1999. He appeared in *Octopussy*, starred on the cover of *Time* magazine, had a cabaret in Las Vegas and was a popular guest on many international chat shows. Once, when TV presenter Richard Madeley insulted his nose, he almost bit his finger off. And who was going to stop him? After all, he stood eight feet tall.

Who am I talking about? None other than Hercules the bear, who died at his home, The Big Bear Ranch, in Perth, Scotland, after a long illness.

His distraught owners Andy and Maggie Robin buried their twenty-five-year-old surrogate son with his favourite possessions near his luxury quarters at Glendevon, overlooking rolling countryside. During their twenty years' touring with Hercules, this was where he always returned, to relax in his forty-five-foot swimming pool or cuddle up with the Robins while he watched TV.

Mr Robin bought Hercules from a Scottish wildlife park in 1974. He soon became a natural before the cameras, although once, while filming a TV commercial in the Hebrides, he escaped from his pen and went missing. During his three weeks of freedom his weight plummeted from fifty-four to thirty-four stones, but after being safely captured he soon put the pounds back on again, getting through 120 pints of milk straight away.

Hercules made friends with everyone he came into contact with, and despite his ferocious appearance he was a true gentle giant. Kleenex once even awarded him the title of 'The Big Softy'.

It was while filming for Disney in 1996 at Pinewood Studios that Hercules collapsed. It was believed that a disc in his back had ruptured, because when he came out of hibernation in 1998, his back legs were paralysed. But the Robins never lost hope that Hercules would recover, and every day they encouraged him during his therapy, which involved swimming a mile. He was recovering well last October but fell ill with a virus and died two days later.

Maggie Robin said, 'He was getting a bit better but he just took a turn for the worse. Hercules was a battler. He fought as hard as he could but it was too much for him.'

Officials at a museum in Stockholm had the ultimate deterrent when a 360-carat blue star sapphire worth nearly half a million dollars went on display. Refusing to trust just the fancy light beams and ultrasonic detectors, they put three deadly saw-scale snakes in the case with it.

Exhibition officials said that anyone bitten by a saw-scale would need at least 80cc of antidote serum in order to survive. The snakes' poison was said to be able to kill someone in less than ten minutes. However, the antidote was kept handy at a nearby hospital, 'just in case'.

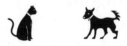

Teachers tired of chasing after unruly children in the nation's playgrounds will be fascinated to hear about an innovative scheme dreamed up by infant-school teacher Wendy Dyble in the Shetlands. She wants to use 'canine teaching assistants'—sheepdogs to you and me—to round up the kiddies and herd them back into class! Far-fetched? The 35,000-strong Professional Association of Teachers doesn't think so. In 1999 they officially endorsed Wendy's plan at their annual conference in Stockport!

Publicists are often asked to arrange weird and wonderful things to promote a new feature film, but probably the strangest publicity stunt in Hollywood history was dreamed up by film mogul Sam Goldwyn. He went to see his studio publicist Arthur L. Mayer and told him about a brilliant idea he'd had to promote his new film starring Mae West and called *It Ain't No Sin*. 'I want seventy parrots all trained to squawk out the title!' he told Mayer. 'It'll be a knockout. It Ain't No Sin! It Ain't No Sin! The papers will love it!' It was a formidable task, but Mayer succeeded in finding seventy of Hollywood's most talented and highly paid parrots and had them coached relentlessly by a team of top animal trainers until they could all squawk out 'It Ain't No Sin!' loud and clear on cue. He called up Sam Goldwyn and asked him to come and see the parrots for himself. 'Forget about that,' said Sam. 'We've changed the title of the movie to *I'm No Angel*.' Mayer quit on the spot.

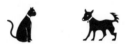

Alfie the Border collie took his job very seriously. Each night, he faithfully guarded the Lynham Inn in Plympton for his owner's father. One day in March 1996 his owner, Laura Knight, left Alfie outside a card shop in Plymouth while she browsed inside. Time passed, and Alfie began to get increasingly anxious. Alarmed that he might actually be late for his job, Alfie ran down the high street, jumped on a passing number 21 bus and set off for the pub all by himself. He tried to get off at the stop outside the pub but the driver wouldn't let him go, thinking he was a stray.

Instead, he called the police and poor old Alfie was carted off to the jug, where he was eventually reunited with his owner. Who says you can't get good staff any more?

Silver King was a horse who made regular appearances in cowboy movies (including the Henry Fonda film *Jesse James*), but he loved to do all his own stunts. He couldn't bear other horses doubling for him and got quite jealous when they did. On one occasion another horse had been brought in to jump off a cliff into water below. The horse did this perfectly, but just afterwards, Silver King broke away from his handler to do exactly the same stunt—the one that had been filmed successfully just moments before.

Because Silver King spent so long under the arc lights he was in danger of going blind. As a precaution a vet prescribed a custom-made pair of sunglasses—equine Ray Bans, if you like. He wore these when rehearsing a scene and took them off when it came to the 'take'. Fortunately, this safeguarded Silver King's eyesight and he continued his acting career for a good many years.

Glasses have also been worn by chickens. The special spectacles were invented at the turn of the century by Mr Andrew Jackson Jr—not to improve the birds' vision but to protect their eyes from each other's beaks.

According to the history books, a dog called Saur was actually King of Norway for three years! Saur was put on the throne after the tyrannical Norwegian king was deposed, and by all accounts ruled quite wisely. He issued his royal commands by wagging his tail to say yes, and by growling if he wanted to forbid something. Legend has it that Saur died more nobly than most 'real' royalty, defending a newborn lamb from a ravenous wolf.

Never mind the long arm of the law, criminals now have to worry about wolves! WOLVES, which stands for the Wireless Operational Link and Video Exploration System, is the brainchild of DC Gil Boyd of the Cambridgeshire constabulary. A miniature video camera is attached to the top of a police dog's head, allowing the handler to 'see' what the dog sees. WOLVES has already proved successful on firearms searches and may play a role in dog-rescue missions in the future. Camera-equipped dogs could be sent into the rubble of fallen buildings to find trapped earthquake victims, for example.

It's not just drugs that dogs are able to sniff out. Those employed by the United States Department of Agriculture are trained to detect fresh fruit, vegetables and meat products which are illegally carried by travellers entering the country, whether knowingly or not.

The Beagle Brigade, as it is known, was formed in 1986 and regularly monitors international flights. Beagles were chosen for their docile nature and keen sense of smell. Each dog strolls with its handler through the baggage reclaim area. If it detects any illegal products then the dog sits down by the suspect, with its head erect. This is the signal for its handler to investigate.

The sense of smell of the beagles is incredible. One of them detected a single clove of garlic wrapped in a sealed plastic bag in the middle of a large trunk, while another dog picked up the scent of lemons carried in a bottle of water inside a very large, hard suitcase.

Did you know . . .
Spain was named after the
Carthaginian word meaning 'land
of rabbits'.

One of the best police sniffer dogs there's ever been was a golden terrier called Trap. He began his career in 1973, aged four. On his first assignment he uncovered more than a ton of drugs, worth $2 million, and by the time he was nine he had sniffed out more than $63 million worth of illegal substances. So keen was his sense of smell that Trap could detect sixteen different types of drugs and eleven separate kinds of explosive.

Like the army, military cadet forces also have regimental mascots, but the 206 Company based in Dudley was a bit different. Their mascot was a full-grown Nile crocodile called Private Caesar and he waddled along with them on parade. After he became too large to handle he was donated to the local Dudley Zoo.

During the 1970s and 1980s, the US Government brought in an unlikely ally to help in a major environmental project—the beaver, a creature often viewed as a destructive pest. In Wyoming, low water levels in the winter threatened the survival of a rare breed of trout. Short of money, the Federal Bureau of Land Management tried an experiment. They deposited some tree trunks on the river banks for beavers to find. The beavers set to work on them quickly, building a number of substantial dams that held water in pools and saved the trout.

Clip-clop, Avon calling! Avon lady Barbara Downes has found a fun way to combine her favourite hobby with her business—she does all her deliveries to her customers on horseback. She leaves Heathcliffe, her horse, tethered to the garden gate before she rings the bell, of course, but admits that he has been known to wander into gardens for the occasional spot of grazing when her back is turned.

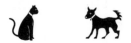

Greedy llamas are the latest recruits to France's fire brigade! Every year, devastating forest fires break out in Provence because of the tinder-dry undergrowth. In an innovative move to tackle the problem, llamas are being brought in to help protect landowners by eating all the bracken and dry grass. A special llama farm has been set up especially to breed this new generation of llama fire-fighters, and you can even hire the beasts for £25 a month or buy your own llama for £4,000—a small price to pay to prevent a raging forest fire on your property!

Should you find yourself short of petrol while driving in Ibadan, Nigeria, there's a service station you just have to visit. The pump attendant there is a pet chimpanzee. Apparently, he's been trained to fill the tank and collect the money. Just to be on the safe side, though, I'd check your change!

Horses are no strangers to hard and dangerous work, but few have worked harder or under more demanding conditions than those employed by America's legendary 'Pony Express', started in April 1860 to carry mail 2,000 miles across the continent to Sacramento in California. Before the Pony Express, letters took at least a month to cross the continent. The Pony Express cut that to just eight days. Horses and their riders rode continuously day and night. One hundred and fifty relay stations were set up along the route where riders could change their exhausted mounts and get going again. The total transfer time was just two minutes. To allow the horses to travel fast over long distances, a rule was drawn up ensuring that no human rider could be over eighteen years of age or weigh more than 126 pounds. Business was good, by all accounts, and a 28-gram letter sent by Pony Express cost the equivalent of £100 in today's money. Although it has worked its way into the mythology of the Wild West, the Pony Express only lasted a year. In 1861, the telegraph came along and made it obsolete overnight!

The world's most unusual racing event was held in Sydney on 27 April 1927, when a leading racehorse and jockey were challenged by a kangaroo. The kangaroo won, easily outpacing the horse with a series of thirty-three-foot leaps! I wonder why kangaroo racing has never caught on . . .

Rinnie the retriever was a police dog at the Wichita Police Department. One night Chuck Smith, a local supermarket accountant, called police to report that he'd been carjacked and robbed of the day's takings.

The police had Rinnie sniff Smith's car to see if he could detect the scent of the robber. After considering the scene for a while, Rinme jumped out of the car—and bit Chuck Smith hard on the backside. The dog was dismissed from the force for making this error of judgement, and his handler, John Judge, was disciplined.

A while later, though, as the result of some further evidence and a lie-detector test, Chuck Smith was discovered to be the robber after all. It turned out that he had invented the carjacking story to throw the police off his trail.

He was arrested and convicted of the robbery—and Rinnie was reinstated and received a commendation.

In the winter of 1999, the Police Federation's monthly magazine published one of the strangest and most controversial articles in its history. In it, PC Garth Coupland of the Norfolk force set out his plans to solve the police recruitment crisis. His suggestion—recruit baboons to do the job. Yes, really. They could be given ranks, just like human police officers, their own uniforms—and special rubber pants in case of 'embarrassing little accidents' while on the job.

PC Coupland believed that baboons could even make police dogs redundant. 'They are smarter and would be able to tackle a wider range of duties,' he said. They could be trained to flush crooks out of their hiding places, recover property from places where humans couldn't reach and use their keen sense of smell to track down caches of drugs or explosives—as well as assist in rescue efforts. 'They could carry medicines to injured or trapped people,' PC Coupland suggested. 'They could be trained to serve a soothing cup of tea or administer a morphine injection with their sensitive and dexterous hands.'

The most controversial part of the PC's innovative idea was to give the baboons firearms training! 'I believe they could be firearms-trained,' he said. 'Imagine the effect on an armed and desperate criminal when faced with a baboon with a pump-action shotgun! This would mean increased safety for police officers, who could stay at a safe distance. This obviously would be a last resort after all negotiation had failed.'

PC Coupland did admit that there were some drawbacks to his idea—like the baboon's tendency to throw its droppings at people if provoked, and its lurid red, purple and blue bottom, which might cause ridicule, but he believed that the special rubber pants he had suggested as part of the uniform would solve both problems.

The article, which, not surprisingly, sparked a national debate, caused a great deal of consternation among senior police officers, who were unsure of how much of it to take seriously . . .

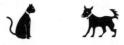

Roman legions used to carry 'psychic hens' around with them to foretell if they would win a battle or not. If the birds ate their grain quickly on the eve of battle, it meant certain victory. If they ate slowly, it would be a close-run thing—and if they ate nothing at all it meant the forthcoming battle would be an absolute disaster.

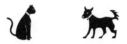

In 1880, the world's first dog-powered car was invented in France by a Monsieur Huret. The car had one small wheel at the front and two huge ones at the back. Inside each of the back tyres was a dog who worked the wheel like a hamster on a treadmill. Happily the idea never caught on, and M. Huret was put out of business by enraged animal lovers.

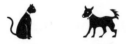

There is only one feature film known to have an all-animal cast. *The Adventures of Chatran*, which was made in Japan in 1987, is the story of the adventures of a farm cat. The cast includes cats, dogs and assorted farmyard creatures—but not a single solitary human. *Jonathan Livingston Seagull* has no humans credited in the cast either—but it's disqualified from the reckoning because some human fishermen put in a brief appearance at the beginning.

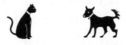

In April 1986 a six-year-old German shepherd police dog named Yerba was awarded a posthumous medal for 'services to humanity' from the Canine Defence League.

Yerba and his handler PC Coxon were investigating a robbery when Yerba disturbed the two suspects. The men were armed, and, despite being repeatedly shot by them, Yerba battled with them until his dying breath. His heroic and unselfish action delayed their getaway, allowing police reinforcements to get to the scene and make the arrest.

PC Coxon said that at least four people, including himself, owed their life to the actions of the brave dog.

Did you know . . .
most mammals are unable to see
colours as humans do. Only the
higher apes like chimpanzees share
man's colour vision.

When Janette Darby collapsed at her home in Rotherham, south Yorkshire, in February 2000, her collie dog Ben knew exactly what to do. He had been given to Janette by Assistance Dogs UK, and now he more than proved his worth by nudging the phone receiver off the hook with his nose and then dialling 999 with his paw! The operator was baffled to hear a fusillade of barks—but police went to check the address. Ben was there to meet them at the door and led them straight to his mistress, who was checked over in hospital and released the next day. The police were every bit as impressed as Ben's owner. 'We think he's absolutely brilliant,' said Inspector Ash Beardmore later.

In Edwardian times, the eccentric (to put it mildly) Princess Radziwill of Poland used to drive around in a chariot pulled by a lion and a leopard.

Did you know . . .
fireflies are not flies and
glow-worms are not worms. They
are both types of beetle.

Landmines are one of the gravest dangers facing people in developing countries. Scattered around from past wars and largely forgotten, they still kill and maim hundreds of innocent victims every year. Now, however, scientists at the University of Montana think they may have discovered the perfect mine detector—the common or garden honey bee!

'We can fly them like miniature bloodhounds,' says scientist Jerry Bromenshenk. 'They're exquisite samplers.'

When honey bees go out foraging for nectar, they return to their hives with all sorts of chemicals on them. Scientists think that by putting sensors in their hive they will be able to pick up the 'scent' of explosives—but the idea doesn't stop there. Apparently bees can be actively trained to seek out explosive chemicals by a system of rewards. Trained bees? Apparently it's perfectly possible. At present, the difficulty comes in working out exactly where the bee found the explosive chemical—a problem which has got scientists working on a special radio tracer which the bee would wear in a tiny miniature backpack as it buzzes around.

'The radio backpack is still a little big for a bee to get off the ground with, but we're working on it,' says Bromenshenk.

A domestic cat named Cayenne gave birth to a rare African wildcat last year after she was implanted with a frozen wildcat embryo. It's part of the conservation work being done by the Audubon Institute Centre for Research of Endangered Species.

Apparently Cayenne treated the wildcat—named Jazz—just like any doting mother would, nursing her and protecting her. The Centre hopes that many more rare species can be helped in this way in the future.

Gulf War veteran Allen Parton was tragically injured in a car accident in the desert while on active service. He suffered severe head injuries and as a result spent three years in hospital, unable to walk or speak, and with no memory of his wife and children. He returned home with, in his own words, no purpose in life.

But all that changed when he was introduced to Endal the Labrador, a dog who has turned his life around.

Endal was trained as an 'assistance dog' by the Hampshire-based charity Canine Partners for Independence, and acts almost as Allen's personal assistant.

Allen says, 'He can fetch everything from my razor to the breakfast cereal or knives and forks on command.' All Allen has to do is say the word 'gloves', for example, and the dog looks around the room until he finds them, before taking them in his mouth and delivering them to his master. If one of Allen's legs slips off his wheelchair, Endal grabs hold of the laces on his shoes, tugs and pulls the leg back into its proper place.

In the morning Endal goes into the kitchen and dutifully takes out his owner's favourite breakfast cereal as well as his bowl. He also gives the post to Allen when it pops through the letter box. One day Endal was watching Allen struggling to withdraw money from a cash machine. Without any prompting—or training—Endal took the card and put it in the machine, and, after Allen had punched in his PIN, took the cash and receipt and gave them to his owner. He even helps in the supermarket, picking things off shelves and putting them in the basket, then taking Allen's wallet and handing it to the cashier.

People are amazed at his abilities. One day Allen boarded a bus with wheelchair access and Endal gave the driver his fare. Allen said that the poor driver was so taken aback, he looked like he needed a stiff drink to get over the shock!

Allen's wife Sandra has said that she can't exaggerate the difference Endal makes to their lives. 'I can trust him to look after my husband, and that means I can have time to myself and leave them together instead of being with Allen twenty-four hours a day.'

As well as helping with the everyday chores, Endal is trained for a far more serious role—as a life-saver. Allen suffers periodic blackouts, and Endal can put his master in the recovery position and cover him with a blanket, then bring him his mobile phone so he can summon help.

Today, both Allen and Sandra work as volunteers for the charity which gave them Endal, who was voted 'Dog of the Millennium' in a competition run by the magazine *Dogs Today*. Deputy editor Carolyn Mentith explained, 'Endal is a very special dog. He has transformed Allen's life. He does things most dog owners couldn't even comprehend. He thoroughly deserves this award.'

A battalion of Coldstream Guards had an unusual recruit in the 1830s—a goose named Jacob. In 1837 he was chased into the battalion's Quebec headquarters by a fox and protected by the sentry on duty at the time, John Kemp. Jacob stayed and became the official camp mascot, accompanying the sentries on patrol.

On one such evening he was waddling alongside John Kemp when French Canadian rebels attacked. They overpowered Kemp and tried to gain entrance to the camp. Fortunately, Jacob was there to sound the alarm, squawking loudly and flapping his wings. This diversion gave Kemp time to recover and ward off the attack. Jacob became famous after his exploits and was taken back to England when the guardsmen returned.

When he eventually died, Jacob was buried

with full military honours.

Even the ancient Romans knew that geese made excellent sentries. In the fourth century BC, geese actually saved the city of Rome from being overrun by the Gauls. A flock was kept at the Temple of Juno and heard the enemy troops coming long before the Roman sentries could. Their furious cackling raised the alarm, and the Roman legions successfully beat off the invaders. The geese were later immortalised by a statue called 'The Saviours of Rome'.

During the Second World War, the Royal Navy also discovered the benefits of goose guards. One British minesweeper carried a goose as its mascot, and the crew soon noticed that whenever the goose cackled and hissed, the lookout would spot an enemy aircraft soon afterwards. Radar was still in development at the time and the goose proved much more efficient!

Geese were still serving in the armed forces as late as the 1970s. During the Vietnam War, the Americans stationed six geese to guard a strategic bridge in Saigon against Viet Cong guerrillas. To show that these were military guard geese rather than just any old geese, they were dyed purple.

Today, the Ballantine whisky distillery at Dunbarton, near Loch Lomond, has a highly effective twenty-four-hour security system—a flock of Chinese white geese. Led by the old gander, 'Mr Ballantine', the geese patrol the 'ageing shed' where the precious barrels are stored. The guard geese recognise all the distillery workers, and when they come across a stranger they emit honks and cackles that bring their human equivalents running.

Did you know . . .
there is only one creature that
sleeps on its back: man.

The most famous elephant who ever lived was probably Jumbo. Standing a massive 11ft 4in high, Jumbo is preserved in the Barnum Museum at Tufts University, Medford, Massachusetts—a university to which the great showman P. T. Barnum donated thousands of dollars in his lifetime. Much of Barnum's wealth came from exhibiting Jumbo; at the time he was the greatest circus attraction in the world.

Jumbo was born in Abyssinia in 1860, but his trip to the United States came via Paris Zoo and then London Zoo. He was the first African elephant to come to Britain, arriving in 1865 after being traded for an Indian rhinoceros. Here he became an institution almost as famous as the Houses of Parliament and Buckingham Palace. Crowds flocked to see him and children rode on his back, accompanied by his keeper, Matthew Scott.

In 1882, on one of his visits to Britain,

Barnum made the zoo authorities an offer they couldn't refuse. He'd take Jumbo off their hands for $10,000—a small fortune then. The zoo accepted but the public got to hear of the deal and there was an outcry across the country. Queen Victoria and the Prince of Wales even tried to intervene, and pleaded with Barnum to reconsider his offer, claiming that Jumbo was 'a national treasure'. A defence fund was set up to try to raise the funds to keep Jumbo in Britain, but a deal was a deal and Jumbo went back to the US with his new owner—and his old keeper, whom the elephant knew and trusted.

Twenty thousand people turned up at the docks to say farewell, and fifteen days later in New York, one of the greatest crowds in the city's history assembled to see him arrive.

Billed as 'the largest elephant ever known to live in captivity', Jumbo drew huge crowds wherever he went. The remarkable thing was that he didn't have to do tricks—people came to see him just to gape at his enormous stature; Jumbo weighed eight tonnes when he was fully grown. He continued giving children rides on his back, though, and in the three and a half years he was with Barnum, he is estimated to have carried over one million children.

Jumbo died in 1885, aged twenty-five. Today he greets students at the university standing as proud as he ever did. The only difference is that nowadays his trunk is full of coins; change thrown for luck, by the students on their way to the exam hall.

The animal star who's appeared in more movies than anyone else is undoubtedly Leo—the MGM lion.

His story goes back to 1916, when Samuel Goldwyn founded Goldwyn Pictures, one of the first Hollywood studios. He needed a trademark for the studio, a gimmick which he could exploit to publicise his new films. The job of finding such a gimmick was the responsibility of adman Howard Dietz, who'd recently graduated from Columbia University. Taking his inspiration from the university magazine, which featured a lion on the cover, Howard presented the idea of 'Leo' to Sam Goldwyn, who loved it. (Dietz also came up with the motto 'Ars Gratia Artis'—'Art for Art's Sake'). In 1924 Goldwyn Pictures merged to become MGM, the entertainment giant we know today, and Leo was retained as a symbol of the new company. Since then, there have been many Leos.

The first Leo was a lion called Slats, who introduced the early silent movie classics. The second Leo, Jackie, was the first MGM lion to roar. His trainer called him 'the Clark Gable of animal actors', and he also made cameo appearances in many Tarzan films. The third Leo was a lion called Tanner; he was the first to appear in glorious colour. His successor was Pasha, who played Leo in the 1940s. Records were lost after that, but there have been many Leos since.

The first Leo toured the country with an entourage, helping to publicise new movies as they opened across the US; he even had his own business manager. In 1927, as a publicity stunt, MGM booked Leo on to the first ever non-stop flight from California to New York (a specially adapted cage was built for him on the aircraft). Unfortunately the plane crashed in Arizona. In the impact Leo's cage burst open and he escaped for several days before being recaptured, hungry but none the worse for his experience.

Leo (in his various guises) has now introduced hundreds of MGM films, including some of the best-loved movies of all times, like *The Wizard of Oz, Gone With The Wind, West Side Story, Singing in the Rain* and *Jailhouse Rock.*

The movie industry is renowned for the trickery used to enhance a picture, and a little of this was used for Leo's unmistakable roar at the start of each film. You see, it's not actually Leo roaring. For the best effect the roar of a brown bear was used—played backwards!

Lassie is one of the most famous animal actors—and probably the best-known dog in the world. But her story goes back to before the first Hollywood movies of the 1940s.

Lassie first made her appearance in a short story called 'Lassie Come Home', which appeared in the *Saturday Evening Post* in 1938. The readers loved it and the author, Eric Knight (a Yorkshireman who emigrated to the US in 1912), was inspired to expand upon it a year later. The Lassie in the story was based on Eric's own dog, Toots. The enlarged story that Eric wrote was published and made into a film by MGM, who bought all rights to Lassie for $8,000. The studio auditioned over a thousand dogs to play the part of Lassie. Although she was a female collie, the dog that got the part was actually a male named Pal.

Pal had been given to dog trainer Rudd Weatherwax by his disenchanted owner. It seemed that all Pal was good for was barking and chasing cars. But Rudd saw that the dog had potential. He found Pal intelligent and quick to learn. Pal had originally been chosen to be an understudy and to appear in scenes as a sort of 'stunt double'. In one of these scenes Lassie had to swim a flooded river. Pal swam perfectly, climbed up on to the bank and dropped down directly in front of the camera with his head between his outstretched paws—not even bothering to shake himself down. The director, Fred Wilcox, was so impressed that Pal was promoted from understudy to star right away. 'It was Pal who jumped in that river, but it was Lassie who climbed out,' said Fred.

The film *Lassie Come Home* opened in October 1943 and starred Roddy McDowell as the young master who is forced to sell his beloved pet, and Elizabeth Taylor as the daughter of Lassie's new owner. To make sure Roddy McDowell and Pal got on together while filming, Pal's trainer let the dog stay at the actor's house, where they built up a good rapport. Of course, for some scenes, the studio had to 'help' Lassie act with Roddy. At the end of the film, Lassie is under a tree waiting for her old master. They run towards each other and Lassie licks his face—inspired by the ice cream that had been secretly smeared over Roddy!

Pal also went on to play Lassie on *The Lassie Radio Show*, dutifully turning up at the radio station to lend his woofs, yelps and snarls, before retiring at thirteen. He lived to be nineteen—a ripe old age for a dog!

When MGM began to film the sequels, a 'lead' Lassie was used alongside several other, similar dogs, each trained for a specific purpose. For example, one dog might have been used for jumping, one for fighting, one for water stunts and so on. Each principal dog was always a descendant of the original Pal, beginning with his son. The 1978 feature film *The Magic of Lassie* starred a sixth-generation descendant of the original Pal.

Looking after this dog was Rudd's son, Bob, and the two of them stayed at New York's fashionable Plaza Hotel during the film's premiere. They had a luxury suite and Lassie was guarded day and night by two private detectives just in case he was 'dognapped'. During this visit, Bob was walking with Lassie in Central Park. According to *Time* magazine, a policeman ordered Bob to put the dog on a leash but Bob protested by saying, 'But this is Lassie—he never wears a leash.' The policeman replied, 'Yeah. Well if that's Lassie, I'm the King of Siam. Now put him on a leash or I'll arrest you!' That was the only time Lassie has worn a leash.

By 1951, MGM had decided that seven Lassie feature films were enough, and they released Lassie from her contract. Rudd bought the rights for a nominal sum; it was the best decision he'd ever make. From 1954 to 1972, 103 half-hour episodes of *Lassie* were sponsored by Campbell Soups—making it one of the longest-running programmes and sponsorships in television history. Rudd Weatherwax went on to write a best-selling book about how to train your dog the Lassie way. His ultimate secret—you can never give your dog too much love, only spoil him with too little discipline. When asked to sum up the career of the original Lassie, Rudd is the master of understatement: 'Not bad for a dog that chased cars and wasn't wanted!'

Arthur, the Kattomeat-crazy cat who ate with his paw, was a stray found wandering in Hemel Hempstead. In the middle of negotiations with the manufacturers of Kattomeat, his owner June Clyne died and a vigorous legal battle ensued between June's husband and Spillers. At one point the husband announced that he had snatched Arthur and rushed him to the Russian Embassy in London, demanding political asylum! The Russian Embassy was besieged by Arthur fans. Extra staff had to be taken on to deal with all the telephone calls flooding in, some from as far away as Australia. 'Arthur Goes Over To The Russians' screamed the newspaper headlines. The Russian press attaché was amused at first, and then increasingly baffled and wound up about it all. 'We haven't seen your damned cat!' he was quoted as saying. 'You can take it from me that we are not interested in capitalistic cats, no matter how much they earn as television stars!'

That Arthur ever was in the embassy seems doubtful. He turned up wandering on Hampstead Heath shortly afterwards.

The husband lost the custody case and Arthur took up residence in an Essex cats' home, working only nine days a year and being sumptuously pampered for the rest of the time. Then, at the ripe old age of fourteen, Arthur was catnapped and disappeared for a second time, but the canny cat proved too bright for his captors and managed to escape, turning up safe and well in a garden in Bedfordshire, over forty miles away. He was returned to the cattery and lived there until he was seventeen—with a security guard posted around the clock.

PC Colin Perks, accompanied by his Alsatian, Rebel, was chasing three suspected villains through the shallow River Dane at Eaton in Cheshire when he slipped and fell backwards. Although the water wasn't deep, it was fast-flowing and PC Perks found it difficult to regain his footing. What's more, weighed down by his water-soaked uniform and boots, he started to slip under the water. No sooner had he got his balance than he was pushed down again. Soon he was exhausted from trying to fight the water and was certain he would drown. Fortunately, Rebel came to the rescue by giving up the chase and running back to his handler. Once he was close, he gripped PC Perks's jacket collar in his mouth and dragged him, against the flow, to the river bank.

PC Perks told a newspaper that without Rebel, he didn't know how he would have got out of the river alive. He was just a few weeks away from collecting his long-service pension and thanks to his dog's quick thinking, the two of them could now enjoy their retirement together.

When the order for the evacuation of Burma was given in March 1944 Lt.-Col. John Williams had a difficult task—how to lead forty-five elephants, eight cows and 198 people to safety over a mountain range.

His fears were allayed, though, due to the invaluable help given to him by Bandoola, a fifty-year-old elephant who, despite his age, was agile and courageous enough to lead the procession.

With his rider seated on his head, using a long bamboo cane to direct the elephant's feet, Bandoola began his ascent into mountains up to 5,000 feet high. Strapped to his back in huge baskets were eight injured children. Despite the weight and the difficulty of the terrain, Bandoola never faltered. At times, the trail was so steep he was almost walking up on his hind legs. With the rest of the evacuees following, Bandoola led them along a narrow ledge, moving one foot at a time to test the ground and keep his balance.

Nineteen days later the whole party arrived safely in India, led triumphantly by Bandoola and the modern-day Hannibal, Lt.-Col. Williams.

Look out, American criminals! Special Deputy Ferris E. Lucas is on your trail. *Very* special deputy, in fact, because Ferris E. Lucas is actually a Vietnamese pot-bellied pig and he's apparently far more skilled at sniffing out drugs than the usual police dogs. 'A bloodhound has the intelligence of a rock,' explains Ferris's police handler. 'A pig, by comparison, is a rocket scientist.'

Did you know . . .
avant-garde Dutch composer
Clemens van de Ven premiered his
latest composition, 'Woolstock', in
front of a specially invited audience
of sheep.

There's probably only one animal in the world who's ever had his own postcode: Smokey the bear, the symbol of the US Forest Fire Service. Smokey lived at Washington Zoo and was so popular that he received sacks of mail every day—the reason for his own postcode.

He was found in early 1950 during a raging fire in the Lincoln National Forest. A fire-fighter, Ray Bell, discovered a tiny orphaned bear cub clinging on to a rock, and took him home. Smokey, as he was named, was treated for singed fur and given to Ray's daughter Judy as a pet. At first, Smokey was in shock and weighed only 4 pounds. He was eventually coaxed back into eating and soon grew into a lively bear, becoming great friends with Ray's cocker spaniel.

Through Ray, the Forest Fire Service heard of Smokey and thought he'd make a great symbol for their fire-prevention programme. In any case, Smokey was getting too big for the family (he eventually weighed 300 pounds). The Fire Service 'adopted' Smokey, but just before he was due to fly to Washington, the bear went missing. He was later found curled up tight inside the family's washing machine— fast asleep.

Smokey joined the zoo in the summer of 1950 and was visited by thousands and thousands of children. He lived to a ripe old age, but now the Fire Service has a successor, Little Smokey. By coincidence, Little Smokey was also found in Lincoln National Forest as a tiny abandoned cub.

Nipper is probably the world's most famous dog. If the name doesn't strike a chord then his picture will—he's the little black-and-white fox terrier featured as the trademark of 'His Master's Voice', a trademark that's over a hundred years old and recognised worldwide.

As a puppy he belonged to Mark Barraud, a successful theatrical-scenery designer in Bristol in the 1880s. Nipper used to accompany Mark to the Princes Theatre where he would play and hide among the props and scenery. In those days theatrical designers often took a bow with the rest of the cast, so when Mark appeared on stage to accept his applause, so did Nipper.

Tragically, Mark died suddenly, and in 1884 Nipper went to live with his brother Francis, a commercial artist with a studio in London. Whenever Francis had to paint a dog, Nipper was his model. Francis had an early Edison phonograph and liked to paint while listening to music. One day, he looked up from his easel and saw Nipper peering into the phonograph's horn, his head cocked to one side, listening attentively for a sound. This pose inspired Francis and he began to capture the image on his canvas, calling the painting *His Master's Voice*. When it was completed, Francis tried to sell it to the Edison Company in London, but they weren't interested. Francis was discouraged and left the painting leaning against the wall of his studio. It was seen, one day, by a friend, who suggested that the black horn be replaced by a more modern brass one. Francis agreed that this might improve the picture, so he visited the Gramophone Company in the Strand to see if he could borrow a machine to use as a reference. When Barry Owen, the manager, saw *His Master's Voice*, he immediately offered Francis £100 for it; £50 for the painting and £50 for the copyright. The painting became the trademark of the Gramophone Company in London and Francis spent the rest of his life making copies for the company's managers. The only change he had to make was replacing the Edison cylinder machine with a more modern, turntable type.

In 1901, the Victor Talking Machine Company of New Jersey (later merged with RCA acquired the US rights to *His Master's Voice* and adopted the painting as its trademark, putting it on to record labels for the first time. The company even had the picture immortalised in four huge stained-glass windows at its headquarters, one of which is kept at the Smithsonian Institute. In 1954 they even constructed a twenty-five-foot-high Nipper statue. It was mounted on top of a four-storey building in Albany, New York, with a flashing beacon on its right ear to alert very low-flying planes.

Today the original painting hangs in the boardroom of EMI, the giant recording corporation that rose from the Gramophone Company. If you look closely enough you can still make out the brush marks where Francis Baxraud painted over the original Edison machine.

Nipper died peacefully in 1895 before he ever became famous, and is buried under a mulberry tree in Kingston, Surrey.

Did you know . . .
mosquitoes prefer to bite blondes.

One of the most amazing stories of bravery exhibited by a police dog concerns a dog named Khan. Khan and his handler, PC Bratchell, were pursuing two men suspected of criminal damage. In the heat of the chase, Khan was hit by a passing car and pinned helplessly underneath. Of course, PC Bratchell immediately broke off the chase and rushed to help his dog. Somehow he summoned up the strength to lift the car single-handedly off the ground, and Khan struggled free. However, instead of giving in to his injuries, the incredible dog set straight off after the suspects again—and he caught them too! When a stunned PC Bratchell caught up with him, Khan had the two suspects cornered and cowering. Only when the men had been arrested did Khan finally give in to his pain and injuries and collapsed on the pavement. He was rushed to a vet and underwent an emergency operation to save his life. Later Khan received an RSPCA plaque for intelligence and courage—but you can bet that it was eventually being able to return to his duties that gave him the most pleasure!

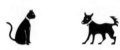

The only official record of a British prime minister making a formal apology to a dog appears in a recent volume of Hansard, the record of all goings-on in the Houses of Parliament. It seems that as Tony Blair stood up to address the house during a particularly heated Prime Minister's Question Time, he accidentally stepped on the paw of Lucy, David Blunkett's guide dog. At least he apologised . . .

Did you know . . .
before stalking their prey, polar bears have been seen to cover up their distinctive black noses with a lump of snow?

CHAPTER THREE

GREAT ESCAPES

Benji, a six-year-old Yorkshire terrier, didn't want to be left out when his owners Steve Hutchinson, Maggie Bundock and their children, Kerry, twelve, and Jonathan, nine, went for a day trip to the Alton Towers theme park in Staffordshire—so he decided to join them.

The family live in Tiptree, Essex, but were staying at a holiday cottage about forty miles from Alton Towers. After they'd left, Benji made his great escape and climbed hills, swam rivers and dodged heavy traffic to find his owners. Once at Alton Towers, he collapsed with exhaustion before he could find them. He was taken in by police who reunited him with his grateful owners.

Steve said, 'I nearly fell over when the police said he'd been to Alton Towers. It either confirms that dogs have a sixth sense or it was a freak coincidence. We are assuming that he somehow knew we were at the theme park and decided he was going to find us.'

Appropriately enough, Benji was named after the film with the same name—the one about a runaway dog!

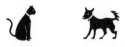

They say that curiosity killed the cat. Well, fortunately, it didn't in the case of Buttons, a four-year-old Persian cross, but she did use up most of her nine lives after spending twenty-five days trapped under a concrete garage floor.

The accident happened when Buttons wandered on to a building site near to her home in Balderton, Nottinghamshire. No one saw her stray in and slip down beneath a wooden framework for a garage floor just before tons of concrete were poured on top.

A few days later residents who had moved into nearby new houses thought they were imagining the distant miaows. These went on day after day, becoming more and more desperate. Workmen called by the residents to investigate eventually traced the cries to the garage—but there was no cat to be seen.

Eventually the penny dropped and the RSPCA, in the guise of Inspector Ian Callingham, was called in. A hole was dug in the concrete where the cries were emanating from and food was laid down—but no cat was forthcoming. The fire brigade used thermal imaging cameras but they didn't have any luck either. Then the rescuers realised that the cat must be on the opposite side of the garage. The concrete was distorting the source of the miaows. This time Buttons appeared as soon as a new hole was dug. She was then reunited with her owners Jamie Boness and Claire Matthews, hungry and thirsty but suffering no real ill effects.

Beaky is a VIT. Not sure what that means? Well, it's 'Very Important Turtle'. The creature was given the red-carpet treatment by the RAF and British Airways as they returned her to the warm waters of Florida after she was washed up 4,500 miles from home on a Pembrokeshire beach last year.

Beaky is actually a rare Kemps Ridley turtle, one of only 900 left in the world and the smallest of all the sea turtles. They can actually live to be a hundred, although Beaky was thought to have been a baby, aged around ten to twelve years old. Experts believed she became trapped in the Gulf Stream, which took her from her home in the Gulf of Mexico. She then became caught in an Atlantic storm, which propelled her all the way to a beach in Broadhaven in Pembrokeshire, Wales. There she was discovered by someone walking, who took her to the nearby St David's Oceanarium. She was covered in seaweed and very weak, but owner Gary Cross took advice on how to look after her before the return trip to Florida. Part of the preparation involved slowly increasing the temperature of her tank to acclimatise her to the warm waters of Florida.

It's believed that her journey to Britain took up to a year. The trip back took just ten hours, and speed was of the essence if she was to survive. To begin with, Beaky had to be covered with Vaseline to stop her drying out. She was then placed in a small foam box and flown 300 miles to Gatwick Airport by an RAF Puma helicopter from nearby 33 Squadron based in Oxfordshire. At Gatwick she was whisked through customs and loaded on to the 11 a.m. BA flight to Orlando. Here she was taken to a sea-life centre, before being put in a breeding programme which aims to restore the Kemps Ridley population to around 10,000 turtles.

Ann and Mike Gammon had the shock of their lives when they opened the door of their home in Dulverton, Somerset, in November 1997. There, staring up at the couple, was their black cat Sodpot, which had disappeared six years earlier.

Mike Gammon said, 'We couldn't believe it when we saw his big yellow eyes looking at us. We were thrilled. He just marched in, acted like he wanted some food and rolled in front of the fire all as if nothing had happened.'

Since Sodpot left home, the Gammons had

become owners of a huge lurcher called Spot. Mr Gammon added, 'I think Sodpot was a bit scared of Spot at first because he's so big, but now they lie on the carpet together. I would love to know where he's been, but he hasn't given us any clues.'

Naturalists were mystified as to how a particular species of green iguana ended up living on the Caribbean island of Anguilla when the nearest colony was on Guadeloupe, 150 miles away. On further investigation, it was discovered that local fishermen had seen at least fifteen of the creatures on a raft of logs heading for the beach.

It was thought that the iguanas had hitched their ride when Hurricane Luis blew through the Caribbean in September 1995, eventually being washed ashore on their new home.

Scientists claim that the iguanas represented the first convincing evidence that animals can start a new population when they reach a new environment.

Did you know . . .
the elephant is the only animal that
has been taught to stand on
its head.

Ever suffer from HRS? Well you might if you

were a cat living in a tall apartment block in the United States. The condition, High-Rise Syndrome, which has been identified by American vets, involves cats, trying to catch birds, falling off the balconies of high-rise apartment buildings and surviving the fall.

A famous case involved Sabrina, a cat in New York who made a dive for a bird into mid-air, and fell thirty-two storeys on to the sidewalk. Her only injury was a chipped tooth. It seems that cats' shape and weight let them fall at a top speed of 60 mph, about half that of a human who might attempt the same stunt.

In 1984, Walter, a cat belonging to David Corr, fell out of an eighteenth-floor apartment window after jumping on to the window sill and losing his footing. David rushed downstairs, with little hope of finding Walter alive. To his astonishment, though, Walter had landed in some bushes and was shocked but not hurt. David honoured his plucky cat by renaming him Chuck Yeager after the famous test pilot in the film *The Right Stuff*.

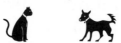

Robert Gill thought the fan belt was going on his van when he heard a ferocious screeching noise as he sped along the motorway. He was wrong. It was actually his beloved black-and-white cat Pepsi desperately clinging to the van roof for dear life. For some reason, the cat had decided to come along with his owner on the seventy-five-mile journey from Indian Queens, Cornwall, to Exeter, but quickly regretted it when the van started reaching speeds of 79 mph! 'I was just coming to the Exeter turn off when the car behind started flashing,' recalls Robert. 'The driver got in front of me and indicated to pull in. The woman then jumped out of her car screaming, "There's a cat on your roof!"' They found Pepsi unhurt but crying, and he completed the rest of the journey safely inside next to his master.

Tabitha the tabby escaped from her cage in an American airport baggage handling area—and sparked an unprecedented cat hunt. Baggage handlers suspected that she had sneaked aboard an aircraft—but which one? A psychic called in to find Tabitha agreed with them, but couldn't be more precise. One American paper had a daily 'cat watch' column with the latest news on the hunt for Tabitha. The tabby meanwhile was clocking up 30,000 air miles between Los Angeles, Miami, Puerto Rico and New York. Passengers reported faint mewing sounds on some planes. Airport staff tried to coax the cat out of her possible hiding place with tuna, but to no avail.

Finally her owner, Carol Ann Timmel, got a court injunction to ground a particular aircraft at New York's JFK airport for an intensive twenty-four-hour search. As time ran out, Tabitha was found in the aircraft's rear ceiling panel behind the passenger compartment. 'We found her under a panel and when I reached out my hand she gave me her paw,' said Carol Ann, who took the cat off to meet the gathered press corps. Hollywood scriptwriters are now said to be interested in turning Tabitha's epic journey into a major feature film.

That great Australian favourite the wallaby is now thriving in Britain! All over Britain, in fact. The New Forest, the Lake District, Somerset, the Isle of Man, Kent, Northumberland, the South Downs—you name the place, chances are they've got a thriving wallaby community close by. How has it happened? Well, it's all Skippy's fault!

In the 1960s, the adventures of Skippy the bush kangaroo were a big hit on British television. People saw how bright and interesting these creatures were and decided to get one as a pet. What the TV show didn't reveal, however, is that the little blighters are also master escape artists. Pet wallaby after pet wallaby made a dash—or leap—for freedom at the first opportunity, and most were never seen again. So many escaped, in fact, that they started to meet up in the wild and form breeding colonies. And now they're set to be as familiar a sight in Britain as the fox or the hare!

When Dino Reardon of North Yorkshire gave one of his prize homing pigeons to a fellow bird-fancier in southern Spain, he thought that was the last he'd see of her. What he didn't take into account was the extraordinary homing instincts of the bird, who flew the 1,500 miles from Algeciras back to her loft in Skipton in 1997.

Her journey was described by the Royal Pigeon Racing Association as 'incredible'. It seems that she was just taking after her father, a racing pigeon called Bluey, who hit the headlines in 1995 after being kidnapped and then escaping. Despite having his wings clipped by his abductors, he managed to *walk* the sixty miles home!

In 1993, two chimpanzees, Al and Akira, escaped from their cage at the Kyoto Primates Research Institute. During their escape, they managed to steal some keys from a security guard and then risked everything by returning to the cages to free their friend, an orang-utan named Doodoo. All three then escaped together.

One of the most unusual rescues in the history of the Wiltshire fire brigade occurred in 1995, when Smudge the hamster fell down a water pipe. In desperation, his family called the brigade to their Swindon home and begged them to find and free Smudge. As you can imagine, there was a good deal of head-scratching and confusion as to where they might even begin to find the hamster. The brigade then tried a scientific approach and calculated the hamster's trajectory down the pipe. They worked out that he must have passed under the foundations of the house and was now probably in the water pipes in the front garden. Arming themselves with shovels, the brigade dug up the front lawn and found the water pipe some six feet down. After removing a section of the pipe, they found Smudge. He was soaking wet—but otherwise unharmed and none the worse for his expedition.

The Canada goose is a beautiful bird and one that's often attracted to cities. It's here that problems start. With their loud honking and frequent and expansive droppings, the geese often get accused of antisocial behaviour.

In one suburb of Toronto the situation was particularly acute, so an animal society captured twelve pairs of geese and transported them 250 miles by truck to a wildlife sanctuary near Lake Erie. All went well and the birds were released in their new home. On the drive back, though, the truck driver was overtaken by twenty-four geese heading straight for a particular suburb in Toronto . . .

Did you know . . .
Persian cats come in over fifty
different colours.

When Sheila the wallaby went walkabout from Edinburgh Zoo, no one expected to see her again. She'd only been at the zoo for four days before tunnelling her way to freedom under a fence. A bus driver later reported seeing her standing in a bus queue as if waiting to get on, and that was the last sighting—until two days later, when staff were astonished to find her waiting patiently outside the zoo gates at opening time. The two-year-old Bennett's wallaby had obviously decided that it was a big bad world out there . . .

Incredible as it might seem, two dogs have

managed to travel 2,000 miles back to their homes.

Jimpa was a Labrador/boxer cross belonging to Warren Dumeshey. Warren moved 2,000 miles from his old home in Pimpinio, Victoria, to a farm at Nyabing, just south of Perth in Western Australia. Unfortunately, one of his new neighbours took a dislike to the dog and used to throw stones at it. Jimpa went out one day and failed to return. After a few weeks Warren was convinced that he was gone for ever. But fourteen months later Jimpa turned up at his old home, having travelled across the country, through mainly inhospitable terrain.

Bobbie was a collie in the US who travelled the same distance but in a much shorter time. His owners lost Bobbie while on holiday in Walcroft, Indiana, but somehow he managed to get back to his home in Silverton, Oregon, in just six months, despite having to cross the Rocky Mountains in the depths of winter. His journey through Illinois, Iowa, Nebraska, Colorado, Wyoming and Idaho was reconstructed by people who remembered feeding and sheltering him en route.

A good soldier never deserts his post, so when Sandy the mongrel, the mascot of the Royal Signals Company, got cut off behind enemy lines, he knew it was his duty to get back to base at all costs.

His adventure started when Mersah Matruh in the Western Desert fell to Rommel's Afrika Korps in 1942. Sandy jumped on board a truck full of Allied soldiers heading home, but the truck was intercepted by the Germans. Sandy made a break for it and got clean away. For the next few weeks he lived on his wits, crossing the battlefield in the midst of intense fighting until he successfully reported in to his home base in Alexandria, 240 miles away.

In 1977 a mongrel called Beauty and one of her puppies were out exploring near their home in Worcestershire when they found themselves trapped in an empty house. They were without food or water for three days before Beauty attempted a 'do-or-die' escape.

She managed to squeeze herself into a forty-foot-high chimney and slowly wriggle her way right up to the top. There, the soot-covered, malnourished dog started barking to raise the alarm. A passer-by heard her and soon police had broken into the house and rescued both Beauty and her puppy, reuniting them with their worried owners.

In the 1930s, London Zoo had a female chimp

called Kiki who was a master escape artist. On taking Kiki her breakfast one morning at the chimp house, her keeper was surprised to see her sitting patiently waiting—outside her cage! She took her breakfast bowl of milk from him and then clambered back into her enclosure again as if nothing had happened. On another occasion Kiki managed to break out of her cage and go off to visit her boyfriend Tarzana in another—much to the disgust of Tarzana's official mate Garufa, who kicked up such a stink that Kiki was swiftly apprehended and sent off to solitary once more!

In 1944, a German man from Magdeburg was at home shaving when he heard a cat howling and scratching at his front door. He stopped what he was doing and went to see what was going on. On the doorstep was a stray cat he had befriended at work—a cat from the other side of the city! The cat bounded up to him and started clawing at his trousers, as if trying to pull him out of the house. Puzzled, the man quickly dried his face and followed the cat outside. The cat set off down the street, stopping to look back every so often as if to reassure himself that he was being followed. They were about half a mile away when the air-raid sirens went and a squadron of RAF Lancasters appeared overhead. Bombs rained down—and one of the very first flattened the man's house. If the cat had not enticed him outside, he'd have been killed for certain!

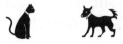

Lola Del-Costa and her husband Ernesto had just been married and were flying from Milan to Spain for their honeymoon in Ernesto's own light aircraft. En route, however, the engine cut out and they had to ditch in the Mediterranean Sea. Ernesto had time to send a Mayday message before the plane crash-landed, badly gashing his throat. Lola was bruised but otherwise OK, and they both abandoned the rapidly sinking aircraft.

They swam for hours, during which time Ernesto was getting weaker and weaker through loss of blood. Eventually he slipped beneath the sea for the last time. Lola kept swimming but her strength was also fading from sheer exhaustion.

Unknown to her, the Mayday had been picked up by the *Lattuga*, an Italian cargo ship under the command of Captain Diego Suni. Daylight was fading as the whole crew scanned the waters for any sign of wreckage or life. Then Rikki, the ship's cat, suddenly ran to the prow of the ship, pacing up and down furiously. Captain Suni ordered searchlights to be pointed towards the prow of the ship, and sure enough, a figure could be seen floating over a hundred yards away.

One of the deckhands leapt into the water and swam back with Lola, who was on the brink of death. She recovered, owing her life to Rikki's incredible 'hunch'.

During 1936–7, a cat spent eighteen months trapped down a forty-five-foot quarry shaft on Idle Moor in Yorkshire. Local people refused to let it perish, and came up to the pit every day to drop toys and tidbits down to the trapped cat. The cat was eventually rescued by a particularly brave RSPCA inspector who went down on ropes and successfully plucked it out of its prison.

Did you know . . .
the chamois, a goat-like antelope,
can stand on an area just a little
bigger than a fifty-pence piece.

In 1984, pigeon-fancier Bill Shillaw of Wentworth, South Yorkshire, had just released his prize bird Cut Throat into the air when the sound of gunshots rang out.

To Bill's horror, Cut Throat was caught in a volley of shots from nearby hunters and plummeted out of the sky into a cluster of trees. Bill was so saddened by the bird's death that he went straight home—he couldn't face finding its broken body.

Two days later, however, he discovered that Cut Throat's homing instinct hadn't left him, even though the bird was severely injured. Bill stepped out of his house to see Cut Throat dragging a wing shattered by shotgun pellets. To get home he'd found his way out of the woods, walking across fields and several roads.

When two terriers disappeared into a rabbit warren in 1999, it sparked one of the longest and most intensive rescue efforts in the history of the RSPCA. The terriers—Candy and Tina—had been out walking with their owner in Thurmaston, Leicestershire, when they decided to explore the warren. Their owner, Colin Clay, contacted the RSPCA, but the first officer on the scene quickly realised the gravity of the situation. The two dogs were trapped under an old waste site and the ground could collapse on top of them at any time. He summoned the fire brigade and they arrived with specialist heat-seeking equipment and a commandeered JCB digger! Then began a tough two-day operation to free the trapped dogs, cutting a way down to them. It nearly ended in tragedy when the digger narrowly missed an electrical mains cable, but the dogs were eventually freed and reunited with their grateful owner.

Trawler captain David Blower sailed back to Torbay with one of the strangest catches the port had ever seen: a barn owl.

David was twenty-five miles out to sea and chatting to a skipper on another boat about a mile away when the other captain suddenly said, 'I've just had an owl fly past the boat.' David thought he was pulling his leg, but the next thing he knew, his mate rushed in to say that an owl had flown into the galley.

The bird was exhausted after being chased out to sea by a huge flock of seagulls and gannets, and used the trawler, *Our Joanna*, as sanctuary.

When he arrived back in harbour, David handed the owl to the RSPCA. It was taken to a nearby refuge before being released back into the wild. Barn owls aren't known for making long flights, so it's still a mystery as to how this example came to be so far from shore.

A goldfish from Northamptonshire must be the luckiest creature alive! Snatched by a hungry heron from a back-garden pond, it managed to wriggle free, only to plunge down a chimney and land in the middle of the fireplace belonging to the Brewin family. Maureen Brewin didn't believe her daughter Jenny when she asked, 'Have you seen the fish that's lying on the hearth?'

'I thought she was joking,' she recalls. 'I didn't know what to do at first. It had obviously fallen down the chimney. It was lying perfectly still, but then its tail started moving.' Quick as a flash, Mrs Brewin scooped up the goldfish and plunged it into a bowl of water. The RSPCA were equally sceptical at first when they heard of the fish's amazing escape, but came round to collect it anyway and to give it a medical examination.

RSPCA Chief Inspector Dave Brown said, 'This was the first time I had been called out to a fish that had fallen down a chimney. Apart from a few superficial injuries to its scales where it had been in the heron's mouth, the fish was unharmed.'

It is now recovering in a pond in Northamptonshire.

A pub called the Drunken Duck, in Burrowgate in the Lake District got its name after the landlord threw away some stale beer, which was promptly drunk by his wife's pet ducks. The next day she found the ducks lying on the floor, apparently dead. Although very saddened by events, rather than let the birds go to waste, she decided to pluck them, ready for the pot and the forthcoming pub 'special' on the menu.

But just as she was preparing them, first one, then another—then another—suddenly came to from what must have been a mammoth hangover by duck standards.

The landlady immediately set about knitting them small woollen vests to keep out the cold until their feathers grew back.

The event was commemorated in the pub's new sign, which depicted a very merry duck staggering about wearing woolly clothing.

Did you know . . .
insects account for eighty per cent
of all animals on earth.

Just what Ernest Mellors needed—a homing pigeon with absolutely no sense of direction. The blue hen in question had been released from Rennes in France for a 365-mile flight back to her coop in Chesterfield, Derbyshire. She promptly flew off course; 5,500 miles off course, in fact. Ernest had given her up for lost when he heard through the enthusiast's magazine, *British Homing World*, that the bird had been found by a fellow pigeon-fancier—in Mexico. 'I don't think I'll be bringing her back though.' says Ernest. 'She's probably having the time of her life there.'

A 3-pound sea bass came back to life just as it was about to be served up for dinner at the Seafood Restaurant in Great Yarmouth in 1998. The chef quickly put it into his lobster tank, where it swam around quite contentedly. Soon after, the fish, nicknamed 'Seabasstian', was returned unharmed to the sea to enjoy its miraculous escape.

Ichijo, the Japanese emperor from 986–1011, was devoted to his cat Myobu No Omoto, so much so that when she was chased by a dog, he exiled the dog—and imprisoned its owner.

British Airways purser John Pearson unwittingly helped to smuggle an illegal immigrant into Canada—his own black-and-white pet cat Katie. When he arrived at his hotel in Montreal after a seven-hour flight from London, he opened his suitcase to find a very disgruntled cat inside. He'd accidentally shut her in the case back home. To add insult to injury, he didn't even recognise Katie at first! 'I didn't realise it was my cat,' he said later. 'It looked so dishevelled, I thought I'd disturbed a stray sleeping under the hotel bed, so I called the hotel porter and told him there was a cat in my room. He was totally flabbergasted!' It was only when John picked up the distressed cat to comfort her that he realised it was Katie. She'd survived the 3,000-mile journey over the Atlantic in the hold of the plane by burrowing deep into the suitcase and wrapping herself up in John's jumper and his big down jacket. Other members of the staff responded magnificently by racing out to buy kitty litter, cat food and some toys for Katie to play with, while the cat clung to her owner for security. Katie returned home in style courtesy of British Airways the next day and the company generously agreed to pay for her stay in quarantine as well.

Nick the Alsatian's owners searched for him for two whole weeks after he was stolen on a camping trip in southern Arizona in 1979. Finally, heartbroken, they had to give up and come home. Four months later, Nick turned up at the door after escaping his captors and making an epic journey of at least 2,000 miles across the Arizona Desert, the Grand Canyon and the 12,000-foot-high mountains of Nevada and Oregon.

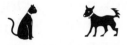

When a little terrier decided to go home to its old place in Staines, Middlesex, it chose not to walk—and took the train instead. The guard on a train saw it jump on board at Bishop's Road station and then get off at West Drayton, where it changed platforms and caught the correct train to Staines!

Alister Bartsch didn't have a tiger in his tank—but he did have a cat under his bonnet. A stray tortoiseshell kitten had made his engine its home. Each day Alister would drive to work from his home in Newcastle to Middlesbrough, completely unaware that the kitten was curled up by the engine. At night, the kitten would sneak out to be fed by neighbours and then climb back in again. Alister reckons he clocked up over 700 miles before he discovered his stowaway. Although his family already have five cats, Alister decided to adopt the little waif and named it Transit. The kitten is now off the road permanently.

Transit isn't the only feline stowaway to have hitched a lift on a passing car recently. In October 1999, holidaymaker Jill Varney and her young daughter and niece befriended an eleven-week-old kitten they called Minstrel on a campsite in Warmwell, Dorset. Setting off back home to Coventry, 150 miles away, they never expected to see Minstrel again. Minstrel, however, knew he was on to a good thing with the Varneys and decided to adopt them. He climbed under the bonnet of Jill's Peugeot and curled up behind one of the headlights. Jill discovered the wandering Minstrel the next day after hearing him miaowing, and the cat now lives with Jill's sister Jackie.

Why do cats stow away in cars? Perhaps Henry Ford understood when he said, 'Do you know why I should like a cat of my very own? Its pleasant purring would remind me of the products of my works. I should imagine myself listening to the distant purring of my motors, and in the cat I should hear the purring of my cars, and in the cars I should hear the purring of my cat.'

A camel finally returned home to its Kuwaiti owner—after going missing for five years. The unnamed beast went AWOL during the Gulf War and finally returned home in April 1996, in good health but pregnant. The camel's owner, Mohammad al-Auwaisheer, couldn't believe his luck when his animal suddenly appeared after all that time, saying, 'Camels are known for their loyalty, but this truly is a miracle!'

When her owners moved to a new home in Bath, Sooty the cat was distinctly unimpressed, especially since her favourite human had remained behind at the old family home in Swansea ninety miles away. So Sooty decided to vote with her paws—and walked out. Seven months later she turned up on the doorstep of her old family home in Swansea, battered and undernourished. The human she'd come to visit, eighteen-year-old Claire Mountford-Davies, heard scratching at the front door and couldn't believe her eyes when she opened it to find Sooty sitting on the doorstep.

No one can explain how Sooty got home. She'd had a sleeping pill to calm her down on the day her owners moved, and had slept through the entire journey. Still, somehow she knew how to find home. To complete her journey, she must have trotted across the Severn Bridge, or else diverted north through Gloucestershire, which would have made her journey even longer and more complicated. You'll be pleased to hear that Sooty is now living permanently with Claire and that there are no plans to send her back to England!

Did you know . . .
a yak has the skeleton of a bison,
the head of a cow, the hair of a

goat, the tail of a horse and grunts
just like a pig.

A very rare bittern, a bird resembling a small heron and which lives on the Norfolk Broads, was blown off course in a big way in March 1996. It turned up 400 miles away in a pigsty in Land's End, Cornwall.

A local animal hospital nursed the bird back to health, but to help it return home, it was flown by British Airways from Newquay to Heathrow, and then chauffeured back to Norfolk by car.

The bittern is an extremely rare breed, having been almost wiped out in the nineteenth century; today there are only twenty breeding males in the UK.

It was a mistake any youngster could make. In the heat of the moment, Purbeck the baby silver-fur seal chose to turn left instead of right—and found himself 2,000 miles away from home. Instead of ending up in the Arctic, where his family would spend the winter, Purbeck ended up lost and alone in Poole Harbour in Dorset. Fishermen spotted him and helped the pup on board their boat, wrapping him up in a flag to keep the youngster warm. Although tired and very hungry from his experience, Purbeck made friends with the fishermen and seemed to enjoy all the attention he got when he was transferred to Cornwall's National Seal Sanctuary where, the last I heard, he was putting on weight and making an excellent recovery. When he's fully fit, Purbeck will be driven up to the Shetlands and released into the sea again—this time probably with a map and a compass.

North Staffordshire police couldn't believe the sheer volume of traffic being recorded on a usually quiet stretch of road while they were conducting a traffic census in 1996. According to the automatic sensors on the road, it was almost as busy as the M1. When they went to check what was happening, they found two wild wallabies jumping back and forth between the sensors!

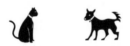

In 1977, Howie the Persian made a spectacular trip of over 1,000 miles across some of the worst terrain in Australia. His owners, the Hicks family, had left their Adelaide home and gone for a long holiday abroad, so they decided to leave Howie with relatives on Queensland's Gold Coast. Nice though they might have been, Howie knew who he really wanted to be with and soon escaped. A year later, he turned up at the Adelaide family home, purring uncontrollably like a little kitten when he found his owners waiting to greet him. He had somehow managed to traverse rivers, deserts and untold miles of wilderness to be reunited.

Hunters on the outskirts of the Polish city of Tarnobrzeg caught a rabbit wearing a tag that identified it as one of hundreds sent from Poland to France for breeding purposes. The shortest distance between France and Tarnobrzeg is over 1,250 miles—an incredible distance for any animal to cover, let alone one without any known homing instincts.

Joe and Marilyn were sick with worry when their eight-month-old Lhasa puppy, Mollie B, went missing on a family trip in Glacier, Montana. While Joe had stopped to take some photographs, Mollie B had jumped out of the car to retrieve a small plastic hairbrush—her favourite toy—which had fallen out when Joe opened the door. Photos taken, Joe drove eighty miles before he realised his dog was missing. He turned back and searched until night fell, but had to return home, empty-handed—and empty-hearted.

The next day, while Joe and Marilyn were sticking up 'missing' posters, a local man was returning to his home in West Glacier when he spotted a small ball of brown fluff lying in the road. What stopped him getting nearer was a large wild black bear. The man also saw a small pink object on the road, and when he went to pick it up, the brown ball of fluff suddenly jumped up. It was Mollie B, and the pink object was her hairbrush!

Keeping one eye on the bear, the man used the hairbrush to lure Mollie B into his car and drove her into town. There, his brother recognised her from the posters and soon Mollie B was reunited with her relieved owners. What was amazing was not that Mollie B had been found, but that she had survived a night of freezing temperatures, walking twenty-seven miles and evading two black bears while all the time clinging to her favourite toy, hoping that her family would return for her.

Vladimir Donsov of Moscow felt sorry for the stray tortoiseshell and took her in, naming her Murka. This was in 1987, but within a year she'd taken a fancy to two of his prized pet canaries. For this crime she was banished—not to Siberia, but to Vladimir's mother, who lived in Voronezh, about 400 miles away. Just over a year later Murka disappeared, and on 19 October 1989, Mr Donsov found her pacing up and down in his Moscow apartment building. She was dirty, hungry—and pregnant. The 400-mile journey had exhausted her so much that after a huge meal she slept for three days straight.

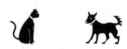

Forget Sir Ranulph Fiennes, Sir Richard Branson or Chris Bonington. The real world-champion explorer is a one-armed lobster nicknamed 'Marathon Man'! The curious crustacean has set a new world record for lobster walkabouts by travelling a staggering 150 miles. That's a lot for a lobster. Most don't venture more than a mile in their entire lives. We know that Marathon Man has the wanderlust, though, because fisherman Brian Lodey hauled him out of the deep in Mounts Bay off the south Cornwall coast in the spring of 1999 and discovered that the six-year-old lobster had already been tagged by researchers. Marathon Man had originated at St David's Head, Pembrokeshire, and had scuttled along the ocean floor to make Cornwall his new home. Along the way, he would have had to descend to seabed depths of 200 feet and then clamber all the way back up again. To a four-inch-long, one-clawed lobster, that's the equivalent of scaling Mount Everest! You'll be pleased to hear that, after making such an epic trek, Marathon Man did not end up in the lobster pot of some swanky restaurant. 'I thought that if he had walked that far, he deserved to have a life,' said Brian Lodey, who returned Marathon Man to the sea.

Did you know . . .
eighty per cent of all freshwater fish
live in the Amazon.

One of the most amazing stories of a cat finding its way home was reported by a French news agency in 1988. The cat in question was called Gribouille, and he showed up on his owner's doorstep almost two years after she had last seen him.

The story starts when seventy-six-year-old Mme Martinet's cat had kittens. She lived in the town of Tannay in central France and she gave a distinctively marked kitten called Gribouille to a neighbour. This neighbour moved with Gribouille to Reutlingen, near Stuttgart, in south-west Germany, but wrote to Mme Martinet to say that Gribouille had gone missing three weeks after the move.

Although both were sad, the neighbour and Mme Martinet soon forgot about the whole thing—until twenty-one months later, when a skinny, malnourished cat turned up on Mme

Martinet's doorstep, looking very sorry for itself. Mme Martinet didn't recognise poor Gribouille at first—but the mother cat did and soon began stroking and licking him in a maternal way.

On further investigation it was confirmed that this scrawny specimen was Gribouille. He'd covered over 600 miles to find his way back home, but soon recovered from his ordeal and went back to his old ways, sleeping in his favourite spot at the foot of a plum tree.

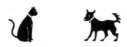

In 1960, Chester the tortoise made a daring bid for freedom from his Cheshire home—and vanished. He turned up again in 1995—thirty-five years later—having travelled all of 750 yards!

A church minister in France received a new posting which meant a move of 140 miles. He owned an Alsatian dog and a cat but decided that although both pets were great friends, the cat would probably enjoy staying in the old village, albeit with new owners. So, taking just his dog, he moved house. Everything was fine until the dog suddenly disappeared with no clue at all as to its whereabouts. Although saddened by his loss, the minister continued with his pastoral duties. Seven weeks later, however, he was astounded to see his dog turn up on his doorstep.

But what was more incredible was that he'd brought the cat back too! Her paws were sore and bleeding from the long journey, but she was otherwise unharmed.

Just one day before she was due to be put to sleep, Sheena the mongrel was selected to be part of America's 'Hearing Dogs' programme for the deaf. Later, she was to prove to be one of the most special dogs the programme had ever trained. One day her owner, Hannah Merker, began to daydream as she crossed a busy road and ignored Sheena's warning signals. As a car sped towards them, Sheena barged her owner to safety and took the full force of the impact herself. The dog was badly injured in the accident, but did recover and eventually resumed her duties with her grateful owner.

Droopy the not-so-wise owl selected a rather unfortunate site for his nest this year. The bird-brain chose to build it on top of an old sewage vent, and accidentally slipped through the grate and plummeted twenty-five feet down the sewer pipe below. People living near the sewer at Gotham in Nottinghamshire were awoken by the tawny owl's quite understandable cries of distress. They phoned the RSPCA, who in turn enlisted the help of the fire brigade and a local farmer. The pipe had to be completely wrenched up and a somewhat subdued Droopy retrieved from inside with a pair of special animal-grabbing tongs. He was covered in oil and sewage, but otherwise unharmed, and after a thorough cleaning-up was reunited with his mate.

Did you know . . .
bears in North America have been known to climb telegraph poles in search of honey. The humming of the wires makes them think that beehives are at the very top.

CHAPTER FOUR

HEROES WITH WET NOSES

Cherry Keaton was a famous big-game photographer in the 1920s. On one expedition she travelled to East Africa to photograph lions, taking with her Pip, a small fix terrier that she'd bought from Battersea Dogs' Home.
    As well as Pip, the expedition included

eleven Masai warriors and four Somali scouts on horseback. A few days in, they reached the plains—and received news that two man-eating lions had been seen near a village.

It wasn't long before the lions picked up the scent of the expedition and attacked. The Masai warriors fought them off but couldn't kill them. One lion was scared off while the other hid in the long grass nearby, watching their every move.

Suddenly Pip disappeared and for a short while there was no sign of the dog. Just a deathly silence. Then the peace was shattered by a huge roar that reverberated across the plain. Just as quickly, the roar ceased.

Cherry ran to see what had happened. In a clearing was Pip, her teeth clamped tightly around the lion's tail. The lion had been killed by one of the Masai when its roar revealed its presence.

The Masai were so impressed with Pip that they renamed her 'Simba', which means 'lion' in Swahili.

In August 1988, JoAnne Saltsman was on holiday with her dog, Bear, and her Vietnamese pot-bellied pig, Lulu. They were staying in a trailer park in Beaver Falls, Pennsylvania, when JoAnne suffered a sudden heart attack and collapsed on the floor, yelling for help.

It was obvious that Bear knew something was wrong, but all he did was bark. Lulu, on the other hand, managed to squeeze through the trailer's dog-flap—a feat in itself considering the animal weighed 150 pounds—pushed open a gate she had never opened before and ran into the street, where she lay down in the middle of the road.

A driver stopped and got out of his car—at which point Lulu got up again and bounded off in the direction of the trailer. Curious as to Lulu's antics, the driver followed her—and found JoAnne. He immediately called the emergency services, who arrived within minutes. Doctors later told JoAnne that if medical help hadn't arrived when it did, she would certainly have died.

Lulu was treated for cuts on her belly that she received after squeezing through the dog-flap. She didn't receive a medal for her bravery. That wouldn't have been of any use to her. No, what she was awarded was far, far better—a bag of jam doughnuts.

In spring 1990, a small fishing boat belonging to Daryl and Gary DeGraffenreid ran into trouble near the Channel Islands off the coast of southern California. As the boat slowly began to sink, Daryl DeGraffenreid decided to swim to an island several miles away to get help. He knew there were sharks in the water, but he was a strong swimmer and confident he could make it. Keeping a careful lookout for tell-tale shark fins, he swam some distance before encountering a very curious baby sea lion who swam right up to him to get a better look. As the little sea lion disappeared, Daryl glanced around—and saw several shark fins breaking the water around him. One was truly huge and belonged to a monster great white shark at least twenty feet long, he estimated. Daryl thought it was all over at that moment— but he hadn't reckoned on the baby sea lion returning with help. Suddenly he was surrounded by sea lions, forming a protective shield between him and the sharks. Considering that sea lions are a favourite delicacy for sharks, Daryl was astounded at their bravery. More and more sea lions kept appearing, until there were at least twenty ringing him, and the sharks backed off. The sea lions stayed with Daryl until he was rescued by a Coast Guard cutter with his brother already on board.

You hear about boys bringing stray dogs home, but in 1992 a dog brought a stray boy home! He wasn't allowed to keep him, though. The little boy, three-year-old Donnie Johnston, had slipped out of his home in Tiny Township, Ontario, apparently with the idea of visiting his mummy in hospital thirty miles away.

Samantha the Alsatian found him trudging through the bitter cold half a mile from his home. Hypothermia was about to set in and the little boy was on the verge of collapse. Samantha went straight over to him and made a big fuss of him. In turn, he gripped hold of her and the dog led him off the road and back to her owner's house and safety.

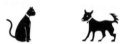

Mrs Clarke was walking along the railway track at Backworth in Northumberland when a dog she had never seen before bounded up and started grabbing at her coat. At first she thought it was attacking her but then she noticed that a small child's shoe had fallen out of its mouth when it gripped her coat. As soon as the dog saw that she had seen the shoe, it picked it up again and set off back down the railway line with Mrs Clarke following behind.

As they rounded a bend, Mrs Clarke couldn't believe her eyes: three small children were playing in the middle of the railway tracks. She grabbed one little boy and carried him clear of danger and had turned around to collect the girls when a train came hurtling around the bend. Her heart was in her mouth as she waited for it to pass. As the last coach disappeared, she saw the other two children standing safely on the other side of the cutting. She also found one of their shoes, which had been wedged between a sleeper and the rail. The other children had been trying to free the little girl when their dog had snatched up the other shoe and, quite independently, set off looking for help.

Did you know . . .
cattle can be identified by their
nose-prints, just as humans can be
identified by their fingerprints.

A British official in India was sitting in his bungalow reading a newspaper when Tom, his cat, came in and started making frantic mewing sounds. The man tried to shoo him off, but Tom wasn't having any of it, advancing again, his fur bristling and his tail furiously flicking the air. Realising that something was wrong, the man got up—and discovered a king cobra lying coiled up under the sofa he had been sitting on!

Jack the Dalmatian was the mascot of a fire station—Brooklyn New York Engine Company 105, to be precise. On every call he would take his place next to the fire-truck driver. On one occasion the crew were answering an alarm call, driving through the city's streets at high speed, when the driver noticed a small boy standing in the middle of the street, too petrified to move. He slammed on the brakes. The wheels locked. Smoke poured from the screeching tyres but he knew he wouldn't be able to stop in time. All the driver could do was keep his foot on the brake as hard as he could, as the distance between the truck and the boy diminished by the second.

Unknown to him, however, Jack had already assessed the situation, and as soon as the brakes were first hit, had jumped out of the moving cab, raced ahead of the truck and, using every ounce of his strength, managed to knock the frightened child clear of the moving truck, rolling to a halt next to the boy in the gutter.

A split second later, the truck swept past before eventually coming to a complete halt. Jack and the boy cheated death by inches, and Jack received a Medal of Valor from the New York Humane Society.

Fluffy was a Persian cat belonging to Margaret Weir of Nottingham. One night Margaret opened the door to let her in for dinner but Fluffy refused to come in—something she'd never ever done. Instead she sat down by the front door, got up, wandered to some nearby bushes and then came back again.

This happened a few times, until Margaret realised that Fluffy wanted her to follow her. This time Margaret went further into the bushes and saw Fluffy sit down next to an old bundle of rags—except that the rags were crying!

When she looked closer, Margaret saw that the bundle was actually an abandoned baby. The baby was quickly rushed to a nearby hospital where she recovered—thanks only to Fluffy.

In 1975, Mark Cooper and his German shepherd Zorro went hiking in California's Sierra Nevada mountain range. While negotiating a particularly treacherous trail, Mark lost his balance and plunged eighty-five feet down a ravine into a mountain stream. The impact knocked him cold. When he came to, he was aware that Zorro had somehow scrambled down the ravine too and now had him by the sleeve, dragging him out of the water to safety. To keep his badly injured master warm, Zorro then lay on top of him until the pair were discovered by other hikers. Mark was too badly injured to be carried off the mountain on a stretcher, so a helicopter was called in to rush him to hospital. In all the confusion, the helicopter set off with the injured man on board—and poor Zorro was left behind! Mark was in no state to enquire about the safety of his dog and so Zorro stayed out in the mountains. It was days before some hikers spotted him, fiercely and faithfully guarding his master's backpack and waiting for him to return. For his bravery and loyalty, Zorro was named American Dog Hero of the Year 1976.

Here's a strange tale about a dog who accidentally shot her owner with a rifle, but then helped him survive.

It happened in 1991 in St Laurent, Manitoba, Canada. Joe Petrowski was cleaning and adjusting a long-barrelled .22 calibre rifle. In the process he had it clamped to a portable work bench and had left the trigger guard off. He was testing the rifle in his garden on a target about thirty yards away, adjusting the sights each time he fired a shot. At his side was his two-year-old German shepherd, Vegas, who was very inquisitive and not at all bothered by the sound of the gunshots.

Petrowski said, 'After my final shot, I reloaded the rifle and went to check the target.' What he hadn't realised was that Vegas had walked under the work bench, and, in doing so, her back had brushed against the exposed trigger.

The rifle went off, hitting her owner in the back as he checked the target. He recalled the events: 'I heard the click. I knew the bullet was coming, but there was no time to duck. I felt the bullet smash into my body and I blacked out for thirty minutes. When I finally opened my eyes, I realised that Vegas was pawing at my face and chewing on my neck.'

There was no one else at home at the time, so Petrowski, who had by now lost a lot of blood, realised that his only chance of survival was to get back inside the house and phone for help. He was helped along by Vegas and managed to reach the phone. Although almost unconscious again, he called the police and told them what had happened.

'The girl on the phone didn't believe me when I told her the shooting involved a dog.' Petrowski recalled. 'So I told her, "Don't worry. The dog doesn't know how to reload."'

Petrowski survived his injuries, which included four broken ribs and a damaged liver and stomach. During his recovery, Vegas would never leave his side. Petrowski doesn't blame his dog for shooting him, since he made the stupid mistake of standing in front of a loaded gun.

The shooting itself was investigated by the Royal Canadian Mounted Police, who described it as a one-in-a-million chance.

Nobody could figure out what Carol and Ray Steiner were suffering from. Their symptoms included headaches, memory loss, nausea and high blood pressure, but doctors couldn't identify this mystery illness.

Then in August 1995 their cat Ringo began acting strangely too, throwing himself over and over again against the back door. Mrs Steiner let him out and sensed that she should follow him.

Ringo immediately bounded over to a part of their garden and began digging. It didn't take long before Mrs Steiner could smell gas. It had been seeping out from a fractured pipe for a long while; enough gas to affect the Steiners but not enough to make them aware of it.

Ringo had saved Carol and Ray, not just from being poisoned but also from a potential gas explosion as well.

Ringo (so called because he loved drumming on the kitchen floor with his paws) was later awarded the American Humane Association's Stillman Award for bravery.

Did you know ...
snails only mate once in their
lifetime. However, the actual act
can last as long as twelve hours.

A dog who really lived up to his name was Hero, a collie who worked the Jolleys' farm near Priest River in Idaho. One day in February 1966 Mrs Jolley and her three-year-old son Shawn were in the barn. While Mrs Jolley was filling the horses' stalls with feed, Shawn was playing in the huge mound of hay at one end of the barn, throwing himself in it and generally having fun. Hero was in the field, rounding up the horses and herding them back to the barn. Mrs Jolley could hear his barks in the distance, but the sound was broken by Shawn's piercing scream. Throwing down her pitchfork, Mrs Jolley turned to see him running the length of the barn, being chased by a wild horse. The berserk animal chased Shawn out of the barn door. Although only three years old, he knew that his only chance was to find shelter under an old tractor.

Shawn's little legs pounded as the horse thundered after him. He reached the tractor, but Mrs Jolley's relief turned to horror when she saw his jacket get caught on a piece of metal, leaving his head and upper body fully exposed.

By now the horse had reached the tractor and was about to trample him. Shawn's mother screamed, but the next thing she knew, Hero was flying through the air, succeeding in getting his jaws around the horse's nose. The horse tried to shake Hero off, but he only let go when the animal flung him against the side of the tractor's cab.

The horse again tried to stamp on Shawn, who was paralysed with fear, but Hero recovered enough to position himself in front of the boy. Despite being kicked and bitten, the dog stood his ground. With the horse distracted, Mrs Jolley rushed over to Shawn and freed his jacket, pushing him to safety. Next she grabbed a stick and helped Hero fight off the horse. Outnumbered, the horse bolted, chased by Hero until the dog himself finally collapsed.

Despite sustaining broken ribs, having both his front paws crushed and losing several teeth, Hero pulled through. Aptly, he was awarded the Ken-L-Ration American Dog Hero of the Year for 1966.

The Second Battalion, US 5th Marines, stationed at Panmunjon at the height of the Korean War, didn't use a jeep or lorry to transport ammunition to their large anti-tank guns—they used a horse, a strong mare whom they named Reckless after the company's nickname, 'The Reckless Rifles'. Reckless soon got used to working with the Marines. She shared their tents if the weather was bad and supplemented her own diet of oats and hay by helping herself to their rations, including chocolate and beer.

She soon became used to working under enemy fire and was officially promoted to corporal. Her bravery was proved without doubt in a battle in March 1953 to retake an outpost held by the Communist Chinese. After the marine who usually led her had been mortally wounded, Reckless carried on to the forward lines on her own—the first time she had done this. Carrying over 190 pounds of shells on her back and disregarding her own safety, Reckless struggled over the difficult terrain despite being wounded in her face and flanks by shrapnel.

During that fateful day, the bold, courageous lone horse made fifty-one runs between the ammunition store and the front lines, entirely on her own, carrying more than four tons of ammunition.

The battle lasted for three days but eventually the post was retaken—thanks mainly to the courage and devotion of Reckless, who was cited for 'her absolute dependability'. After the war, she lived the rest of her days at Camp Pendleton, California, where she was allowed further indulgences of chocolate and beer.

For her courage and loyalty shown in combat, Reckless was made a marine staff sergeant—the only horse with this rank in the Marine Corps.

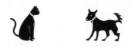

During the London Blitz, Beauty the wire-haired terrier was a PDSA mascot. Over the course of her career she managed to find and save sixty-three people and animals trapped in ruined buildings, and earned herself a Dickin Medal. Her human colleagues bought her two pairs of little leather boots so that her paws were protected when she dug in the ruins. She became so famous that the authorities decided to train other dogs to find missing people. Five of these went on to win Dickin Medals for their heroism, including Jet, a gorgeous black Alsatian who once found twenty-five people trapped under a bombed building and Irma, another Alsatian, who ignored her handler's instructions and located two little girls trapped in a building thought to be deserted.

It was a freezing night in December 1964, and Marvin Scott was concerned that the frost might damage his boat, which was moored to a floating dock near to his home in Washington State. He thought he'd better check on it, so, dressing up warmly, he and his malamute/collie dog Patches walked down to the dock.

Marvin tried to see if the boat was OK, but

as he was pulling it towards him he slipped on the sheet ice that covered the short pier, smashed into the floating dock and fell into the icy water.

He was in agony. Although he didn't know it at the time, hitting the dock had torn nearly all the tendons in his legs. The heavy weight of his winter clothing made Marvin start slipping under the water. He tried repeatedly to make for the surface, but each time he got nearer, he started descending again. Since he couldn't move his legs, he couldn't make any headway.

Marvin knew he was going to drown, but just as his strength and will were about to desert him, he felt something grab his hair and pull him towards the surface. He was aware that it was Patches who had jumped into the water and was now trying to pull him to safety, swimming towards the dock with all the strength he could muster.

When they reached the dock, Marvin managed to push Patches on to it but his own legs were too badly injured for him to climb out. He made one last attempt before the pain and cold became too much and he fainted, slipping into the freezing depths once more.

Again, with total disregard for his own well-being, Patches leapt back into the water and pulled Marvin up by his hair until he reached the floating dock once more. This time Patches got on to the pier on his own and, using his teeth, grabbed hold of Marvin's heavy winter coat. Somehow he managed to pull Marvin up to safety. With Marvin dragging his battered body, and Patches pulling him, the two managed to cover the 300 feet to their house, where assistance was at hand.

It took months for Marvin to recover from his injuries. His survival was down to his dog, who refused to give up or consider his own safety. That year Patches was named the Ken-L-Ration Dog Hero of the Year.

Stephen Spielberg didn't think to include him in *Saving Private Ryan*, but one of the true unsung heroes of Omaha Beach on D-Day was Sergeant Fleabag. As American troops stormed ashore on 4 June 1944, Sergeant Fleabag—a Pomeranian—hit the beach with his owner. They were met by a lethal barrage of mortar and artillery shells, while machine-gun fire raked the sand around them. Nowhere seemed safe. As men fell all around him, Sergeant Fleabag seemed to possess an almost psychic sense of danger. It was as if he knew where the next shell would fall. He would dodge from foxhole to foxhole, pausing to listen for incoming shells. Desperate soldiers, pinned down by the murderous fire, soon realised what the dog was doing and started to follow him up the beach! When he ducked, they ducked. When he thought it was time to leave a foxhole, they got out pretty quickly as well. Sergeant Fleabag and the men following him finally reached a rocky promontory and dug in, but Sergeant Fleabag kept urging them to leave. Convinced they were finally safe, the soldiers ignored him. Deciding that it was every man—or dog—for himself, Sergeant Fleabag abandoned the position. The troops looked at each other and finally decided to follow their leader. As they spilled out, a shell from a German 88mm howitzer slammed into the position. Most of the men escaped, but the Pomeranian's owner was too slow and was badly wounded by the shell. That was it for Sergeant Fleabag. He was no longer interested in leading the assault on the beach. Instead he stayed beside his owner until the battle ended and he could be evacuated to a field hospital.

Because his owner was so badly wounded, he was transferred from the hospital to a waiting medical ship bound for England. Sergeant Fleabag rode in the ambulance, but was refused permission to board the ship. Dejected, he just slumped down on the quayside and howled.

By now, though, the dog's leadership on the beach had become something of a legend— and word of how he had helped to save many lives had even reached the ears of Field Marshal Montgomery himself. A real animal lover, 'Monty' decided he wanted to meet

Sergeant Fleabag for himself and was told he was down on the dock. He was driven there by jeep, to find Sergeant Fleabag sitting staring up at the hospital ship, looking lost and bewildered. The Field Marshal immediately gave orders that the brave dog be allowed on the hospital ship to join his wounded master— and even issued further instructions permitting Sergeant Fleabag to stay with his master in hospital in England!

Did you know . . .
the hummingbird is the only bird
that can fly backwards. It achieves
this feat by beating its wings at an
incredible speed—up to eighty
beats per second.

Who needs a burglar alarm when you've got Pikoy the parrot? In September 1999, a burglar successfully broke into the Philippines home of Pikoy's owner, Fando Santos. As he tiptoed through the living room, the parrot woke up and began to squawk, 'Fando, Fando, there's an intruder!' The burglar turned on his heels and fled, but was later caught by police.

Thirty-year-old Charlene Camburn owes her life to a group of seals who helped her keep afloat for hours when she swam for assistance after her partner and son were marooned on a sandbank.

Their ordeal began when Charlene, her partner Chris Tomlinson and their son Brogan, seven, decided to spend a Sunday afternoon watching a seal colony off Donna Nook sandbanks on the Lincolnshire coast last February.

After their Jack Russell terriers started frightening the seals, they decided to head back home, only to discover that they had been cut off by the rising tide, about a mile from the shore. By now, fog was drifting in. Neither Chris nor Brogan could swim and Charlene knew that their only chance of survival would be if she could swim to the shore and raise the alarm. Stripping to her underwear, Charlene jumped into the freezing sea and set off for the coastline, desperate to save her family. She told reporters, 'About two minutes after getting into the water I noticed this seal in front of me, it was facing me and swimming backwards. I looked around and there were about six or seven seals circling around me. At first I thought they saw me as a threat because of the way the dogs had behaved. But within seconds I knew they were friendly.'

With the fog now closing in, Charlene could only see three feet in front of her. She thought she was heading for the shore but there was no way she could tell. 'I was disoriented and there was nothing to focus on to know I was going in the right direction,' she said.

Whenever she started sinking, the seals would nudge her and keep her afloat. 'I wanted to grab hold of them, to use them to keep me up, but my hands were too frozen to stretch out,' she said. 'They surrounded me and seemed to be protecting me from the force of the tide.'

Eventually, however, the freezing water and exhaustion began to get the better of Charlene and she found herself sinking under the water.

'I kept praying to God, and all the time the seals went under my feet. They were nudging my leg. I'm sure this was to try to keep me up. All the time the seal in front was swimming backwards and staring at me. I was thinking it was telling me to follow it.'

As Charlene struggled in the water, Chris, Brogan and their dogs were jogging along the sandbank to keep warm. Suddenly they discovered a route back to shore and met someone with a mobile phone, who alerted the coastguard.

A lifeboat was launched, and by the time it eventually found Charlene at 6.30, she had been in the water for two and a half hours. She was still a mile from the shore, and had actually been forced by the tide to swim in circles. When she was eventually pulled aboard the rescue boat she had hypothermia and was close to death. The next thing she remembers is waking up in hospital.

At the family home in Cleethorpes, Lincolnshire, she is convinced that the seals played a part in saving her, saying, 'You can't get any closer to death than I did and get away with it. I know from my experience that seals are intelligent creatures. I believe I owe them my life.'

When fire broke out in a farmyard in Leominster, Massachusetts, in August 1994, the firemen on the scene had time to free and rescue a prize sow, but thought it was much too dangerous to try to rescue her piglets. The sow disagreed, however. Completely disregarding her own safety, she plunged into the burning pen to save her babies. Astonished firemen turned their hoses on her to help keep her from burning as she ran in and out of the flames five times before all her piglets were safe.

Clem Brase was walking to his bedroom on 15 September 1998 when he suffered a stroke, collapsing to the floor, unable to move. He was alone in the house apart from his cat Buffy, who, on hearing Clem fall, rushed to his side. There she kept purring and fussing with him to try to keep him conscious.

In the middle of this Clem became aware of the telephone starting to ring, but he was unable to rise to pick up the receiver. Buffy, though, leapt on to the table where the phone was and knocked it on to the floor. Using her nose, she then pushed the phone close to Clem so he could speak to the caller. It was his daughter, just making one of her regular calls to catch up on news. He managed to tell her what had happened and she immediately called one of his neighbours, who summoned help.

Thanks to Buffy, Clem received quick medical attention and made a full recovery. Buffy won the Whiskas Vitalife Award for the most heroic cat of the year. Commenting on the award, Clem told company representatives, 'Without little Buffy I would have been who knows where.'

Sultan the Alsatian proved he was a real bright spark when he prevented his owner, Alex Flemming, from being electrocuted on 1 January 1994. The dog was watching his owner vacuuming out his car at their home in Bloemfontein, South Africa, when the electric cable extension spool Alex was holding suddenly became live. As the electricity surged through him, Alex collapsed and started to pass out on the ground. Immediately Sultan sprang forward and wrenched the spool from his master's hands, taking the full force of the electric shock himself through his jaws. The brave dog received terrible burns to the inside of his mouth in the process, but undoubtedly saved his master's life. For his courage, he was awarded a gold medal by South Africa's Society for the Prevention of Cruelty to Animals.

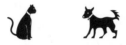

Almost thirty years before the first Lassie feature film captured the hearts of the world, another dog named Lassie was also proving herself a heroine.

On New Year's Day 1915, the *Formidable*, a Royal Navy battleship, was hit by a torpedo from a German submarine off the South Devon coast, with the loss of more than 500 men. One of the ship's life rafts, containing the bodies of many men, was blown by the wind to Lyme Regis. Here, the cellar of the Pilot Boat pub was turned into a makeshift mortuary. The corpses were laid out on the stone cellar floor, and although Lassie, the pub dog, was called away from them, she refused to leave, and began licking the face of one of the victims, Able Seaman John Cowan. To the landlord's astonishment, she wouldn't leave him and stayed by his side for half an hour. It was then that Cowan began to stir.

He was rushed to hospital, where he made a full recovery. Soon he and Lassie made headline news, and although the loss of a battleship like the *Formidable* was a crushing blow to the war effort, the Navy exploited the story of the seaman and the dog who had saved him as a great morale booster, making sure it was sent around the world.

Author Nigel Clarke uncovered this story, while researching a book about shipwrecks, and is convinced that this is the dog that the Lassie books and films were based on. Eric Knight, author of the Lassie books, was then a serviceman in America and would almost inevitably have heard or read the reports.

Paramount now owns the *Lassie* film rights, and although there is no definite proof of which dog inspired the original, they are open to suggestion that it was the Lyme Regis Lassie, stating, 'The British claim is as good if not better than any other theories. We would love to think she could be the original. It certainly is a great tale.'

As for Lassie herself, well, she was reunited with Able Seaman John Cowan when he returned to the Pilot Boat to thank her for saving his life. Now, eighty-five years later, the pub is still adorned with newspaper cuttings, photographs and personal anecdotes of everyone who met her. The current landlord, Bill Wiscombe, is proud of her legacy, saying, 'We've always known about the story, which is part of our history here,' and adding, 'If they're thinking of doing a Lassie sequel, then we'd be very pleased if they filmed it here.'

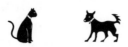

They say that rats always desert a sinking ship, but Fido the pet rat didn't run away when fire broke out at his family's home in Torquay, Devon, on the night of 12 April 1998. Instead, discovering that his cage had been left unfastened, he jumped out, scuttled out of the room, climbed up fifteen stairs each eight inches high and started furiously scratching at one of the bedroom doors. Nine-year-old Megan Gumbley was woken up by her pet rat and—none too pleased—scooped him up and carried him downstairs again. It was only when she opened the living-room door and was met by a wall of smoke and flames that she realised the danger and ran to call her family. Everyone escaped safely, including Naseem, the family's Alsatian, who'd slept soundly through the entire episode.

Did you know . . .
whales don't actually spout water,
they exhale air through their blow-
holes and this creates a mist or fog
that looks like a water spout.

Mopsy the orange rex doe rabbit turned crimebuster in June 1998—and bagged herself a burglar! On the night of 30 June, two intruders broke into the Jenkins family home in Fetcham, Surrey. Shreddie, the family's Airedale, slept soundly on, but in the garage below Mr and Mrs Jenkins's bedroom, Mopsy was all too aware of the burglars and started using her big paws to make a furious drumming sound. 'Suddenly I was awakened by a noise coming from the garage below our bedroom,' Mr Jenkins recalls. 'Mopsy was thumping like mad on the floor of her hutch. I jumped out of bed to see what the matter was and saw two people with a flashlight. I immediately dialled 999.' Police arrived swiftly on the scene and caught one of the burglars. While there was no official reward for the capture, Mopsy did receive a rather large carrot from her family for raising the alarm.

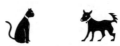

There are many recorded cases of dogs rescuing their masters—or even complete strangers—from drowning, but in December 1993, Cujo the Rottweiler actually saved a puppy who had fallen into some water. The puppy, a three-month-old Rottie named Delta, had tumbled into a weir and was too small and weak to fight the fierce currents. Cujo, who belonged to a neighbour, had either seen the puppy fall in or had heard its frightened yelps.

Either way, he came bounding down to the bank, plunged into the turbulent waters and seized Delta by the back of his neck. Holding the puppy's head safely out of the water, the adult Rottweiler then struck out for dry land and scrambled back up the bank to safety.

Smokey the baby hedgehog owes her life to a kindly cat by the name of Whiskers. The Naylor family of Godalming in Surrey were planning to have a garden bonfire in the evening, but had noticed their black-and-white cat Whiskers fussing at the pile of leaves and old garden refuse all through the day. Whenever they went outside, Whiskers would run up to them, miaowing frantically and desperately trying to get them to follow her back to the bonfire. When night came and the family lit their bonfire, Whiskers went absolutely crazy, digging in her paws and hissing at her owners as they struggled to pull her away from the flames and lock her indoors. It was only when Tracy Naylor returned from shutting Whiskers in that a slight movement at the bottom of the bonfire caught her eye. It was a tiny hedgehog. Whiskers had been trying to warn the family that the baby was inside the woodpile. Tracy reached down and snatched up the pathetic little thing just as the flames began to crackle

125

around her.

Tracy looked after the hedgehog until she could take it to nearby Hydestile Wildlife Hospital for a check-up. Apart from the effects of inhaling some smoke, Smokey—as the baby hedgehog became known—was completely unhurt, and, in a specially arranged meeting at the sanctuary, even got to thank the cat who'd saved her life.

In 1937 an apartment block caught fire in Boston, Massachusetts, sending adults and children stumbling into the streets in their nightclothes, suffering from the effects of smoke. One of the residents was blind, but his guide dog, Bruce, a sheepdog, guided him safely out as the fire caught hold.

As he was being led out, he heard a woman from an upstairs apartment screaming that her baby was trapped in his room. The apartment was now blazing away and fire-fighters had arrived to try to contain the fire. They stopped her from rushing back into the flames—and certain death—but before they could make an attempt to rescue her child, Bruce rushed past them, almost knocking them over in his haste.

They looked on, astonished, as he disappeared into the inferno. By now glass was splintering in the intense heat and wooden floors were collapsing. There seemed no hope that Bruce would ever get out alive, but to the astonishment of all concerned, he appeared out of the smoke carrying a tiny baby in his mouth.

The baby was unhurt, but Bruce received burns to his coat and face in what must be one of the most amazing dog rescues ever. Even the fire brigade admitted that they couldn't have done a better job.

It started as just another trip to the park near their home in Newhaven, East Sussex, for Sharon Fossey and her four-month-old daughter Jordan. Accompanying them was Ben, their seven-month-old Labrador/pit bull terrier cross. Sharon let Ben off the lead as usual and followed him a little way. Then Ben stopped. His hackles went up and he started barking furiously back in the direction they had just come from. Sharon turned around and saw that someone had grabbed her little daughter in her pushchair and was making off with her towards the park gates. She was rooted to the spot—but Ben wasn't. He flew into action, covering the fifty yards to the child snatcher in a matter of seconds. He sank his teeth into the man's leg and kept on biting him. The man screamed and tried to kick him away, but there was no way on earth Ben was giving up.

Eventually the man let go of the pushchair and fled, hobbling on a badly torn leg. When Sharon caught up with Ben, he was standing guard over Jordan in her upturned pushchair, ready in case the child snatcher tried again.

'Ben looked very proud of himself. He knew he had done a good job,' Sharon said later. 'I would have lost my little daughter if it hadn't been for Ben. I've never seen him act like that before. He was wonderful.'

Barbara was puzzled when she heard someone at the door of her home in Thomaston, Connecticut. It was late and she wasn't expecting anyone. No sooner had she opened the door than she was knocked to the ground by a drunken stranger who was there to rob her—or worse. She screamed but knew that it was unlikely anyone could hear her.

What she didn't realise was that her cries *were* heard—not by a neighbour but by her African grey parrot, Samantha, and Gomer, her little chihuahua.

As she tussled with her assailant, Samantha flew at the man's face, scratching him with sharp claws and pecking him viciously. At the same time, Gomer sank his fangs into the man's leg, causing him to yell out in pain.

The two pets kept up their attack despite Barbara's assailant striking out at them.

Eventually their onslaught became too much. He let go of Barbara and ran staggering back into the street, clutching his bloody face. He was never seen again.

The combined weight of his two attackers was only a few pounds—proof that bravery can come in very small packages.

Did you know . . .
moths don't eat clothes; their larvae
do. Moths lay their eggs on clothes
and when they hatch, their larvae
have an immediate food supply.

When grizzly bear fights grizzly bear you can be sure the fur will fly. What makes this next story so special is that one of the grizzlies was a dog—a St Bernard called Grizzly Bear, who lived with his owner, Mrs Gratias, in the small town of Denali in Alaska. One morning, with her husband out and her two-year-old daughter asleep, she was preparing lunch while the twenty-month-old St Bernard lazed happily by the stove.

Just then his ears perked up and he tilted his head at the back door. Mrs Gratias thought she heard a sound too and decided to take a look. The noise was a sort of low growling and it came from the end of the back yard. As she walked down the yard she saw a bear cub rummaging by the dustbins. It looked so cute and was as startled to see her as she was by its sudden appearance. But what Mrs Gratias suddenly realised was that although the cub wasn't much of a threat, its mother would be.

She rushed back to the cabin as fast as she could, but as she turned the corner her way was blocked. She just had time to register that it was the cub's mother before a huge paw knocked her to the ground. Another swipe and Mrs Gratias's face had been cut open. Then it clawed her shoulder and she lost more blood. Mrs Gratias was aware of the bear's sharp teeth and warm breath inches from her face, but just before she lost consciousness she saw a flash of brown fur get between her and the bear. It was *her* Grizzly Bear.

The two beasts fought ferociously and although at times it seemed that the dog's teeth were no match for the bear's paws, it refused to give up. When Mrs Gratias came to she was first aware of how quiet it was, then of something licking her face. It was Grizzly Bear the dog, who'd somehow chased off the giant bear. Dragging herself to her feet, she struggled back to the cabin, where she collapsed again.

Both she and her St Bernard recovered. Ken-L-Ration named Grizzly Bear the 1970 Dog Hero of the Year and Mrs Gratias awarded him a great big hug—a bear hug!

A prime example of 'dogged' determination has to be Jess the Border collie's epic pursuit of a motorcycle thief in April 1996. Everyone was fast asleep in the lonely farmhouse in Dumbarton, Scotland, when a burglar broke into the barn and stole a motorbike. Everybody, that is, except Jess. As the thief sped off on the bike, Jess the collie bounded after him in hot pursuit. She ran. And ran. And ran. Eventually, after an incredible forty miles with the dog still hot on his trail, the motorbike ran out of petrol and the burglar fled empty-handed. Jess arrived on the scene and took charge. 'We couldn't believe it when the police called and told us they had found Jess on top of the bike,' said her owner David Muirhead. Apparently, after successfully recovering the bike, Jess refused to let it out of her sight again and insisted on sleeping next to it every night!

Sir Henry Lee's new valet seemed amiable enough, but Sir Henry's mastiff guard dog didn't like him one little bit. He refused to let the new valet out of his sight, padding behind him everywhere he went. The valet tried to shoo him away, but all he got was a beady look and a low, rumbling growl. When his master retired for the night, and his valet joined him in the bedroom, the dog howled outside the door and scratched at it incessantly. After the valet had left, Sir Henry decided to let the dog into the bedroom with him for once—and it was a good thing he did. In the dead of night, the bedroom door slipped open and an intruder swiftly crossed the carpet to Sir Henry's bed. As Sir Henry awoke, his dog sprang from under the bed, knocking the intruder flying and then pinning him to the ground. It was the valet. With the giant dog on top of him, he admitted that he'd planned to murder Sir Henry and then loot the antique treasures in his house.

Sir Henry realised that his dog had known something was wrong from the very start, and to mark his loyalty, he had a full-length picture of him painted with the inscription, 'More faithful than favoured'.

Rifleman Khan started life as a perfectly ordinary Alsatian. He was the much-loved pet of the Railton family from Tolworth in Surrey, and would very probably have enjoyed a happy and undistinguished life if war hadn't broken out. The Railtons heard an appeal on the radio for dogs to serve with the armed forces and reluctantly decided to offer him for service. Now he was officially 'War Dog 147' and, after training, was assigned with his handler, Corporal Muldoon, to the 6th

Battalion of the Cameronian Regiment.

On the night of 2 November 1944, Rifleman Khan and his handler climbed into a small assault boat to take part in an attack on German positions on the other side of an estuary at Walcheren in Belgium. As the boats slipped stealthily through the pitch-black waters, the German lookouts spotted them. Powerful searchlights swept across the water and the British boats came under heavy fire from machine guns, artillery and mortars. Almost immediately, Rifleman Khan's boat was hit and cut in half. Both dog and handler were flung through the air into the water and separated. Rifleman Khan managed to scramble up the far bank to safety—and then realised that his handler was missing. As the battle raged all around him, he padded up and down the shore looking for Corporal Muldoon. There was no sign of him. The dog stopped, pricked up his ears and somehow heard his handler's cries for help out in the estuary. Corporal Muldoon couldn't swim . . . Fearlessly, the Alsatian plunged back into the water and, ignoring the shrapnel and bullets landing all around him, swam out through the darkness to where Muldoon was floundering. He clamped his teeth around Muldoon's collar and paddled frantically for shore. As they emerged from the water, Rifleman Khan continued to drag his handler over the treacherous mud banks and up on to firmer ground before letting him go. For his heroic life-saving act, Rifleman Khan won the 'animal VC'—the Dickin Medal. His citation read: '. . . for rescuing L/Cpl Muldoon from drowning under heavy shell fire at the assault of Walcheren, November 1944, while serving with the 6th Cameronians'.

Did you know . . .
caterpillars have over 2,000 muscles
in their bodies compared to less
than 700 in humans. However, the
human neck has the same number
of vertebrae as the neck of a giraffe.

Carlo was more 'dogtor' than doctor, but he seemed to know what he was doing when his companion, Dick the cat, swallowed a needle and cotton. The needle got wedged in Dick's throat but Carlo wouldn't let his master do anything about it. Instead, this little dog nuzzled up to the cat and started licking the fur on its neck furiously. This lasted for hours; Carlo was obviously trying to dislodge the needle from inside the cat's throat, trying to move it upwards.

Eventually Carlo gave a yelp of triumph and snapped his head back. In his teeth was the needle and thread, which he'd managed to pull through from the inside.

Dick made a full recovery, all thanks to Carlo.

In July 1985, golfers on the Forest of Arden golf course in Warwickshire were privileged to see one of the most amazing rescues of all time. According to witnesses, a baby rabbit suddenly shot out of bushes on the tenth green with a hungry stoat close behind. Just as the stoat caught the baby rabbit, a gaggle of Canada geese swooped down and made straight for them, hissing and flapping their wings aggressively. The stoat bolted in terror and the birds then formed a protective circle around the baby rabbit until it hopped away into bushes. The stoat, regaining its composure, tried to start the chase again, but the geese stood their ground, forming a wall between it and the rabbit until the baby was long gone.

Ten-year-old Josh Carlisle Coffey lives in Cassville, Missouri, and suffers from Down's Syndrome, so he needs more attention than most boys his age. Imagine his parents' worry, then, when on 6 March 1996 he failed to come in for supper when called. When his father, Johnny, had last seen him, Josh was playing outside with a couple of stray dogs, but by evening snow had started to fall quite heavily—and Josh was nowhere to be seen.

Soon 150 local residents were combing the nearby Ozark hills with torches, and during the next seventy hours over 700 would-be rescuers joined in the search. At night the windchill made the temperature drop down to minus 34 degrees and most people had privately given up Josh for dead. His parents, however, refused to abandon hope.

Johnny said, 'My mind was telling me there's no way he can be alive, but my soul kept telling me, "Don't worry, he's alive. Somewhere."'

Remarkably this turned out to be true. Josh *was* alive, being cared for by the two stray dogs he was last seen playing with.

One of the volunteer searchers was Oscar Nell, who was riding on horseback through a thick forest about a mile from Josh's home. He came across one of the strays—a small mongrel—barking loudly and looking agitated. Oscar followed the dog through the forest until it stopped—and there, lying face down with his coat pulled over his head, was Josh. Standing guard next to him was the other stray, a beagle/dachshund mix.

Sheriff Ralph Hendrix thought that both dogs had curled up next to Josh, keeping him warm so he stayed alive. They also probably pulled his coat over his head, since Josh wasn't wearing a hat when he went missing. Experts have claimed that dogs instinctively sense when people need special care.

Josh was released from hospital after treatment for frostbite, but he can't remember—or can't describe—what happened while he was missing. What he has done, though, is name the two loyal dogs that stayed by his side and saved his life. They're now called Baby and Angel and the family have adopted them. Josh's mother Lynn Coffey said Josh is happy to be home with his family, 'but I doubt he really understands all the fuss.' She added, 'There's no other way you can look at this than as God's way of protecting him. Those dogs were angels.'

Rex Beach was a horse who belonged to Walter Devereux. On this particular night he was grazing deep in the Washington woods near to Port Angeles. This was unusual, because he should have been asleep in his corral!

That night Walter had a premonition that Rex Beach had escaped from his pen, and some sixth sense told him to get up and look in the woods. After a few minutes he saw his tall horse in a moonlit clearing. Rex Beach picked up Walter's familiar scent as he approached— but then detected another scent, also familiar, but this time deadly. It was a mountain cougar he could smell, and it was heading into the clearing.

A few seconds later the cougar revealed itself, crouching low to the ground on its powerful haunches. Its eyes were fixed on its prey—not Rex Beach but Walter, who was oblivious to its approach.

In a split second Walter saw the cougar about to pounce—but in that same split second, Rex Beach gave a loud snort and reared up. Distracted, the cougar was caught off guard—but only for a moment. Next thing Walter knew, horse and cougar were locked in combat—claws and teeth against hooves. Walter was frozen to the spot, helpless to intervene, as the battle went on. Time after time the cougar clawed Rex Beach—only to be kicked away by his powerful hooves. Seizing his moment, Rex Beach caught the cougar's neck in his teeth and threw him to the ground. The two creatures faced each other in a stand-off. Both were bleeding and fighting for breath but neither one would give ground. Rex Beach struck out one final time—and the cougar turned tail and ran up a tree.

Wasting no time, Walter grabbed Rex Beach and they made their escape. The horse's exploits in rescuing his master from the cougar led him to be nominated for the Latham Foundation's Gold Medal, awarded for animal heroism.

More Victoria Crosses were awarded for bravery at the battle of Rourke's Drift than during any other battle in British military history, but one unsung hero was Dick, the surgeon's dog. As the mission at Rourke's Drift was assaulted by a huge Zulu army some 5,000 strong, Surgeon Reynolds fought relentlessly to save the wounded. He was alone in the field hospital operating on a seriously injured soldier when a Zulu warrior broke through the defences and came running in, assegai spear at the ready. Surgeon Reynolds was defenceless, and if the Zulu killed him, he would then be free to massacre the wounded men inside the hospital. Quick as a flash, Dick the dog—who was only a little fox terrier—ran at the Zulu and started biting him around the shins. The Zulu retreated, yelping with pain and with Dick barking for all he was worth in hot pursuit. His pluck and bravery had saved over forty lives. His master, Surgeon Reynolds, was awarded the Victoria Cross and Dick himself received a mention in dispatches for 'his constant attention to the wounded under fire where they fell'.

An Indian woman was carrying her baby across

a rickety old bridge over a river when part of the trelliswork gave way. The baby slipped from her hands and plunged into the river below. Almost immediately, a wild monkey leapt down from a tree on the river bank, snatched up the baby in its arms and swam to shore. In front of incredulous witnesses, it then gave the baby back to its mother and seemed to be telling her off before jumping back into the tree again!

The first dog to win a medal for valour during the Second World War was Chum the Airedale terrier. Chum found Mrs Marjorie French trapped in a makeshift air-raid shelter at her home in Purley, Surrey, after a bomb had exploded nearby, collapsing the house on top of her. Furiously, Chum dug his way through the rubble and uncovered Mrs French's head. Then he seized her unconscious body by the hair and dragged her from the ruins. Having saved her, he ran off. It took the Our Dumb Friends League ages to track the shy hero down to his home with the Chant family, who lived streets away, but they persevered, and when Chum was eventually identified, he was awarded the 'Dogs' VC'—the Bravery Medal of Our Dumb Friends League.

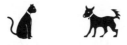

In June 1971, Yvonne Vladislavich was thrown overboard into the Indian Ocean when her yacht exploded. Out of sight of land, she feared she was going to drown—until three dolphins swam up. One helped her to stay afloat while the other two circled around her to keep marauding sharks at bay. The dolphins stayed with her as she drifted some two hundred miles with the currents, eventually climbing up on to a marker buoy. Their job done, they simply headed off out to sea again.

Did you know . . .
the wandering albatross has the
largest wingspan of any bird and
can glide on air currents for up to
six days without ever beating its
wings, sleeping in mid-air as it
does so.

One pet who certainly failed to live up to her name was a Siamese cat who lived with the Carter family in South Wichita, Kansas. Her name? Dumb-Dumb.

The house where the Carters lived had an integral garage where Dumb-Dumb and her companion, Che-Che the chihuahua, slept. One day in 1972, a burglar had gained access to the garage and was quietly forcing the door to the kitchen.

The burglar felt that Che-Che was more of a threat to him than the small Siamese cat crouched on a shelf, and so he didn't pay her any attention. That was his undoing. At last he'd opened the door to the kitchen, but just as he was about to enter, Dumb-Dumb leapt on to his head, clinging on for dear life with her sharp claws as the burglar staggered around, crashing into ladders, cans of paint and a host of other things stored in the garage.

Hearing the noise, Mrs Carter rushed into the garage to see the burglar trying to dislodge the hissing cat, who by now had sunk her teeth into his ear and was hanging off it! The burglar eventually stumbled out, with the cat still attached, and was last seen by Mrs Carter running down the road, howling.

After a while Dumb-Dumb returned— unharmed. She was given the Cat Hero of the Year award for 1972 by the Carnation Company. She might not have earned her name but she'd definitely earned the honour.

Ron and Mindy Wynne of Trotwood, Ohio, were a bit nervous when it came to introducing their collie Papillon to their newborn baby, Rachel. They'd owned Papillon for two years and he got along fine with their two older children, Matthew and Mandy. However, when

Mindy brought her baby home from the hospital in 1993 Papillon started acting strangely. It's not unusual for pets to be jealous of new arrivals in a family. After all, it's someone else (and someone cuter) to share the love and attention with. However, Mindy felt very uneasy about the whole situation. She and her husband Ron even discussed giving their dog away, but events a few weeks later showed just how wrong they had been.

Mindy had just fed Rachel and had put her in her crib for her usual afternoon nap. The baby was soon sleeping soundly so Mindy decided to take a quick shower. A few minutes later she heard Papillon barking loudly. Mindy shouted at him to stop—he'd wake the baby. But Papillon wouldn't stop. In fact he barked more furiously and even howled at the top of his voice. Next thing Mindy knew, Papillon was banging the door to the shower room with his paws.

Grabbing a towel, Mindy knew that something was wrong. Maybe there was a fire or an intruder. She couldn't smell smoke and there was no sign of forced entry, so Mindy followed Papillon upstairs into the baby's room. As soon as she caught sight of the infant she let out a scream. Rachel was lifeless and a deep blue colour. Mindy grabbed her out of the crib and started giving her the kiss of life. Her other daughter, Mandy, who had been in the garden, heard Mindy scream and also ran in. As soon as she saw what her mother was doing she called the emergency services.

By the time an ambulance arrived, Rachel was breathing—albeit irregularly. She was rushed to hospital and thanks to Papillon made a full recovery.

Mindy and Ron are so thankful they didn't give Papillon away—what they took for jealousy was the small collie's natural instinct to protect the young baby. Papillon's deed became well known and he was awarded numerous doggy gifts by well-wishers. That year he led the town parade, a local hero.

The 5th Western Cavalry Canadian Expeditionary Force were given strict instructions not to bring any pets or mascots with them when they were shipped overseas to Europe in 1914, but the men decided to make an exception for their favourite—Bill the Goat. He was smuggled aboard ship and soon found himself at the front line. Bill seemed to share his fellow soldiers' lack of respect for authority. At camp, a sergeant major discovered him trying to eat up the roll call and wrenched it off him. As he stooped to pick up the tattered remains, Bill gave him a ferocious butt in the behind that sent him cartwheeling! When he pulled the same trick on a superior officer, though, he found himself in serious trouble. He was suspected of being a German sympathiser and nearly found himself court-martialled.

Amazingly, Bill survived through some of the most terrible battles of the Great War. He was unofficially made Sergeant Bill after the battle of Neuve Chapelle, and during the second battle of Ypres, distinguished himself by single-handedly taking a Prussian guardsman prisoner even though he had been wounded. His comrades found him in a shell crater, glowering down at the cowering German soldier, almost daring him to move. Soon after, Bill was declared missing in action—and there were rumours spread around that the Bengal Lancers, being partial to curried goat, had stolen him away in a night raid. Happily, he turned up again and a special celebration was held in his honour.

In April 1917, he went over the top with his regiment at Vimy Ridge and was credited with saving three soldiers' lives, head-butting them into fox holes and safety just before a shell exploded nearby.

When the war finally ended in November 1918, Bill was one of only a handful of survivors of all those who had set off with him in 1914. To mark his distinguished service, he was awarded the 1914/15 Star for his heroism and the British War Medal and Victory Medal. On returning to Canada, immigration officials wanted to impound and quarantine him, but his comrades found a way of smuggling him through. They had to. Bill was going to lead the battalion's homecoming victory parade!

In January 1992, John Culbertson of Tullahoma, Tennessee, was on his way back home after walking his Labrador, Sparky, when he felt a sharp pain in his chest and rapidly began to lose consciousness. The fifty-year-old farmer recalled, 'I began to black out. Something was wrong and I didn't know what. As I fell down I remember grabbing Sparky's collar, not wanting to lose him.'

But loyal Sparky did more than stay by his master's side. With John's hand firmly gripping his collar, he began dragging his master up a long country road, right up to his front door— no mean feat when you consider that John weighed over sixteen stone!

Reaching the door, Sparky was out of breath but managed enough energy to bark until John's wife Dotty opened the door.

John was still alive but barely breathing and was rushed to hospital, where he underwent a triple-bypass operation. Doctors told him that Sparky had saved his life—he would have died from oxygen starvation to his brain if his loyal dog hadn't dragged him home.

John told reporters, 'Sparky saved my life. He's worth millions to me. Anything Sparky wants, he's going to get!'

For his quick thinking, Sparky was named the Ken-L-Ration Dog Hero of the Year.

In 1371, a French nobleman called Aubri de Montdidier was murdered by his companion Macaire while out hunting in the forest just outside Paris. Macaire waited until Montdidier's huge faithful Irish wolfhound was off chasing deer, and then swiftly killed his companion and buried his body in a shallow grave. The first anyone knew of this was when the frantic wolfhound turned up at the home of another of Montdidier's friends. He seized the man by the sleeve and dragged him off towards the woods. Realising that something was wrong, the friend went willingly and the massive dog led him straight to Montdidier's grave. After the funeral, the friend adopted the wolfhound and he was a regular sight around the court of Charles VI. Then, as the pair were going about their business one day, the wolfhound clamped eyes on the murderer Macaire—and flew at him. He was only restrained with the greatest difficulty. Whenever the two met after that, the dog would attempt to attack his master's killer— and eventually the nobles decided there must be something in the dog's behaviour. Charles VI decreed that the truth could only be decided by 'trial by combat'—man versus dog. The fight took place on the Isle de la Cité in the centre of Paris. Macaire was given a club and the wolfhound a barrel to retreat into if he needed to rest. But the dog had no interest in anything save attacking. Avoiding the swinging club, he lunged at Macaire, knocking him to the ground and pinning him there. Then he stood on him, his huge jaws around his throat, and waited. Macaire screamed out that he had indeed murdered the dog's owner and pleaded for help. He was taken away and in due course executed. The remarkable dog had succeeded in avenging his master.

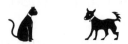

Mules are famous for being stubborn. Now whereas this can be frustrating when trying to get them to carry loads or go where you want them to, in the case of Pal it was a trait that was to save the life of his owner, Oregon rancher J. Campbell.

When Mr Campbell, a sprightly sixty-year-old, saw that a bull had broken into the field where his Jersey cows were grazing, he thought he could chase it off himself. As he headed towards it, shouting and shooting, the bull raised its head and glared. Next thing Mr Campbell knew, the ground was vibrating as the angry bull stampeded straight towards him. He was caught in the open without any form of defence, and there was only one thing to do—run!

As healthy as he was for his age, Mr Campbell was no match for the charging bull, who was soon just fifty yards away from him. As he headed for the safety of the ranch fence he was aware of a brown blur moving in the opposite direction. It was Pal the mule, who'd decided that if the bull could charge his master, then he could charge the bull! The two creatures collided and the bull was winded, giving Mr Campbell the precious seconds he needed to climb over the fence to safety.

No one had told Pal that he was no match for a charging bull, but he decided that this beast wasn't going to make an ass out of him! No matter how many times the bull charged at him, Pal was able to dodge out of the way at the last moment, turning and kicking the bull with his powerful hind legs as it went by. Time after time this happened, with Pal managing to stay just out of reach of the bull's deadly horns.

Mr Campbell had now recovered enough from his ordeal to see that Pal was getting exhausted. Grabbing a large piece of wood from the fence, he jumped into the field again, shouting loudly and waving his makeshift weapon. Faced with two opponents—one of them now armed—the bull turned tail and retreated.

Pal's obstinacy had saved the life of his master, and for his heroism, he was awarded the Latham Foundation's Gold Medal for the State of Oregon, which he received in 1931.

Mary Meredith accidentally slipped while taking a bath, hitting her head on the taps and knocking herself unconscious. She ended up face down in the water and was starting to drown when help came in the form of Katie, her retriever.

Fortunately, the bathroom door had been slightly open and Katie, who was normally downstairs, must have sensed that Mary was in danger. She bounded up the stairs, leapt into the bath and somehow manoeuvred herself under Mary's chest, holding her mouth above the water-line.

That was how Mary found herself when she came to. She had no idea how long she'd been like this—just that Katie had saved her life.

Did you know . . .
the pharaoh hound is the only
breed of dog that blushes. Its nose
and ears change colour to a rosy
red whenever it's excited or happy.

Andrea Andersen loved the big soppy Newfoundland dog who lived next door to her, and the dog—whose name was Villa—seemed equally besotted with her. One day in February

1983, the little girl sneaked out from her home to play in the snow. She wandered further and further away, oblivious to the storm that was rapidly approaching. A ferocious blizzard suddenly engulfed her and she stumbled over, plunging into a deep snowdrift up to her neck. Andrea screamed for help but no one could hear her above the howling winds—no one, that is, except Villa. He barged his way outside, jumped a five-foot-high fence and went charging to the rescue. While his owners, Dick and Lynda Veit, were still wondering what on earth was going on, Villa had found Andrea and was desperately scrabbling at the snowdrift, scraping the snow away from around her with his massive paws. When he had freed her arms, Villa then lowered his head and she flung them around his neck. The massive dog turned and pulled, dragging her clean out of the drift, and then proudly escorted her home. His owners were amazed—and immediately treated him to a slap-up meal with the largest steak they could find. A special ceremony was also later held in his honour in Washington DC, where he was awarded a Ken-L-Ration medal for his 'outstanding loyalty and intelligence'.

It looked to his owner like a discarded rubbish sack floating in the water, but Rex the Alsatian knew differently. He dived into the lake, grabbed the sack and towed it back to shore gripped firmly in his mouth. Inside were five tiny puppies. Someone had tried to drown them. Rex and his owner took the puppies home, and, from then on, Rex took extra special care to guard them as they grew up.

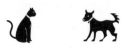

Abby the Rottweiler took her babysitting duties just as seriously as her teenage mistress did. The two had gone over to mind the Gelfand family's six-month-old baby girl at the family home in Pound Ridge, forty miles north of Manhattan.

Both Abby and her mistress were immediately suspicious of the thick-set ponytailed man who came knocking at the door. He said that the baby's mother had asked him to come over and collect the child because her father had been in an accident and rushed to hospital. Not believing a word of it, the teenager wisely slammed the door straight in his face. But as she turned away, the stranger smashed the door down, knocked her to the floor and, picking up the baby under one arm, raced down the driveway towards a waiting van. Abby set off in pursuit. Ninety pounds of none-too-happy Rottweiler landed on the abductor's back, slamming him face down on to the drive. The dog then clamped her teeth around his arm, forcing him to let go of the terrified infant. Screaming with pain, the man managed to scramble free and run off, leaving Abby standing protectively over the baby, baring her fangs in warning at the would-be kidnapper.

For her heroic deed, Abby has since been proclaimed Westchester County's Canine Hero of the Year. A special ceremony has been held in her honour and police have rushed to praise her. Abby deserves a medal and a lifetime's supply of Milk Bones,' one officer said. 'It proves beyond a doubt that dogs are man's best friends.'

Ten-year-old Penny Grantz of Niles, Ohio, was out burning some rubbish on a bonfire in 1961 when a gust of wind caught a lighted paper and blew it on to her skirt, catching it alight. Terrified, Penny ran screaming towards the house, but as she did so, the wind fanned the flames and soon her whole skirt was ablaze.

Her dog, a collie called Duke, saw this and ran towards her, grabbing the end of the skirt and ripping it off her. By now, however, the flames had spread to Penny's blouse. Despite suffering burns to his face and mouth, Duke barked as loudly as he could, attracting the attention of Penny's father, who ran outside, tore the rest of the burning clothes off his daughter and rushed her to hospital.

Penny recovered from her terrible injuries. One of her doctors said, 'If it wasn't for Duke's heroic action she would have died.' Because of his bravery, Duke was honoured by being declared Ken-L-Ration Dog Hero of the Year.

In the United States, Dalmatians are often associated with the fire service, sort of unofficial mascots. You'll usually find them in fire stations rather than at the fire itself—but Spuds, a four-year-old Dalmatian who lived with the Tanis family in Rock Hill, South Carolina, liked to do things differently.

Fifteen-year-old Dirk Tanis was tired and hungry from his Saturday job when he got back home. He decided to make a snack and heated some oil so he could have a fry-up. But while waiting for the oil to get hot he dozed off, only to be woken up by Spuds biting his hand—something he'd never ever done before. Dirk jumped up. He could smell the smoke right away, and, when he dashed to the kitchen, the flames from the burning oil had already caught the ceiling and the wooden kitchen cabinets alight.

Covering his face, Dirk ran in, turned off the cooker and called the fire brigade. He then dashed outside, not realising that Spuds had remained behind. The dog had seen the family's other pet, a small kitten called Gizmo, run into the kitchen, unaware of the danger. By now, the whole room had filled with smoke and Gizmo was coughing, her eyes weeping.

Just as the fire brigade arrived, they saw Spuds carrying Gizmo to safety, holding her collar firmly in his teeth.

Fortunately, the fire burned itself out before any serious damage was done to the house. The fire chief at the scene recognised the bravery of Spuds, who was later awarded the 1991 William O. Stillman award for animal bravery by the American Humane Society. This is usually given for pets who save their owners. It was the first time it had been awarded for a pet rescuing another pet! Incidentally, if you're wondering why Dalmatians and fire stations traditionally go together, it goes back to when fire tenders were pulled by horses. As a breed, Dalmatians tend to get on well with them, and were used to keep other dogs from nipping at the horses' hooves.

In wartime, dogs have often displayed a strange ability to sense danger, a sort of sixth sense. One such dog was Bob, a collie/Labrador cross and the first ever recipient of the Dickin Medal.

Bob served with 'C' Company of the 6th

Queen's Own Royal West Kent regiment in North Africa, where his duties included guarding stores, carrying messages and going on reconnaissance patrols. For this duty, the white patches on his fur were covered in washable camouflage paint.

One moonless night in 1943, Bob was patrolling in enemy lines when he suddenly froze—refusing to take another step further. The soldiers behind him hesitated for a moment, then prepared to move on. Bob still stood rooted to the spot—and a moment later, a glimpse of movement was observed about 200 yards further on. The Germans were up ahead—and in considerable force. The patrol ducked down and went unseen—Bob had saved them from being captured or killed.

Brave Bob served with distinction throughout the war in Italy and Sicily. When the war was over, however, he decided he preferred the Italian sun to the British weather and ran away in Milan.

Did you know . . .
a Japanese remedy for gastritis was
to put a live black cat on the
patient's stomach and keep it there
for four hours.

Two young friends, Hannah Stubbs and Michel Felli, were playing in the garden of Hannah's house in Colorado Springs,

Colorado, when a stranger approached the back fence and started talking to them.

Hannah's mother Susan was inside the house and didn't see this, but another member of the family did—their American spitz, Nori. She'd been watching through the window, and as the man approached became agitated.

By now the stranger had enticed the two children over to the fence, then suddenly grabbed them and pulled them over to his side.

Nori started yapping and pawing at the back door to go out. This was odd because she was normally quite docile, but Susan let her go. Before she had time to open the door fully Nori had bounded past her, nearly knocking her down, and run round the side of the house.

Susan sensed that something had disturbed Nori and followed her out. She just had time to comprehend that Hannah and Michel were missing when she heard a shrill scream. Looking over the fence she saw a man carrying both little girls under his arms. However, the scream hadn't come from them, but from the stranger; Nori had sunk her teeth firmly into his backside! Despite the kidnapper trying to shake her off, Nori wouldn't let go. In desperation the kidnapper dropped the two girls and made good his escape, but not before Nori had taken another sizeable chunk out of his trousers—and his bottom.

The man was last seen running down the street crying out in pain. Meanwhile Susan had caught up with the frightened girls and was comforting them as Nori bared his fangs in the direction of the departing would-be abductor.

Airedale Jack was a stray terrier that had been taken in by Battersea Dogs' Home but adopted by the Sherwood Foresters Battalion. During the First World War, Jack went with the company to France, where he served as a messenger and guard. It was 1918 and the Foresters were at the front, in the thick of the action. During a heavy bombardment they found themselves surrounded by German troops with no communication back to their headquarters. Unless they could get an SOS for reinforcements back to their base, they were doomed. Enemy soldiers were advancing inch by inch, covered by their own artillery. None of the Foresters could ever hope to get back with a message; their only chance of salvation was Jack. A message was attached to his collar in a pouch, he was given a reassuring pat and then set off.

Jack kept low to the ground as shells exploded nearby and machine-gun bullets whistled just inches overhead. But the bombardment was intense and Jack was wounded several times by shrapnel in his jaw, his shoulder and his paws. He collapsed about two miles from the battalion's headquarters but dragged himself the final distance to deliver the message on behalf of the Foresters, dying soon after from his injuries.

Reinforcements were sent and the troops were saved—all thanks to the devotion of Airedale Jack, one of the bravest dogs in the world. His courage was recognised by the award of a posthumous animal VC and a monument in his honour at the Imperial War Museum.

Little Arron Wines was having the time of his life at a holiday camp in Wales in 1991. One day he was having a picnic on the beach with his parents, Dean and Cherie, when he decided to wander off to explore a nearby tidal pool. Still a toddler, Arron stumbled at the water's edge and fell in. The shock, and the fact that his little arms weren't strong enough, meant that he couldn't pull himself back out.

Fortunately, at the same time, Heather Hodder was out walking Tess, her black Labrador. The dog suddenly started barking loudly, and, before Heather knew what was happening, Tess had taken off and dived into the pool where Arron was now floating face down, motionless.

Heather told her local newspaper, 'Tess dived straight into the water and I realised she had hold of a little boy. She dragged him out by his trousers. The child's lips were blue and he didn't appear to be breathing.'

Heather's screams alerted Arron's parents, who'd been looking for their son. They rushed over and managed to revive him with the kiss of life. After the incident Dean Wines told reporters, 'There's no doubt my son would be dead if it wasn't for that heroic dog. She was really wonderful and I can't thank her enough.'

Everyone teased Liz Hutton about the size of her six-year-old Labrador, Eva. Like all over-loved and over-spoiled Labs, Eva was really starting to pile on the pounds and she waddled when she walked. However, when Liz got lost out in the bush during a holiday in Auckland, New Zealand, it was Eva's puppy fat that saved her life! One night Liz decided to take Eva for a quick walk, wearing just an oilskin over her pyjamas, but she soon became disorientated and completely lost.

The next morning the alarm was raised, and hundreds of people began an intensive search for the pair. After three bitterly cold and rainy nights, the searchers had almost given up all hope. It was Liz's own father who eventually found her—cold, wet and hungry, but otherwise unhurt. Her dog Eva had saved her from dying of exposure by lying on top of her every night, her big tubby body keeping Liz warm and dry!

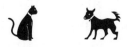

Burglars usually think twice about breaking into a home with a dog. Perhaps they should also steer clear of homes with cats! One burglar, in South Shields, Tyne and Wear, recently went to jail because he made the mistake of underestimating Suki, the misanthropic moggy. Suki, according to her owner, David Brown, dislikes people at the best of times, and someone trespassing on her territory was the last straw. When she heard the burglar breaking into the garden shed in the middle of the night she leapt up, arched her back and began spitting and scratching at the bedroom door, her hackles raised. 'The cat is very grumpy and can't bear people,' admits David. 'It's taken me the last four years to be able even to stroke her! When I let her out she raced into the back garden and I noticed that someone had opened the door to our shed and that the hedge trimmer was missing. The cat was prowling around near our greenhouse and when I went over this man ran off.'

Stupidly, the burglar returned the next night and Suki went crazy again. This time David called the police and the burglar was apprehended. In court Judge Geoffrey Vos praised Suki's actions, saying, 'I have never been a cat lover in the past, but after hearing this perhaps my views have been misguided!' The prosecution also admitted its debt of gratitude to Suki, saying, 'It was as if the cat could hear and sense things that humans couldn't. Without this animal, the defendant might never have been caught!'

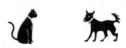

Most humans wouldn't dream of running straight in front of a herd of stampeding cows, but Rusty the cross-breed collie didn't even think twice. After all, a toddler's life was at stake. The little boy, Philip Stevens, had been out playing with some older boys, including Rusty's owner, in fields near their homes in St Austell, Cornwall. His mother was there too, but Philip, eager to explore, had wandered off some distance and was inspecting a gap in the hedge between two fields. Suddenly the cattle in one of the fields began to panic and surged towards the gap in the hedge where Philip stood. Everyone saw what was going to happen—and knew they could never reach Philip in time. However, by the time the humans understood the danger, Rusty had already run almost the length of the field. She swept past the frightened little boy and straight at the cows, who were almost on top of him now. Barking and snapping at them, she managed to turn the herd aside just in the nick of time, taking a vicious kick on the shoulder from one of the cows in the process. Her courage and quick thinking had saved Philip from almost certain death, and she later received a special medal and certificate from the PDSA.

PAT dogs are chosen by the charity PRO-Dogs for their exceptionally good temperaments, and bring great pleasure to the sick and elderly people they visit with their owners—but at least one PAT dog has proved they can still be tough when they need to. Jacob the Alsatian was out practising his training exercises in a local park with his owner, Mrs Betty Harris, when she was attacked. Jacob was practising an 'out-of-sight stay' command at the time and the mugger thought Mrs Harris was alone. He punched her to the ground and then ran off with her handbag. 'Jacob! Come!' yelled Mrs Harris. The Alsatian bounded up, checked on his owner and then set off in pursuit of the mugger, refusing all commands to come back. The mugger and Jacob both disappeared from sight and Mrs Harris staggered home. She was just telling her husband what had happened when Jacob came swaggering proudly through the door, his owner's handbag dangling from his jaws!

Did you know . . .
bats aren't really blind at all.
They've evolved as nocturnal
hunters and can see much better in
half-light than in daylight. In pitch-
blackness they use their sonar to
detect prey.

Sheep aren't the brightest of creatures—so it's a good thing that sheepdogs are among the smartest animals around. A flock of sheep on Hathersage Farm were out feeding on the moors when they got in a bit of a panic. Charging about, several of them fell thirty feet down a gully and were trapped on a rocky ledge. Below them was a seventy-foot drop and certain death. When Mr Priestly, the farm's owner, discovered them, he began an ambitious rescue attempt. He and a friend were lowered down the gully on ropes—along with his two Border collies, Jaff and Moss. Mr Priestly was worried that the frightened sheep would panic and dash straight off the ledge, so the two dogs played a vital part in the rescue by penning in the sheep and not letting them get anywhere near the edge. Each sheep was then individually tied to a rope and hoisted up the gully in turn. After all the sheep had been safely rescued, Mr Priestly tried to send the dogs up—but they refused to go. After all, their master was still on the precarious ledge and in danger. Only when the humans had gone would the dogs leave their post—a dedication to duty which earned them both a PDSA silver medal.

John and Cassandra Kraven had not intended to bring their cat Jasper on holiday with them. They had planned to leave him with a friend, but when she had to decline at the last minute, the Kravens dutifully packed Jasper into the car with their two-year-old daughter, Janie, and the rest of their luggage, and headed off for their summer holiday in the wild Adirondack Mountains of America. Four nights later, Janie was playing in the garden of their remote holiday cottage when a large black bear emerged from the woods. Her parents seemed frozen to the spot as it advanced on the toddler, picked her up in its jaws and started to shake her. Jasper appeared from nowhere, shrieking fiercely as he jumped on to the bear's head. He dug his back claws in hard and then leaned forward, slashing at the bear's face. The bear howled in pain and surprise, dropping the little girl and swiping up at its head to try to dislodge the cat. The cat jumped clear and for a moment the two animals just stood staring at one another. Then Jasper ran, plunging into the forest with the enraged bear in hot pursuit. The Kravens bundled their little daughter into the cottage and closed all the doors. Miraculously she was completely unhurt—the bear's teeth had sunk through her loose nightdress. Trapped in the cottage, the family began to fear for their brave cat, but there was no way they could go into the forest to search with the bear out there.

Then, at last, there was a scratching at the door. It was Jasper, tired and ragged but unhurt.

The most special guest of honour was missing from Canada's 1999 Annual Purina Animal Heroes Hall of Fame ceremony. Caesar, a Rottweiler serving with the Edmonton Police Force, had been killed in the line of duty, protecting schoolchildren from a crazed gunman. In June 1998, Caesar and his handler, Constable Randy Goss, had raced to a school after emergency calls reported a man with a shotgun threatening children in the playground. As the maniac turned his gun on the police, Caesar didn't hesitate. The powerful Rottweiler went straight at him and was almost within reach when the gunman opened fire, fatally wounding him. Police officers on the scene returned fire and dropped the gunman, but nothing could be done to save Caesar's life. His handler, PC Goss, paid a moving tribute at the awards ceremony to the dog he had raised from a puppy. 'To define accurately what it feels like to work with an animal so closely, and the flattering feeling it is to know he'd lay down his life for you at any moment in time, it's indescribable,' PC Goss told the audience. 'I considered it the greatest honour I've ever had in the ten years of my work with the Edmonton police service.'

Did you know . . .
elephants never stop growing
throughout their entire lives.

While Ann Paul slept in her home in Waterloo, Ontario, she was bitten by a venomous spider. Her life was saved by the family's American Staffordshire terrier, Norton, who worried her husband awake and alerted him to the problem. Ann was rushed to hospital and spent several days in intensive care. Without Norton's warning, she would almost certainly have died in her sleep from the poison.

CHAPTER FIVE

IT MUST BE LOVE

Susan Duncan of Bellvue, Washington, suffers from multiple sclerosis and today she can only get about with the aid of a cane or a wheelchair. In 1990 she had trained the family dog, Casper, to help fetch her cane, pick up small objects and do other simple chores. When he died unexpectedly the following year, she visited her local animal shelter where she found Joe, a 170-pound Great Dane/Alsatian mix who was only a few days away from being put to sleep.

Susan trained the dog herself and Joe has now given her back some freedom.

In the morning, when Susan's MS is at its worst, Joe removes her bedcovers. He then grabs her pyjama legs gently in his mouth and slowly pulls her towards the edge of the bed. Susan can then swing into a sitting position and Joe takes this as a sign to pull the drawers open in her dressing table. He then brings Susan any clothes that she points out to him.

Whenever the phone rings, Joe picks it up and brings it over to her. And if Susan falls over, Joe is always there to help. He lies down so she can put one arm around his neck, then he raises himself, pulling Susan part of the way up, so it's easier for her to stand.

Joe also helps with household chores and shopping, and carries anything she wants in a backpack that he wears.

Susan says of her clever and loyal helper, 'Joe keeps me more functional and increases my accessibility and decreases my reliance on other people.' She told reporters, 'Everybody thinks I gave Joe a second chance by rescuing him from an animal shelter, but Joe gave me a second chance at life, too.'

In 1913 a woman in Massachusetts, Ann Wigmorem, broke both her legs just above the ankle. She was taken to Middleboro hospital to have the bones set, but after a few days the news was broken to her that gangrene had set in and both legs would have to be amputated.

Ann couldn't believe what she was hearing. Her grandmother had cured many cases of gangrene by recommending a special diet and applying packs of herbs and grasses to the wounds. She refused to give her consent to the operation and was taken home to die.

Ann's parents were enraged by her refusal to undergo the operation, but her uncle gave her his full support. Every day he carried her out into the sun and sat her on a bench. There Ann used to reach down and pull up clumps of the long grass, which she ate. She was very lonely, though, and one day she prayed for a companion.

Shortly afterwards a companion did appear—in the form of a small white dog that seemed to come from nowhere. Ann named it Little Angel, and every day it used to visit her, sitting in the shade cast by her bench and always within petting distance.

169

Every so often the little dog would reach up, and without putting pressure on Ann's legs, would lick the greenish gangrene patches.

This 'treatment' continued for quite a while, and eventually Anne found that the pain had diminished and that the gangrene was actually slowly vanishing.

One of her neighbours was a surgeon, who used to stop by every now and then. On this particular day he looked at her legs and couldn't believe his eyes. The gangrene had completely disappeared. Neither he nor any of the doctors at the hospital could explain the 'miracle cure'.

Did you know ...
the world's smallest mammal is the bumble-bee bat. It lives in Thailand and is, quite literally, the size of a large bumble-bee.

American President Calvin Coolidge had a pet canary, Snowflake. One day, Washington reporter Bascom Timmols came to the White House to interview the President, accompanied by his cat. Rather than acting like Sylvester and Tweetie-Pie, the cat and the bird loved each other on sight. Shortly after the interview, the President sent Snowflake over to the newspaperman's house to live with his new feline friend. According to Timmols, his cat was enchanted by the canary's singing.

170

In return, the canary would walk up and down on the cat's back, and was allowed to rest between his paws.

Peter the macaw was a tough old bird, but there was one thing that worried him—the over-amorous advances of Prudence, another macaw that shared his home at the Frome Pets and Aquatic Centre run by Jayne and Angus Hart. The final straw was when Prudence snuggled up to Peter in the shop's aviary. So desperate was he to escape her clutches that he flew straight out, smashing through the pet-shop window into the wild beyond.

After his break for freedom Mrs Hart said, 'I knew they weren't getting on very well and Prudence made him a bit nervous, but I didn't think it was this bad.'

Mrs Hart bought the South American green-winged macaw, worth £1,000, in 1998 to cheer up lonely Prudence. She took an instant liking to Peter—but the feeling wasn't mutual. When the birds were introduced to each other in the aviary, Peter would always fly back into his own cage and stay there. Recounting his dramatic escape, Mrs Hart said, 'He just shot across the room and through the window like a bullet. It was like something out of a cartoon.'

Peter actually has quite a good chance of survival in the wilds around Frome. His thick feathers will keep him warm and his size is likely to discourage predators. He could feed off the bark of oak, pine and apple trees.

According to animal expert Emma Magnus, macaws are actually 'choosy' lovers who can be just as selective in choosing their partners as humans are.

Melvyn and Sara Scott's two pets are the best of friends—which is quite unusual because Brandy is a Jack Russell and Smurf is a ferret.

The pair are best pals and like to chase each other around the garden, but their friendship really paid off when Brandy went missing after being let off his leash while out walking with Mrs Scott in Graves Park, Sheffield.

He ran off into thick undergrowth and, just as Mrs Scott caught sight of him, scampered down a hole, thought to have been dug by foxes. Mrs Scott shouted for him in vain for half an hour and then ran home to call her husband. He enlisted neighbours and friends to help search for Brandy but not a sign was seen or heard of the dog.

The search went on for twelve hours. 'We feared the worst because there hadn't been a whimper from Brandy,' said Mr Scott. 'We tried digging down, but that was no good.'

The terrier was believed to have been trapped about thirty feet along the narrow tunnel, one of a network thought to be running underneath the park. The fire brigade was called and they suggested bringing in a mechanical digger. Then Mr Scott had an idea—enlist the help of Smurf. Dashing home, Mr Scott returned with Smurf and a long washing line, which was tied around the animal. The ferret was placed at the entrance of the hole where Brandy was last seen. Immediately his natural instincts took over and he ran inside.

After a while, Smurf reappeared, safe but alone. Then, just when they were about to give up, he was followed out by Brandy, who was wearing a broad grin.

Mrs Scott said, 'I couldn't believe it when Smurf came out of the hole with Brandy right behind him. I was in tears. I thought he was trapped or buried alive. We were so relieved when he eventually came out.'

Fire brigade sub-officer Peter Mathias said, 'We thought the only alternative was to try to bring in a JCB and dig him out. Then Mr Scott had his brainwave and went home to get Smurf.'

Jana and her family, who lived in Montana, had two great cats, Chubby, a young orange tabby, and his mother, Christmas, named because of her beautiful snow-white coat.

Chubby was an inquisitive cat, always getting into scrapes and on one occasion breaking his tail. Then one day his inquisitiveness got the better of him and he literally walked out of the family's lives. At first the family were very sad, but always thought that he'd be back. After the months began to pass though, they accepted he was gone for ever, and would wonder what he was doing and who he was living with.

Then, one tragic day, there was a house fire which destroyed their home and killed Christmas. The family were even more devastated, but once they got their lives back in order they decided to get another cat. In the local evening news 'Pet of the Week' spot, Jana saw a beautiful grey cat that was up for adoption. By a strange coincidence, the cat, named Smokey, had been saved from a cabin fire. Jana decided that Smokey was the cat for her, and the next day went to the cattery to adopt her.

There she was shown Smokey's cage, but the cat that really caught her eye was in the cage next to it. Here was a very familiar-looking tabby: Chubby. It was definitely him; the bump on his tail from the earlier fracture meant there was no doubting the fact.

Jana brought Chubby back to the family's new house, eighteen months after he disappeared and none the worse for his travels.

During the nineteenth century, Dr W Sturgill, a physician for the Norfolk and Western Railroad, once treated a dog he found caught in some barbed wire near one of the tracks. The dog recovered and was released and that was the last Dr Sturgill saw of him.

Well, until a year later, that is. One day there was a scratching at the door. The doctor went to investigate, and standing there was the same dog he had treated, this time with another dog whose paws were bleeding. Both dogs looked up plaintively at the doctor as if asking him for help. Somehow the first dog had remembered where he went for treatment and had communicated this to his friend. Dr Sturgill treated the second dog's injuries, which were relatively minor, and watched them walk off together down the street.

Mrs Roundtree's dog Duke was an old cocker spaniel who was sadly almost blind. With barely any sight left, he was confused and unable to find his way about once past the front door.

One day Mrs Roundtree was looking out of a window when she noticed her cat, Bos'n, in the street with the bewildered dog. As she stared in amazement, she saw Bos'n nudge Duke from one side to the other, gently guiding him back to the house.

From that momentous day onwards, Bos'n took control as Duke's 'guide dog', helping him navigate and keeping an eye open for obstacles in his path. He helped Duke get from place to place and even made sure he didn't step too near the edge of Mrs Roundtree's porch, where there was no guard rail. Duke might have been old and blind, but Bos'n ensured he still had a quality of life in his remaining years.

I've heard of a similar thing happening at a donkey sanctuary, where a blind donkey was helped by two sighted donkeys who positioned themselves either side of him.

Incidentally, Charles Darwin also reported several crows who fed one of their own kind after it had lost its eyesight.

A pet store in Fresno, California, featured a large glass-walled aviary containing a tree. The aviary was filled with all sorts of exotic parrots, who'd each marked out various branches as their own territory. One day a small green parrot was introduced into the aviary, but was immediately shunned by the older and bigger birds. Every time he tried to find a space on one of the branches, the other birds forced him off by flapping their wings, squawking and pecking him. This happened every time he tried to alight on a new branch. Soon there was only one space left for him to try—and this was next to a large long-billed macaw.

The little parrot reluctantly climbed on to the macaw's branch and began to edge sideways, closer and closer to the macaw, which was now studying him intently. Suddenly the macaw raised his wing and the small green parrot was rooted to the spot. But instead of signalling the start of yet more territorial screeching, the macaw continued to hold his wing up.

Wasting no time, the little parrot nervously moved closer and took shelter under the macaw's welcoming and friendly wing.

The whole scene was witnessed by Becky Long, who said she had never seen such a 'moment of pure sweetness', adding, 'Before this I never really gave a lot of thought to the expression "taking someone under your wing".'

Did you know . . .
ants have demonstrated that they
can lift stones fifty times their own
weight and pull loads three
hundred times their own weight.
Their brains are also proportionally
much larger compared to their
bodies than any other animal.

When an elderly Budapest couple lost their dog down a ventilation shaft, they were thrilled when a stranger volunteered to climb all the way down and rescue him. He was as good as his word, ushering the dog to safety. So thrilled were the couple that they immediately went home with their dog, leaving the man trapped down the ventilation shaft. He spent four days alone at the bottom of the shaft before the owners realised what they'd done!

No one knew who owned him, where he came from or what his name was, but it was very obvious that the golden Labrador sitting by the roadside was waiting for someone. There he sat, rain or shine, summer or winter, on the side of a little B road between the signposts for Corsham and Trowbridge in Wiltshire. Eventually the local villagers took an interest in him. They nicknamed him Winston, fed him and even built a roadside shelter for him to make those long winter days and nights spent waiting just that little bit more bearable. He lived there until he died—and no one ever found out who he belonged to or who he was waiting for so devotedly.

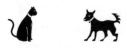

It was possibly the strangest story of unrequited love ever, when Dylan the raccoon fell in love with *Coronation Street* landlady Bet Gilroy. Until he clamped eyes on Bet, played by Julie Goodyear, Dylan had been nothing but trouble at the animal sanctuary near Litchfield in Staffordshire where he lived. Diagnosed as hyperactive, he would be into everything—until he heard the *Coronation Street* music start. Then he would sit mesmerised in front of the telly. 'He just sits there all gooey-eyed when Bet is on the screen,' sanctuary owner Rob Smith told reporters. 'We've taped several episodes . . . and when we want a bit of peace and quiet we just play Dylan a videotape.'

Mark Twain reported a very unusual friendship he observed at the zoological gardens in Marseilles; that between a cat and an African elephant. The cat used to climb up one of the elephant's rear legs to reach his back so it could lie in the sun. Time and time again the elephant would pick the cat up delicately with its trunk, and deposit it gently back on the ground. The cat, though, refused to go away and climbed up again, and again, and again. Eventually the elephant gave in and let the cat climb up whenever it liked, and the two became firm friends.

Louis XIV of France loved dogs but suffered from ailurophobia—the fear of cats. He spent 200,000 gold francs on the construction of royal kennels at Versailles and reserved seventy forests and 800 royal parks for the training of more than a thousand of his hounds. Although there were hundreds of royal retainers, Louis is believed to have personally fed his dogs himself. This usually took place under the huge dining-room table in the Versailles Palace Hall of Mirrors, much to the annoyance of his wife and mistresses when they were present.

The dogs probably never went hungry, considering that Louis's average dinner consisted of four plates of soup, one whole pheasant, two slices of ham, salad, mutton, pastry, fruit, hard-boiled eggs and ice cream.

In 1676 Louis was presented with a meal prepared by one of the foremost chefs in the whole of France, Le Grand Valtel. The King could not finish all of it and requested what was probably the world's first doggy bag. Valtel was so mortified by the thought of his creation being fed to some dogs that he committed suicide.

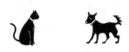

Fidget the cat belonged to a Bournemouth pensioner, who set off one day to visit friends in Southampton. Tragically, the pensioner was knocked down by a bus and severely injured. He lay in a coma for several days before dying.

During this time, Fidget was looked after by a neighbour, but on the day of the funeral, the cat was nowhere to be seen. The neighbour had to give up looking to get ready for the service, but when he arrived at the cemetery, there was Fidget. The groundsman said that the cat had arrived early that morning and had just waited patiently by his master's open grave.

The cat remained like this until the coffin was slowly lowered, then, as if his respects had been paid, turned around and ambled sadly home.

Ralph Helfer changed the way animals were trained in Hollywood. Before he got involved in the industry, cruelty was often used to 'persuade' an animal to perform. Ralph recognised the importance of using the carrot rather than the stick and developed what he called 'affection training', using love and a gentle approach with his animal actors.

Proving all his critics wrong, Ralph soon demonstrated how his technique paid off, managing to get even fierce creatures like lions and tigers to work safely alongside small children. One day, though, his method was put to the test following an accident on the Hollywood freeway. Ralph was in a car towing a fully grown lioness named Tammy in a specially designed trailer. They were nearly at the studio when the hitch on the car snapped. The trailer broke loose and slid across the freeway on its own, eventually overturning, rupturing one of its sides. Ralph could only watch helplessly as Tammy crawled out of the wreckage, dazed and confused, with blood streaming down her face, making it almost impossible for her to see. She staggered about the freeway as cars zoomed past her. There was a great danger that Tammy would either get hit, or, if she made a break for it, would reach the residential area nearby.

Ralph got out of the car and slowly approached Tammy, calling out to her in the sweetest, calmest voice he could muster. By now cars had stopped to watch the drama; terrified drivers were cowering behind locked doors as Tammy wandered within feet of their vehicles. Ralph slowly reduced the distance between them, all the time calling out to Tammy to stay calm. Slowly but surely Tammy made her way towards him, resisting her fear and the instinct to run away.

Ralph described the scene in his book, *The Beauty of Beasts*: 'A lump was forming in my throat. Here was this blind lion on the freeway, battered and nearly unconscious, limping towards the sound of my voice. To this day I have never been more proud of our affection training.'

Ralph comforted the lioness until a veterinary van arrived to take her away for treatment . . .

Did you know . . .
a butterfly's eye has 17,000
different lenses.

Eleven-year-old Richard Beale from Erdington, Birmingham, loves his five-year-old golden retriever Chad. The two are inseparable but the relationship goes much deeper than just playmates. Richard suffers from epilepsy and has seizures on average twice a month. Somehow Chad knows instinctively when Richard is about to have a fit, and attracts the attention of Richard's mother Ruth, allowing her to take precautions, such as placing Richard in a certain position so that he doesn't injure himself.

She says, 'On many occasions, Chad and Richard have been together in the dining room while I am in the kitchen. Chad had suddenly come running in to paw at me and bark, letting me know that a seizure is on the way.'

Dogs are known to be extremely sensitive to the body's electrical activity, which is highly affected by epilepsy. It's thought that Chad is somehow able to detect changes in the electrical impulses generated by Richard's brain. Whatever the explanation, Chad is an invaluable early-warning system.

'Chad is my best friend and it's great that he helps me,' says Richard.

King the German shepherd was devoted to Philip Friedman, the grandfather of the family he lived with in Brooklyn, New York. But sadly, the old man was in ill health and passed away in the summer of 1975. At the moment of his going, King somehow knew and began to howl inconsolably, even though he was in another part of the house. When the family attended the funeral, King took the opportunity to escape. The family came home to find him gone. For three weeks they searched everywhere for him, trying all his favourite haunts, but there was no sign of him. In desperation, they tried the cemetery where the grandfather had been buried and asked the groundskeeper if he'd seen a German shepherd. The groundskeeper said he had. At two o'clock every day for the past three weeks, as regular as clockwork, he'd seen a German shepherd walk up to the old man's grave and lie down on top of it, whimpering and moaning. At first he'd tried to scare the dog away, but King had snarled at him and seen him off. He then realised that the faithful dog was doing nothing wrong—he was just paying his last respects to someone he loved very much.

The ancient Egyptians thought so much of cats that they could not bear to see harm come to them. There was no such thing as a stray. All cats were fed and looked after and loved—and woe betide you if you harmed one. The penalty was death! Playing on this, their sworn enemies the Persians once marched into battle holding cats in their arms. Rather than risk any harm coming to the cats in the ensuing battle, the Egyptians immediately surrendered.

If a fire ever broke out, the ancient Egyptian equivalent of the fire brigade were told to save the cats first—and worry about the people later. Should a cat actually die, it would often be buried with little pots of milk to lap up in the afterlife.

Evidence of how precious cats were to the Egyptians can be seen in their law that forbade the export of any cat (although some did find their way abroad, probably smuggled out by Phoenician traders).

If you're wondering what ancient Egyptian moggies looked like, the closest counterpart today is the Abyssinian, or a breed

185

unrecognised in Britain but thriving in America called the Egyptian Mau.

During the Second World War, Bobs, a fox terrier, was the ship's dog on board HMS *Tornado*. One day the ship was attacked by a German U-boat and started sinking. All the crew abandoned ship and Bobs found himself in a drifting life raft with ten men who were all unconscious. The raft was taking in water and the men were in danger of drowning, but Bobs saved their lives by barking persistently until he was heard by the crew of nearby HMS *Radiant*, who steamed to the rescue.

Cats have been kept as pets for at least 4,500 years. You can even see a picture of a house cat proudly wearing a lotus-blossom collar on an Egyptian tomb dating back to 2600 BC. In fact, the relationship may go back even further than this. Remains on Cyprus have suggested that people were keeping pet cats as long ago as 6000 BC! Dogs, on the other hand, have probably been our constant companions for the last 10,000 years.

One of the grandest dogs' homes must be the one that puppies Nicki and Carla live in. It's a $100,000 furnished three-bedroom house in Memphis, Tennessee—and they live there on their own. The house used to belong to their owner, Helen Walsh, who lived there alone apart from her two canine companions. The trio would sleep and even watch TV together. Before Helen died in 1987, she left provision in her will to make sure the dogs were well cared for. After they die, the house will be sold, with the money going to charity.

In the meantime, Helen's niece, Sister Mary Greaber, stops by the brick house twice a day to feed the dogs and take them for walks. She told reporters, 'To be perfectly honest, a lot of humans don't live as well as Nicki and Carla, but anyone who knows these two dogs can't begrudge them a thing. They're two of the most lovable pets in the world.'

It was the wedding of the year—for frogs at least. On 13 March 1999, hundreds of (human) guests assembled at a Hindu temple in Gauhati in India to bless the union of two frogs. A third frog acted as bridesmaid. In this case froggy didn't go a-courting—it was an arranged marriage. The couple were fixed up in a bid to please the rain gods when the expected seasonal monsoon was delayed. The couple enjoyed a full three-hour ceremony, presided over by two Hindu priests. 'There was no other option,' explains Mrs Nizara Pathak, who became the bride's foster mother, in keeping with tradition.

The change in Bobby was dramatic. Only a few years earlier he had been a grade-A student in his Boston high school; now he was suffering from severe depression, withdrawing so much that his friends left him. Worse still, his condition deteriorated so that he became vegetable-like, unable to talk or move. Psychiatrists were unable to offer any explanation or hope. All Bobby would do was sit motionless in a chair, staring blankly ahead, not even moving his eyes.

Then one day, out of the blue, he responded to a picture of a cat in a magazine—nothing significant, but his eyes moved for the first time in months. This reaction happened whenever Bobby was shown a picture of a cat, so the family decided to go one better—they bought him a small kitten.

Immediately Bobby was introduced to his new companion, he turned to look at it, then started to stroke it. A couple of hours later, Bobby spoke to the kitten—slowly at first but improving more quickly every day. Playing with the cat was the best therapy Bobby could have hoped for. The same psychiatrists who had given up on him a few months earlier were baffled by his amazing recovery—it was nothing short of a miracle.

Bobby's progress continued at such an amazing rate that soon he was able to go back to school and catch up on the education he'd missed. Although he was reintroduced to his friends, his greatest pal would always be the cat that helped him to get his life back.

Benny Subo wanted everything to be perfect when he proposed to his girlfriend. He took her to their special place, a marina in Los Angeles, went down on one knee, produced the ring, began, 'Will you—' and then a pelican relieved itself on his head. Benny wasn't amused. He sued the marina's owners.

Humans often propose with a diamond—and penguins do something remarkably similar. If a male penguin finds a female attractive, he presents her with the largest, shiniest rock he can find. If she 'accepts', they're officially a couple.

In 1992, a study of 5,000 men at Australia's Baker Research Institute revealed that owning a dog actually lowers a man's cholesterol levels, making him less susceptible to heart disease. The researchers claimed that the benefits come from the relaxing effects of stroking a pet.

A similar study carried out by the University of Pennsylvania showed that heart patients with companion animals showed a higher rate of survival. The American Heart Association reported that blood pressure and heart rate were reduced by simply petting a dog.

Did you know . . .
tigers absolutely hate the smell of
alcohol! Keepers who work with
tigers should never drink, because if
the tiger can smell it on a human's
breath they are far more likely
to attack.

In 1921, a real-life Tarzan emerged from the bush near Grahamstown, South Africa. Lucas, as he was later christened, was twelve, and had been raised since he was an infant by a troop of baboons. Slowly but surely he adapted to living in the humans' world and became a farm worker. Now able to speak both Afrikaans and English, he later revealed a tantalising glimpse of what life was like living as a baboon. 'I can recall only a few incidents of my life among the baboons,' he said. 'My food consisted mainly of crickets, ostrich eggs, prickly pears, green mealies and wild honey. I was kicked on the head by an ostrich while raiding its nest and was often stung by bees while robbing their hives, and once fell and broke my leg. While with the baboons I walked on all fours and slept in the bush entirely naked.'

Even stranger, in 1931 a man was reported to have been found living with a pride of lions in South Africa.

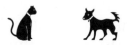

Spot was a cheery mongrel who lived in North Chingford, and was very, very restless. He hated staying at home all day and made friends with a road sweeper, accompanying him on his rounds in the town. Eventually the road sweeper retired but Spot didn't seem to get on as well with his replacement. Looking for someone else to attach himself to, Spot made friends with the postman instead, and after that, accompanied him delivering letters all round the streets.

Mademoiselle Dympny was a great harpist in the seventeenth century and claimed she owed her success to her cat. Whenever she played, she constantly looked for her cat's signs of pleasure or displeasure—and reacted to this feedback accordingly to improve her performance.

Ignace Paderewski, the famous Polish pianist and composer, also loved to have his cat around him when he played. He claimed that one of his compositions, 'Cat's Fugue', was inspired by his own cat walking up and down the keyboard one day.

Paderewski's debut in London was at St James's, where he was nervous and disappointed to find only about one hundred people in the theatre. Just before he went on he whispered in the ear of the house cat, 'Wish me luck.' The cat responded by jumping up on to his lap and purring.

The performance was a huge success, and to thank the cat for being such a good omen, he performed the 'Cat's Fugue' for it alone after the show.

One of the strangest Victorian fairground attractions was 'The Happy Family'—a diverse collection of animals who were traditional enemies but who had learned instead to live together happily. The Happy Family was invented by a poor labourer from Lambeth called Charles Garbett. His cat had lost her kittens and—quite amazingly—she'd adopted some orphaned baby rats as her own. It was such a sight that Garbett found he could charge people money to see it. Realising he was on to a good thing, Garbett turned his cat and her adopted rat babies into a fairground show and then carefully started adding other natural enemies to the family.

By 1860, when the show was displayed in a booth at the Windsor Onion Fair, it was reported to have included three dogs—Rose, Tom and Lumpy—a raven, four monkeys, two cats, four pigeons, three hawks, two ducks, four guinea pigs, two ferrets, two rabbits, thirteen rats, one cock, two hens, one badger, two 'kangaroo opossums', one hare and one raccoon!

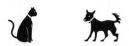

When Dan and Marilyn Walland noticed that their goose Sheila was feeling lonely and unloved, they did what any caring pet owners would do—they advertised for a boyfriend for her in the lonely-hearts column of a local newspaper. 'Goose recently widowed,' ran the advertisement, 'seeks gander for meaningful relationship.' Sheila had been off her food and fading fast since she lost her boyfriend Fred, and Dan and Marilyn had had no luck in finding any suitable partners within a hundred-mile radius of their home in Gammergill, North Yorkshire. Every gander they came across was spoken for. The lonely-hearts ad was their last hope—and it worked! Within an hour, they got a call from a local man whose gander had recently become a widower. A blind date was swiftly arranged for Sheila and her prospective boyfriend—also called Fred. Nerves were frayed. Would they like each other, or would Fred honk Sheila off? They needn't have worried. One look at each other and it was love. Sheila and Fred have now settled down together and are expected to start a family soon.

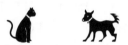

Billy Thomas couldn't take it any more. He liked cats, but sharing his Wakefield home with 129 of them was driving him round the twist. So he gave his wife Christine an ultimatum: 'Either they go or I do.' The very next day Billy was looking for a new home. 'I don't mind him going,' Christine said. 'He's just made room for me to adopt more cats!'

An orphanage in Nairobi, Kenya, is looking for some very special foster parents for the little ones. They have to be mature, skilful, well balanced—and elephants! The David Shelton Elephant Orphanage takes in baby elephants that have been orphaned by poachers before they've had a chance to learn the skills they'll need to survive in the wild. By pairing the babies up with adult elephant foster parents, the orphanage has found that they quickly learn from their elders and can safely be released after a year into one of Kenya's protected wildlife parks.

Purdey the cat got into a terrible scrape one night when she accidentally became impaled on a two-foot-long iron spike left carelessly lying about on some waste ground. Despite the pain, she somehow dragged herself home, the spike still embedded in her, but collapsed just after pulling herself through the cat-flap, dislodging the spike in the process.

Her owner, Karen, was unaware of the accident until the morning, but everything was all right. Her Labrador Max had licked the wounds clean and had kept Purdey warm. Karen told reporters, 'I could tell by the way her fur was wet that he had looked after her.'

Purdey was rushed to the vet, where she recovered from her ordeal—all thanks to the care and attention given to her by Max.

Pensioner Frank Mattingley lay in a coma in a Southampton hospital, motionless and silent— apart from occasionally whispering the name

of his collie, Tipper. The doctors felt they had nothing to lose, so Tipper was brought to the hospital and allowed to see his master lying still in his bed. Tipper took one look at him and barked; Frank stirred and sat up—and from that moment on made a miraculous recovery.

Did you know . . .
camels can drink up to twenty-six
gallons of water at a time.

Jim Bull of Newport on the Isle of Wight hit on an ingenious plan to scare off a heron that turned up now and again to eat the fish and frogs in his garden pond. He installed a large plastic dummy heron to frighten the real bird away. Things couldn't have gone more wrong, though. Instead of being intimidated, the real heron fell hopelessly in love with the dummy and started turning up every single night to perform a mating dance—before eating the contents of the pond!

It was love at first sight when Scott Brand stumbled over a little lost puppy while out walking near his Minnesota home. The puppy waddled over to him, licked his hand affectionately and then started rubbing at his legs. How could Paul resist? He scooped the animal up and took it home, giving it a big meal of hamburgers and milk before bed. The puppy was given the freedom of the house, but soon proved to be unusually destructive—even by puppy standards. One day, for instance, Paul came home to find that his three-piece suite had been almost shredded. He really didn't want to get rid of the puppy, however, so in desperation he called in the vet, who took one look at the puppy and was straight on the phone. Half an hour later, two zoo keepers arrived to recover their lost four-month-old lion cub!

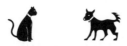

Sophie was the perfect bridesmaid at Yssanne Wheatley and Senior RAF Aircraftsman Gut Bentley's wedding in April 1998. Like any eight-year-old, she was as pretty as a picture, with a garland of flowers adorning her hair, standing dutifully beside the bride throughout the ceremony and being as good as gold all through the reception. Afterwards, the happy couple left for their honeymoon—and Sophie retired gracefully to her dog basket. It had been a big day for the lurcher, who had been rescued from a dogs' home by Yssanne's parents four years before. 'I didn't know which of my four best friends to choose,' Yssanne recalls. 'Sophie seemed the perfect answer. The two of us are great pals and the vicar didn't mind, so that was that.'

Linda Reischel of Flushing, New York, finds homes for stray animals. She was out in the severe blizzards of February 1996 with her friend Helen Scher when they spotted a small black terrier near a tree in a local park (they later named him Sparky). They put a leash round his neck and tried to coax him into Linda's car, but the dog wouldn't come. He strained against the leash to get back to the tree, and all the while the snow was getting heavier.

When they got close to the tree they found a rope tied around the trunk—and tied to the other end was another dog, heavily pregnant, now buried up to its nose in the snow. Once the girls released this second animal, Sparky came willingly with them. The bitch later gave birth to seven puppies and all were fine— thanks to Sparky, who'd refused to leave without her.

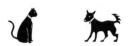

Little Romana Strasser lived in Aurolzmuenster in Austria with her family and their two pets—a 700-pound prize boar and a five-year-old Alsatian, Afra. She was playing in the garden in March 1974 when the boar broke loose from its pen and charged her, hurling her up into the air and trying to gore her as she lay helpless on the ground.

Hearing her screams for help, Afra leapt on to the boar's back and grabbed its ear, pulling its head back and giving Romana vital moments to crawl to safety. While Afra distracted the boar, Romana's father managed to restrain it and quickly called an ambulance. Romana underwent several operations but recovered from her injuries—only thanks to Afra, who took on a 700-pound boar to save her.

When her keepers decided it was time for Koko the gorilla to become a mum, they even let her choose her mate, by the wonders of video-dating. Koko was provided with ten different videotaped 'interviews' with prospective suitors so that she could judge them on appearance, body language and general 'hunkiness'. Koko eventually chose Ndume, a ten-year-old from Cincinnati Zoo.

After Howard M. Chaplin's black cocker spaniel, Peter, died, he decided to start a collection of books about dogs in his memory. By 1920 he had more than ninety titles at his

Rhode Island home, and by 1937, the collection had grown to nearly 2,000 volumes. There were books in ten different languages, including the first ever published in England about dogs, *De Canibus Britannicus.* There are now over 3,000 books in Mr Chaplin's collection and each one has a bookplate featuring the little dog who inspired the library.

They say an elephant never forgets. Perhaps the same is true of dogs. In 1988 John Rayner, who was disabled, was at home in St Petersburg, Florida, when he heard a screech of brakes followed by a dull thud and a whimper. He hobbled out to see a car driving off into the distance and a battered stray dog lying in the road. He took in the dog, whom he named Sheena, and nursed her back to health. It was a gesture that Sheena wouldn't forget; she repaid this kindness four years later when John was attacked by muggers.

John had left Sheena in his car as he went food shopping, but on his way back, he was confronted by two youths. The first hit him and grabbed his wallet, but John managed to lash out with his walking stick and hit his accomplice, temporarily winding him. The first mugger then pushed John against his car and began beating him. As he was being punched and battered John knew there was only one way he could save himself. Dropping one of his arms that was protecting his head, he managed to undo the car door. Sheena, who'd been watching the whole attack, had been waiting for this moment. She threw her whole weight against the door, knocking the youth to the ground, then bit his face while he desperately tried to knock her off. The mugger was in agony as her teeth sank in, and his shrieks attracted attention. In minutes the police had arrived, but not before both muggers had fled the scene of the crime. John owed his life to Sheena; just as she owed hers to him.

In January 1996, London Zoo had a very special arrival—the first tiger cub born there for more than thirty years. Sadly, Hari—a very rare Sumatran tiger—was abandoned by his mum at birth. Keepers took to hand-raising the feisty little cub, but they were worried that he'd miss out on playing with others of his own kind and grow up thinking he was human rather than tiger. They searched all over for a companion cub for Hari, but there was none of the right age. Keepers then fell back on Plan B and introduced Hari to a very special playmate called Liffy, a Japanese Akita dog. The Akita is a tough breed, more than able to stand up to a tiger cub's rough play, and the two quickly became the best of friends, tussling and wrestling like two regular cubs. 'He's not a tiger,' said one of Hari's keepers, 'but at least he's got four legs and a tail!'

Pigeon-fancier John Elsworth from Houston, Texas, thought up a novel way to propose to his girlfriend. He decided to deliver his proposal by homing pigeon. However, the bird strayed off course and flew to the home of one Rita Williams instead. Rita read the note and invited John to call her. When he met Rita, John fell in love at first sight, and the couple got married very shortly afterwards!

It'll never catch on here. The Japanese have gone completely crazy over giant beetles and are keeping them as pets. There is even a magazine devoted to beetle owners called *Gekkan Mushi* (*Beetle Monthly*). Top specimens can reach quite staggering prices too. You could expect to pay £26,000 for a pair of rare Okuwagata beetles from Tokyo's exclusive Tobu department store, and in 1999, a company president paid a staggering £52,000 for a giant stag beetle! If your pockets don't run that deep you can get more common-or-garden varieties of beetle for just £2.10—from

202

special vending machines. Yes, vending machines. Japanese newspapers have reported that the beetle vending machines are selling out every day of the week, with people travelling over a hundred miles just to drop their 400 yen in the slot and pick up their new pet. Japanese animal groups have complained about sticking beetles in the machines as if they were cans of fizzy drinks or chocolate bars, but the company running the machines insists that the cool, dark, quiet interiors are perfect habitats for the insects.

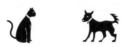

Beauty the tortoiseshell cat was the perfect loving mother. She was already nursing three kittens, but didn't say no when her owner, John Paling, introduced her to a very unusual orphaned baby—Sammy the squirrel. She fed and groomed him too. As the kittens grew up, they just saw Sammy as a brother and readily accepted him, allowing him to join in their games. John described him as a 'squitten'!

Despite being raised alongside three cats—or perhaps because of it—Sammy took being released back into the wild very well. A dominant local male squirrel, nicknamed Ivan the Terrible, tried bullying Sammy, but all that fighting practice with the kittens had made him pretty tough. He flipped Ivan over and pinned him down with ease!

Did you know . . .
humans spend one third of their
lives asleep, while domestic cats
and koalas are officially two of the
doziest animals on earth, spending
two-thirds of their lives sleeping.

M. Desroches, a prosperous French baker, loved his cat and was heartbroken when it went missing. He spent hours searching nearby streets with a recent photograph of his pet, asking anyone he came across if they'd seen it.

Unfortunately no one had, and M. Desroches had to resort to some drastic measures. He closed his bakery and spent a small fortune on producing 80,000 'wanted' posters featuring his cat and offering a large reward.

He then walked the streets sticking them on lamp-posts, fences, trees—as many places as he could find. He worked his way outwards from his bakery, often walking several miles in a day, but even months later, no one had reported seeing his beloved cat.

Worse was to come. Since he'd closed his bakery, a rival shop had opened and had taken all his customers.

Even after that M. Desroches continued his lonely walks. Now that his business had failed, it was only the hope of finding his cat that kept him going. One day he was walking past a wooded area when out jumped his cat! He was overjoyed. Even though he'd lost his business, he'd found his cat—and she was worth more to him than anything in the world.

Jean Ricord of Nice in France was devoted to Coco, her dog. They were a popular pair and travelled everywhere together. Of course, when Jean died suddenly of a heart attack aged fifty-nine, her loss was mourned by all her friends—but none more than Coco.

The week after her mistress died, Coco refused to leave the balcony of their fourth-floor apartment, spending the day looking down on the street where she used to go walkies every day.

At the end of that week, Jean Ricord's funeral cortège went by, at which point Coco seemed to perk up. As the procession passed beneath her, she launched herself off the balcony and plunged to the ground. It was as if she'd decided that although separated from her mistress in life, she'd be reunited in death.

The mourners were so taken aback by Coco's suicide that they buried her with her owner so that they'd never be parted.

The doctors had a huge medical file on little

Arran Taylor, but none of them could work out what was wrong with him—or how to cure him. At seven years of age, the youngster from Belfast refused to speak to anyone and had extreme learning difficulties. Arran's family had all but given up on the medical profession finding a cure when his grandmother read about a girl with a similar condition who had been treated at the Dolphin Research Center in Florida by swimming with the dolphins. The treatment wasn't cheap—it cost £5,000—but Arran's family determinedly set out to raise the money by holding raffles and quiz nights. It took them a year, but finally they were able to set out for Florida. At the Dolphin Research Center they met Dr David Nathanson—or 'Dr Dave' as everyone soon came to call him—who had been working with children and dolphins for eight years and who is convinced dolphins want to help children with special needs.

'Dolphins love playing with children,' he explains. 'I have no doubt that they sense and see that these children are less independent than others. I've seen dolphins watch children with cerebral palsy and then use their mouths to help move the children's legs.'

At first little Arran was scared of the dolphins, but he soon got the hang of the reward scheme. Dr Dave showed Arran a picture of a cow and the little boy uttered the first word he had ever spoken—'cow'. Two weeks into the therapy, Arran was riding on the backs of the dolphins, roaring with laughter and having a brilliant time.

The dolphin therapy couldn't cure Arran, of course, but doctors back home were impressed by the improvement in him. It was as if the dolphins had switched him on somehow, making him more receptive to learning—and open to the day-to-day teaching which can help him further.

When a woman tried to snatch nineteen-month-old toddler Joseph Walters from his garden in Wolverhampton, his dog Pluto leapt to his defence. He grabbed Joseph's trouser leg and clung on for dear life, refusing to let the child go at any price. His snarling alerted Joseph's mum and she rushed out. The woman fled—without Joseph. Wolverhampton police praised Pluto's action, saying that without the faithful dog, Joseph would almost certainly have been abducted.

'Man bites dog' is a cliché, but how about 'Woman kisses dog'? It happened in a poodle parlour in Massachusetts in December 1988. When Escape, a greyhound, suffered what appeared to be a heart attack, the owner of the parlour, Patricia Lopez, leapt into action to revive him, giving the dog heart massage and the kiss of life.

After a few minutes Escape started coughing and then regained consciousness. The episode was reported in the *New York Times*, which quoted Patricia as saying, 'I don't mind kissing dogs but would rather not perform mouth-to-mouth again.'

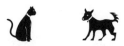

A walk in the wilds would almost certainly have ended in disaster for the Harger family if it hadn't been for their scruffy old mongrel Scotty. On 27 December 1997, twelve-year-old Misty Harger became hopelessly separated from her parents while they were out walking in woods bordering the Buffalo River Canyon in Arkansas. While police helicopters with heat-seeking cameras, and a hundred searchers with bloodhounds failed to locate her, Scotty sneaked away from home and tracked her down himself within a couple of hours. He stayed with the girl as she wandered disorientated in the forest, and when she took her shoes off after they'd got wet, he seized the opportunity to run off with them and hide them, preventing her from going any deeper into the woods. As night fell, the temperature dropped to minus 8° centigrade, and Misty, who was only wearing light clothing, began to feel the effects of hypothermia. Scotty did the best he could, snuggling up to her and keeping her warm, and preventing her from falling asleep by barking incessantly. Just ninety minutes before a snowstorm broke, Misty and Scotty were finally found by searchers. While a helicopter dashed the little girl to the nearest hospital and safety, Scotty slipped away and trotted home to a hero's welcome.

Koalas do not make good pets. In fact, it's illegal to keep one as a pet, but in 1937, Mrs Oswin Roberts was given special permission to raise an orphaned baby koala in her home at Cowes on Phillip Island, Victoria. The baby, named Edward, slept in a cot and even joined the family at mealtimes, sitting up in a highchair and nibbling his plate of eucalyptus leaves. His favourite activity, apparently, was sitting on Mrs Roberts's head and being taken for a ride around the garden.

It was a classic case of unrequited love. He was a fit, handsome, all-American man. She was a six-foot 150-pound emu. When the emu first set eyes on Ed Stuardi of Mobile, Alabama, it was love at first sight. The besotted bird followed Ed everywhere trying to charm him with her winsome ways. Ed responded by trying to shoo her off with a canoe paddle and by firing his gun in the air. After three days of this somewhat one-sided relationship, Ed swallowed his pride and admitted that this was one female he couldn't handle. He called the Mobile Animal Rescue Foundation and they captured her with nets. The emu, who had been callously dumped by her previous owner, was later given a new home on a farm with plenty of male emus. 'It was the emu mating season and she had her heart set on this man,' said an amused official from the Rescue Foundation.

Rikki, a twenty-month-old corgi, was a devoted mother who refused to leave her four young puppies when a fire broke out in the shed where they lived in Warborough, Oxfordshire. Alerted by the smoke, her owner Dorothy Richards pleaded with Rikki to come out, but she stayed, moving her dogs around to try to keep out of the way of the approaching flames.

Dorothy was beaten back by the blaze, but Rikki was found alive, though quite badly burned, lying over her four babies—three of which had survived the inferno, thanks to their mum. The dog was later awarded a bravery medal by the National Pets Club of Great Britain.

Did you know . . .
it costs approximately £15 to feed
an ant for a year at London Zoo,
compared with over £6,000 for an
elephant.

When Jubalani the baby African elephant was abandoned by his mother, he was inconsolable. Staff at the Hoedspruit Breeding and Research Centre for Endangered Species in South Africa didn't know how to cheer him up—but another one of their animals did. Skaar the sheep adopted him as her own baby and the pair quickly became inseparable, spending all day, every day together.

'Skaar is very good with young wild animals,' says Lente Roode, the owner of the research centre. 'She's always there with Jubalani and she's always friendly, even if he pushes her.'

Jubalani isn't the first exotic baby animal the sheep has adopted. She's also helped to raise baby white rhinos and water buffaloes.

Dinah the red setter was sent away from her beloved home in Cookstown, Ireland, to go to live with a new owner in Lurgan, some twenty miles away. She was pregnant at the time. While at her new home, she gave birth to a litter of five lovely puppies. A couple of days later she disappeared—and the puppies with her. Everyone assumed they'd been stolen—the puppies were much too tiny to have walked off anywhere—but ten days later, Dinah's old owners found her fast asleep in the backyard with all five puppies snuggled around her. She was gaunt and haggard and her feet were red, raw and bleeding. She had brought her puppies all the way home, carrying one in her mouth for a short distance, putting it down, returning to collect the next, then starting the whole long and laborious process again. To get home, she'd have had to swim numerous times across the River Blackwater at Mahery Ferry, which is treacherous, very deep and over eighty yards wide. Each time she would have crossed it with a puppy in her mouth, deposited it safely on the far bank and then returned for the next. After such a heroic effort, it would have been completely heartless to send them back to their new home—and it was agreed that Dinah—and her litter—could stay in the old home she obviously loved so much.

CHAPTER SIX

JUST LIKE ONE OF THE FAMILY

If you're cunning, street smart and a master of disguise, then it's not too difficult to evade police while on the run. Animal trainer Arlan Seidon managed to do it for five years before finally being arrested in Jefferson, Texas. But what made his exploits even more unbelievable was the fact that he was on the run with two fully grown elephants! Each beast required 600 pounds of food a day and was responsible for 500 pounds of droppings—so it's amazing that the police weren't on his scent.

Arlan's 'crime' had been to kidnap the two elephants from their owner in New Jersey because he suspected that they were being abused. The creatures knew him well, having been raised by him before they were sold to their current owner.

The trio spent their first four years as fugitives travelling around the northern United States and Canada before moving down to Texas. Each winter Arlan would load the elephants in a truck and take them down to Florida using the back roads.

In one of my previous books I told you about a bra for cows. Well, not wishing to be outdone, the Dunlop-Enerka factory in Drachten, Holland, has started manufacturing water beds for cows. Costing about £120, these allow the creatures to have a better posture while sleeping, giving them a more comfortable sleep—which in turn results in a higher milk yield.

You could have forgiven the police dispatcher for disbelieving the report filed by Florida Department of Law Enforcement officers Tom Colbert and John Halliday. They had spotted a car being driven erratically on Highway 19, in Clearwater, Florida—and on closer inspection they could see a three-foot iguana in the driving seat, its front feet resting on the steering wheel.

Still thinking they were dreaming, the officers followed the car for several miles before pulling it over. Sure enough, there was a three-foot iguana at the wheel, but slouched right down in the driving seat was the car's owner, John Ruppell, drunk. It turned out that he was driving the car (well, just about), with his pet iguana providing assistance.

He was later charged with drunk-driving (you could almost say he was as drunk as a newt!).

If you see something wriggling beneath Sue Lightfoot's blouse, don't be alarmed. It's only a baby bat that she's adopted. He's kept under her blouse—hanging from her bra strap, to be precise—because the bat, thought to have been accidentally dropped by his mother, needs warmth and the comfort of being next to a heartbeat.

The creature, known as Batty, is a pipistrelle. This breed is Britain's smallest bat but the most common in towns and cities. Mrs Lightfoot's German shepherd found the abandoned bat lying on the floor of her cottage at Exford on Exmoor. He spends most of the day asleep, peeking out for a feed every four hours—milk or water taken from a teaspoon.

Mrs Lightfoot manages a travel agency in Barnstaple in Devon, and her colleagues there have got used to Batty. 'They thought it was a bit strange at first, but now they are totally used to the idea and even get involved in feeding him,' she says.

Sue might be in for a bit of a surprise, though. Bats like Batty can live for up to sixteen years and develop a lifelong bond to their mother, even if she is only adoptive. He might be hanging around for quite some time.

Did you know . . .
giant pandas eat so much bamboo
they have to go to the toilet over
forty times a day.

British lorry driver Tom Gillen refused to listen to friends when they told him that Kathy, his little puppy, would grow into a very, very large dog.

They were right. Kathy was a Pyrenean mountain dog and soon stood nearly a metre high and weighed over 130 pounds.

Despite her size, Tom took Kathy in his cab everywhere. One day, however, he was made redundant and realised that he would have to give her away since it cost too much to care for her. He took her to an animal sanctuary in Kent and warned the carers that Kathy must never be fenced in or put in a kennel—she needed space, and lots of it.

Kathy was soon placed with a new family, but they ignored Tom's warnings. They left her in a room in the house and Kathy ended up jumping through the window. She was later found wandering towards the motorway that led to Tom's house.

This made Kathy famous and she appeared in the national press and on the BBC's *Blue Peter* in a story about just how expensive it can be to look after large dogs. Unable to cope with her bids for freedom, her new owners returned her to the sanctuary. Shortly after the programme went out, the sanctuary received a letter on regal stationery that asked them to put Kathy on a flight from Heathrow addressed to 'The Duchess of Alba, The Palace, Madrid'.

Kathy's new home is a hundred-room castle in Madrid where she has the run of a twenty-five-hectare garden with the other royal dogs.

This next tale sounds too fantastic to be believable, but it is true. Documented in books and in *Life* magazine, it concerns a baboon called Johnny.

The story starts in 1955. Lindsay Schmidt was driving down an Australian country road when he saw a truck up ahead with an engine fire. He stopped, grabbed his own fire extinguisher and managed to put the blaze out before too much damage was done.

The truck driver was so grateful that he offered Lindsay part of his cargo. He happened to own a travelling circus and on the truck were ten baboons. Lindsay wasn't sure if he wanted a baboon. In fact, the idea had never entered his mind. But one of the creatures stepped forward in its cage and looked up with wide eyes as if to say hello, and

Lindsay was immediately smitten. He decided there and then to adopt the baboon and name him Johnny.

They drove back to Lindsay's farm that evening and Lindsay prepared dinner, serving his own on a plate on the table, and putting Johnny's share in a bowl on the floor. Johnny looked at Lindsay's plate, and at his own bowl on the floor. Then he frowned, took his bowl and put it on the table. This was the first of many indications that Lindsay hadn't just acquired a pet, but an equal.

During the days that followed, Lindsay went about his chores on the farm, followed by Johnny, who kept a close eye on what was going on.

One day Lindsay turned round to see Johnny carrying a large bucket of chicken feed, lumbering around with it and distributing it expertly. From then on, feeding the chickens was one of Johnny's jobs. Lindsay wondered if Johnny could help him in other ways. One of the slowest jobs was feeding the sheep. This involved driving out to the pastures in a tractor pulling a trailer full of hay bales. On his own Lindsay would drive the tractor, stop it, clamber on to the trailer, throw off the hay, clamber down again, get back in the tractor and drive on a bit—only to repeat the procedure. Johnny picked the idea up very quickly, riding the trailer and throwing the hay bales off expertly on Lindsay's signal.

One day the tractor hit a hidden rock and Lindsay was thrown out of the cab, landing in its path. He looked up to see the tractor heading straight for him—but then it stopped, a foot from his body. Slowly Lindsay got up, relieved at his lucky escape. As he came round to the cab, there was Johnny in the driver's seat, holding the ignition key in his hairy hand. As soon as he'd seen Lindsay thrown out, he'd jumped from the trailer to the tractor and turned the engine off, something he'd seen Lindsay do a hundred times before.

The two became inseparable friends, and Johnny even learned to drive the tractor around the fields by himself, with reliable witnesses as proof.

Lindsay went on to list Johnny as an employee on his tax returns, which amused the Australian tax authorities, to say the least. However, they investigated the claim and sure enough accepted the description. From then on, Johnny's official status was 'baboon field hand.'

When the Abbey National Building Society was floated on the stock market in 1989, the organisation received a very unusual enquiry from a lady in Eastbourne, who wanted to know whether her pet poodle was entitled to buy shares. The confusion came about because the Abbey's leaflet on share ownership showed a dog digging up a share certificate . . .

In 1991 Optik Paradies of Munich launched a range of designer spectacles and sunglasses—for dogs. The spectacles, which cost around £100, could apparently be made to prescription—though how you get a dog to sit an eye test baffles me. They were held on by three supports on the dog's nose and an adjustable band tied around the head. Optik Paradies claimed that they had the full support of vets and that the glasses were also useful for protecting a dog's eyes if it enjoyed sticking its head out of the car window while driving along.

We're used to hearing stories about eccentric owners leaving fortunes to their pets. Normally these are cats and dogs; however, one pet that would be pampered for the rest of his life was a thirty-year-old tortoise called Fred. Tortoises are one of the least expensive pets to look after and it's estimated that the £25,000 left to Fred would keep him in cabbage and lettuce for five hundred years!

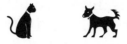

Andy the poodle starred in the London production of *42nd Street* and had a contract that stipulated a supply of dog biscuits in his dressing room and first-class rail travel to and from the theatre. After performances he ate at Flounders restaurant, where staff escorted him to and from his own table.

Did you know . . .
British Lassie-type collies are the descendants of Roman sheep-dogs.

A salon in Lyons offers a special DIY dog-bathing service. They supply the tubs of water, shampoos and special 'dog driers'. All you have to do is bring your dog along and spend most of the day struggling to get it into the tub.

The feline answer to Bill Gates was a white cat named Charlie Chan. In 1978, he inherited $250,000 when his mistress died. He also inherited a house full of antiques and seven aces of land in Joplin, Missouri.

When Calvin Coolidge became President of

the United States, he stayed true to his country roots and his real friends from back home. Once elected, he decided to host a dinner party especially for his friends. Being simple country folk, they were very, very intimidated by the plush surroundings of the White House and were terrified that they would commit a shameful breach of etiquette around the table. The best thing to do, they all decided, was to copy whatever the President did. This went very well until coffee was being served. The President poured half his coffee into his saucer. The guests exchanged glances, then copied him. The President added some milk and sugar. Hastily his guests did the same. Then President Coolidge picked up his saucer and put it on the floor for his cat . . .

The ruler of the Indian state of Gujarat, Sir Mahabat Khan Babi Pathan, was truly one of the world's great dog lovers. He owned over 800 of them, all pedigrees. Each dog had its own private room in his palace, complete with a personal servant and electric light. How many of his people had electric light we can only guess. It's estimated that he spent £32,000 a year on the upkeep of his dogs—and that didn't include all the elaborate doggy state weddings and funerals he staged. A typical wedding would see trumpeters and parades of elephants, while the dogs would be dressed in the finest silk clothes encrusted with jewels.

Horse-racing and royalty have always been inextricably linked, but never more closely than in the case of French Prince Louis-Henri. In 1719, he suddenly became convinced that he was going to be reincarnated as a racehorse—and set about creating the finest stables in the whole of France so he wouldn't have to rough it when he came back. To this end, he built a magnificent new wing on to the French stately home of Chantilly that dwarfed the original medieval chateau. The new stables were built with stunning classical architecture both inside and out and adorned with intricate statues and carvings, so that the prince would have something nice to look at while enjoying his morning feedbag.

Certain that he'd come back to earth as the crème de la crème of thoroughbreds, Louis-Henri gave strict instructions that only the best horses could live here. Whether he actually ever was reincarnated as a horse is, of course, one of history's great unknowns.

A client of the prestigious Coutts Bank received a letter enclosing income-tax forms for signature and requesting 'the date of Sebastian's birth for the tax inspector'.

The client duly advised Coutts that Sebastian was born on 1 July 1988, but she was worried about claiming him as a dependant since he was a basset hound.

The embarrassed banker who'd sent the letter replied, 'Oh, dear. I had such a clear image of Sebastian as a six-year-old boy.'

Lulu, a dog belonging to Haile Selassie, Emperor of Ethiopia, was one of the most pampered dogs in the world. Night and day, Lulu's every need was attended to by her own personal 'Dog Man', whose sole responsibility was her welfare and well-being while at home, or accompanying the Emperor on diplomatic trips abroad. According to the *Daily Mail*, one of the Dog Man's specific tasks was to mop up any 'indiscretions' with a satin cloth (apparently, Lulu liked to urinate on the shoes of foreign dignitaries).

Francis Henry Egerton, the eighth Earl of Bridgwater, had two great passions in life— footwear and dogs. He wore a new pair of boots or shoes every day. Each night his new shoes were placed beside those he had previously worn. This way he could count them and use them as a calendar. But his love of fine shoes also extended to his pets. He provided each of his dogs with little hand-made boots, made by his own cobbler from the softest leather. The Earl preferred the company of his dogs to that of humans and often dined with them. He would have his grand dining-room table set for twelve guests. Servants would then bring in twelve of his dogs, each dressed in fine doggy clothes comprising little silk coats and satin breeches with a crisp linen napkin around their necks. They ate from the finest china while the Earl conversed with them. The Earl claimed his dogs behaved with 'decency and decorum, as could be expected from any gentleman'. If, however, they misbehaved, then they would be dressed in servant's clothes and made to eat in the kitchen for a week.

Baker was one of the original squirrel monkeys blasted off into space to pave the way for human astronauts. In 1959 she was launched 300 miles in a sub-orbital flight on board a Jupiter rocket, and then brought safely back to earth.

The normal life span of a squirrel monkey is about eight years in captivity, and twelve years in the wild. Scientists don't know exactly what happened up in space, but Baker lived to be over twenty-five years old!

To celebrate the twenty-fifth anniversary of her space flight, she was guest of honour at a bananas-and-jelly celebration.

Most people are content with a weathercock on the roof of their house, but John and Ida Mole of Guildford, Surrey, have something far more impressive: a twenty-seven-inch tall eagle owl with a wing-span of five feet.

Named Edwina, the bird escaped when its owner, Peter Taylor, accidentally left the door to her cage open. Edwina had been hand-reared and Peter was concerned that she would not be able to survive in the wild. Various animal welfare groups tried to recapture her, but with no luck. Wildlife experts say there is now little point in putting her back in captivity. She seems happy and healthy exactly where she is and is thought to be living off rats, mice and other small mammals she catches in nearby fields.

Mr Mole said, 'She has become quite a celebrity in the neighbourhood and everyone stops to take photos of her.'

Maggie Peterson set up the world's first doggy

diner next to a large dog park in Plymouth, Michigan. Owners take their pets along for a wide choice of snacks including 'doggy cheeseburger' and chips. Diplomatically, Maggie has left hot dogs off the menu. The idea is now catching on. Ohio has its own Puppy Hut, where canine customers can snack out on veggieburgers or chilli sausages. All dog food is guaranteed salt-free and extra healthy. Puppy Hut also holds special film nights, with *Lassie* usually top of the bill.

In July 1986 Coco's Sidewalk Café opened in Florida to cater for the snobs of the doggy world, or—as they prefer to call them—canine connoisseurs. The menu offered a choice of rare roast beef or turkey breast and a selection of mineral waters. That's a place where 'doggy bag' takes on a whole new meaning . . .

In AD 999, in Japan, a cat gave birth to the five loveliest kittens the Emperor had ever seen. They were snowy-white, with perfect, alert blue eyes. So beautiful were the kittens that the Emperor officially made them all Royal Princes of Japan. The idea soon spread that all cats were princes and, as royalty should be pampered, the cats could not be expected to do a stroke of work. It was a golden age for cats! But it couldn't last.

Japan was plagued by mice, as cats were

forbidden to be put to work as humble mousers, and the entire silk industry was near to collapse as the mice kept dining on the silkworms. The Japanese tried to drive the mice away by painting pictures of cats and showing them to the mice, or sneaking up on them with stuffed toy cats—but nothing seemed to work. There was only one solution. By royal decree, cats were no longer princes— and had to earn their living once again.

Did you know . . .
most gorillas have a phobia about
water and may refuse to cross even
the smallest of streams.

Apparently it's twice as exciting as *EastEnders* and the characters are far more sympathetic and likeable too. I'm talking about a special all-chimpanzee soap-opera film made at Stirling University in 1998. It wasn't intended for us humans to watch—which is a shame— but researchers made the soap to see if zoo chimps could be cheered up by a daily dose of their favourite television serial. Apparently, younger simian viewers liked the playful scenes best and would often copy them. Older female chimps became the real hardcore viewers, though. According to the researchers, they turned into 'couch potatoes' and had to be literally dragged away from the TV screen when their favourite soap was on!

Zak, a twelve-year-old ginger tom belonging to Neville and Anne King from York, spends most of his time asleep in the garden or curled up on the sofa.

Well, it's not surprising given that Zak is a monster moggy who weighs in at a huge 34 pounds. Zak wandered into the King household nine years ago. Today they serve him fourteen separate meals a day. 'He won't eat normal cat food,' said Mr King. 'I tried him on diet food once and he hated it. The vet used to read me the riot act about Zak's weight but doesn't bother any more. What can I do? I can't see my pet waste away.'

Zak eats a diet of minced lamb, fish, shrimps and biscuits, all washed down with lashings of milk, but despite his colossal intake, his owners don't think he eats that much. 'I think he's just a bit like me,' added Mr King. 'He just eats all the wrong things. He is simply a gorgeous big cat, if a touch overweight. Some people are big-boned. I think he's just well padded.'

(Incidentally, there is no current official fattest cat in Britain or the world. The previous world-record holder was a 46-pound Australian cat named Himmy, but he died in 1986. *The Guinness Book of Records* commented, 'Zak is the fattest cat we know about. We will be contacting the owner with a view to getting Zak entered into our next edition.')

Zak might be heavy for a cat at 34 pounds, but Kell, an English mastiff, definitely leaves her in the shade. She weighs in at a massive nineteen stones, but is really a soppy dog, according to her owner Tom Scott of East Leake, Nottinghamshire. 'She's a real old softie. She would only go for somebody if she saw anyone she knows being attacked.'

Tom first realised he had a record breaker on his hands when he saw a TV show that featured the previous title holder at a mere 242 pounds. At 270 pounds, Kell is still growing and is likely to make twenty-one stone. She is currently thirty-five inches high and six feet long. Keeping a dog this large doesn't come cheap, as Tom knows. She eats 15 pounds of fresh mince, four pints of goat's milk and half a dozen eggs a day. 'Basically she's on a boxer's diet. Lots of protein to build her up,' Tom said. Having a dog like Kell is also a good way for Tom to keep fit. He takes her on a two-hour run every day.

Sammy the squatting seal has set up home illegally in a navigation buoy at the entrance to the River Exe, near Exmouth in Devon—but no one seems to mind. With its beautiful sea view and easy access to the river, it's a highly desirable residence. The buoy is hollow, so Sammy can climb inside and shelter from the wind, and if he fancies a snack he can jump out of his front door straight into the river and snatch up a fish—or pop along to the local takeaway (nearby rows of lobster pots set on the seabed by fishermen). When Sammy first took up residence in the buoy, locals worried he might be ill. The RSPCA sailed out to the buoy, gave Sammy the once-over and pronounced him as fit as a fiddle. It seems he simply prefers the buoy to an exposed, slimy, seaweed-covered rock . . .

Every year, a wild mountain goat is crowned king of the town of Killorglin in County Kerry during its annual Puck Fair. The goat is crowned by the town's beauty queen and gets to reign for three days before he is deposed and returned to the wilds. No one really knows why . . .

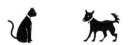

Theodore Roosevelt, who gave his name to the teddy bear, kept quite a menagerie at the White House. It included Jonathan the bear; Bill the lizard; Eli Yale the macaw; Baron Spreckle the hen; Dr Johnson, Bishop Doane

231

and Fighting Bob the guinea pigs; Josiah the
badger; Maude the pig; and Emily Spinach, his
daughter's garter snake.

When Webby the five-year-old Jack Russell
was discovered abandoned on Dartmoor,
things looked as bleak as the landscape. He
was shivering and close to death, and although
he was nursed back to health by rescuers at the
Woodside Animal Sanctuary in Plymouth, the
tendons in his front paws had been
permanently damaged by the freezing
conditions.

Debbie Blackmore, deputy manager at the
sanctuary, said, 'He was very thin and
traumatised when he came here, but it was his
feet that mainly worried us.' The dog's
damaged paws had developed a webbed
appearance, which gave rise to the name the
sanctuary staff gave him. Debbie added, 'His
feet got hurt because they weren't used to the
cold and rough terrain of the moor. They then
became sore because he ended up walking on
a part of his feet he wouldn't normally use.'

Just when it looked as though Webby would
have difficulty in walking for the rest of his life,
salvation came in the form of a pair of custom-
made leather doggy-shoes, made by a company
of specialist shoemakers. He found his first
pair, which were fastened with Velcro, a bit

heavy and they kept slipping off. The second pair have bright blue laces. Debbie says he's quite happy with them and bounds along. He's a very contented dog, especially with his new owners, Rick Wilkinson and David Neale of Tomes, who adopted Webby after he captured their hearts on a television appeal. Mr Wilkinson said, 'When Webby was picked up he had lost all faith in humanity. But now he has made a terrific recovery and is really one of the family.'

Because of his tailor-made shoes, Webby has now become a local celebrity in Totnes and his owners even produced his own pin-up calendar. With the aid of computer wizardry, he stars in twelve comical pictures, including one of him surfing! All proceeds go to the Woodside sanctuary.

Have you ever wondered who first thought up the idea of special food for pets? According to legend, it was one James Spratt of Cincinnati, Ohio. He emigrated to Britain in 1851 to sell lightning conductors, and as his ship arrived in Britain, he is supposed to have noticed that a pack of stray dogs had gathered expectantly at the quayside. He soon found out why. The sailors on his ship lined up along the rails and threw them stale ship's biscuits. This gave him the idea of setting up the world's first pet-food business, making biscuits especially for dogs. They were called Spratt's Meal Fibrine Dog Cakes. In fact, special dog food had been around a lot longer than that. The eleventh-century Domesday Book refers to three thousand cakes of 'dog bread' being produced in Cheltenham in Gloucestershire. Historians don't know a lot about 'dog bread', but it's a pretty safe bet that it was food made *for* dogs rather than—perish the thought—food made *from* dogs. James Spratt does have one claim to fame, though. He gave a job to a young office junior named Charles Cruft—and it was selling Spratt's Dog Cakes that gave Cruft the idea for the world-famous dog show that still bears his name.

Incidentally, although tinned cat and dog food was invented in 1926, unbelievably it still didn't catch on until the late 1950s. Before then, pets usually ate table scraps.

Margaret Chamberlain was rather worried about her black cat Basil. He was getting decidedly plump, despite the fact that he spent most of his day out and about. A few streets away from Mrs Chamberlain's home in Bromley Cross, near Bolton, Linda Berry was having similar worries about her cat, Tom. He was getting plenty of exercise, staying out half the time, but was piling on the pounds like nobody's business. Just before Christmas 1997, the Chamberlain family moved to another house a hundred yards away and decided to keep Basil in for a week to get him used to his new home. At precisely the same time, Linda's cat Tom mysteriously went missing. After a week of fearing the worst, Linda was delighted to see Tom when he finally turned up again. She'd learned her lesson and decided to fit him with a smart cat collar and a shiny disc with his name and number on it. Imagine Margaret's surprise when her Basil came home wearing a disc saying 'Tom'. Of course, they were one and the same cat. For years, Basil/Tom had been leading a devious double life, commuting between the two homes, getting two sets of owners to fuss him and eating double helpings of food every day. 'I believed he was spending nights out on the tiles,' said Margaret. 'Instead, from the age of one, he's been at Linda's relaxing in his favourite rocking chair and special cat basket!'

Did you know . . .
giraffes can run at a top speed of
around 35 mph and can beat
champion racehorses over a short
distance.

President Ulysses Grant suspected that one or more of his staff were poisoning his son's dogs. When he acquired the latest pet, a

Newfoundland puppy, he announced to the staff, 'Jesse has a new dog. You may have noticed that his former pets have been particularly unfortunate. When this dog dies, every employee in the White House will be at once discharged.'

The honour of being the first and only cat to have its obituary in *Wisden* went to Peter, a moggy who lived at Lord's cricket ground for twelve years. Peter watched every game with interest and would often walk on to the edge of the pitch to get a closer look at the action. The entry stated, 'CAT, PETER. His ninth life ended on 5 November 1964.' His obituary included a warm tribute from the then secretary of the MCC, Billy Griffith, who described Peter as 'a cat of great character who loved publicity'.

Bath-time fun is the secret of getting along with shy birds, according to aviculturalist Uschi Birr. She says that the Amazon and grey parrots, Conure, Lory and Macaw all love to take baths and showers and enjoy 'singing and dancing in the rain'. So, if your bird isn't responding, try spraying it daily, at the same time of day, and it'll soon perk up.

Pigs might fly—and indeed they did. Pigs took to the air sooner than most other flightless creatures. The first pig known to have flown in an aircraft shared the cockpit with J. T. C. Morre-Brabazon on his flights over England in 1909—just six years after the Wright brothers invented powered flight.

So you think that the story of Clyde the orang-utan who kept trucker Clint Eastwood company in *Every Which Way But Loose* was a trifle unrealistic? Not so! When Swiss lorry driver Fernand Montendon was stopped en route to London from Dover in November 1975, police found a three-foot ape sitting next to him in his cab—and no, it wasn't his co-driver. They didn't mind the company he kept, but they did mind that he'd ignored the anti-rabies regulations, and fined him £200.

Manfred von Richthofen was better known as the Red Baron, the fearless German air ace of the First World War, credited with eighty kills. Although his flying skills were legendary, what's not so well known is that he performed some of his most impressive aerial manoeuvres accompanied in the cockpit by Moritz, his Great Dane. (Perhaps that's why they called air-to-air combat 'dog-fighting'!)

Able Seacat Second Class Lucky Fred Wunpound was a fully signed-up member of Her Majesty's Royal Navy. His shipmates on board HMS *Hecate* even filled in a census form for the cat, who was recorded as being 'born in England, of doubtful parentage, single and male'. Fred set sail in 1966 and travelled over a quarter of a million miles before retiring from duty in 1975. The *Navy News* recorded his retirement, and Vice Admiral Tait wrote him a glowing reference. In his ten years of service, according to his records, he gained promotion from 'Junior He-cat' to 'Ordinary He-cat' to 'Able Seacat'. He also earned two good-conduct badges and had only one stain on his otherwise unblemished record—a temporary moment of insanity in Brixham fish market!

Because of his rather unfortunate facial resemblance to a certain mad German dictator, the black-and-white Australian cat who came visiting the American Air Force in

1945 quickly got the nickname of 'Adolf'. Despite this, Adolf proved himself to be a true friend of the Allies. Pilot Ed Stelzig found him stowing away on his Dakota transport aircraft after a stopover in Darwin and decided to adopt him. From that moment on, Adolf was an official crew member with the United States Fifth Air Force and flew everywhere with his human crew. Somehow he could tell the particular engine sound of Ed's plane and would jump on board the moment the engines started to go off on another adventure. He only got the plane wrong once—and was returned from foreign climes a week later. In total, it's estimated that Adolf flew over 92,140 miles with his aircraft, spending most of the time snuggled up in the cockpit enjoying the heat coming off the radio set.

To some horses, a treat means a sugar lump. To others it's an apple. But Kizzy the horse's favourite treat is to watch television! Twice a week, Louise Ersser brings Kizzy from her stables to the family home near Hockley in Essex to roam around the garden—and then settle down in the living room for a good goggle at the box. 'When the TV's on, Kizzy relaxes so much that sometimes she lies on the floor and lets you tickle her,' says Louise. 'It's just like having a dog.'

Louise's husband Shane isn't so sure about Kizzy making herself at home in the living room. 'He thinks Kizzy's a bit smelly and that I'm mad for letting her in,' Louise admits, 'but he doesn't mind really.' Which is a good thing too, because apparently Kizzy gets quite sulky now if she can't watch TV. 'If the television isn't on, her ears go back and she gets in quite a mood,' says Louise. And Kizzy's favourite programme? Why, it's *Neigh-bours*, of course!

If you ever doubted that too much junk food is bad for you, consider the case of Arnie the five-year-old blue and grey macaw. Arnie's indulgent owner raised the parrot on a diet of coffee, hot chocolate and cola—and spawned a monster. Arnie was bad-tempered, aggressive and loved to bite anyone and everything he could get his beak into. Luckily, however, the staff at Parrot Line Rescue knew exactly what to do. They put him on a special detoxification diet of fresh fruit and herbal tea, and now—by all accounts—Arnie is a completely reformed character with a very sweet disposition.

Did you know . . .
you can tell the age of a fish by
counting the rings on its scales, just
as you can get an idea of the age of
a tree by counting the rings in its

trunk. You can also tell a bear's age by counting the rings in a cross section of its tooth. However, it's not recommended that you try this . . .

There's a donkey sanctuary with a difference in the west of England. Founded by Dr Elizabeth Svendsen, who also operates refuges across Britain and Ireland, it's for the treatment of alcoholic donkeys. It might sound amusing, but a large number of irresponsible owners have been teaching their donkeys to down pints of beer as a sort of party trick. Donkeys are more likely than humans to get addicted to alcohol, and, when they do, these normally placid creatures can become really aggressive and dangerous.

A donkey that belonged to a pub landlord was actually fed on a diet of Guinness and crisps. One day it attacked his wife when she refused to serve it any more beer. The reason she stopped wasn't that she thought it was cruel to get the animal drunk—but because it was after closing time.

Beverly Sharpe, who lived in a small town on the German/Dutch border, awoke in the middle of the night, convinced she could feel something pressing down on the pillow next to

241

her head. After reassuring herself it was just a bad dream, she turned over to try to get back to sleep, only to come face to face with a six-foot-long boa constrictor that was coiled up right next to her head. The snake, called Feathers, had escaped from a neighbour's house several weeks earlier and was thought to have been trying to find its way back. A hurried call to the authorities had Feathers safely removed and reunited with its rightful owner.

A lot of people like the company of pets but don't want the full-time responsibility of owning them—or can't keep them because their accommodation is unsuitable.

Pet-shop owner Masahito Kobayashi provides a service to these people—by renting out pets to customers. He originally started renting animals out to film and TV crews, but later extended the service to ordinary customers. A four-hour walk with a cat or small dog costs around £15, while larger dogs cost £25 for the same time.

Diplomat and statesman Henry Kissinger would often stay at the exclusive Bohemian Grove resort in California, but while he was sitting in the gardens or by the pool, the local frog population would go berserk, croaking loudly and incessantly, disturbing not just the statesman but all the other guests.

A herpetologist—a reptile expert—was called in by the resort's management to investigate the problem, and after making tape-recordings and analysing them he came up with the answer.

It seemed that Kissinger's deep baritone voice sounded exactly like a male frog in heat.

CHAPTER SEVEN

KIND HEARTS

Quick-thinking Steve Marsden of New Mills in Derbyshire saved the life of a drowning sheep by jumping into the swollen River Goyt in Derbyshire, dragging the unconscious animal to the bank and then giving it the kiss of life.

The incident happened just before Christmas last year when Steve and his wife Janet were out for a stroll with their collie Spot, on moorland near Whaley Bridge. The dog started barking at what Steve thought was a plastic bag floating in the water. It was only as they got closer that they realised it was a sheep. Janet insisted that Steve jump in and save the poor animal, and he managed to chase it downstream and drag it over to the bank while Janet ran to a nearby farm to summon help. It was when he reached dry land again that Steve realised that the sheep had stopped breathing. Steve is a member of a local cave rescue team and immediately set about making use of his first-aid training. He cleared the sheep's airway of grass, tilted her head back and started to give her mouth-to-mouth resuscitation.

Steve said, 'I was also pummelling her to massage her heart, but when that didn't work I took another deep breath and blew. All of a sudden she started coughing and spluttering and came back to life.'

By this time Janet had returned with the farmer's daughter and the sheep was up on its feet, a bit unsteady but otherwise all right.

Of the miraculous rescue, Janet said, 'It was a million-to-one chance that we were out walking in that area because the path is rarely used. It was also fortunate that the sheep was spotted by two people who were daft enough to get involved like we did. But we are a family of animal lovers and we couldn't ignore what was happening.'

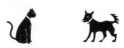

When Kellie the border collie lost her hearing in an accident at just seven weeks, her owner, breeder Lesley Bustard, was advised to have her put down. But Lesley knew that with perseverance and love, disabilities can be overcome. She herself had been fighting cancer for most of the dog's life and she knew what could be achieved.

She also set herself a goal, and remembers telling her specialist, 'I can't die yet. I've got to get this deaf dog to Cruft's.'

Lesley aims to get Kellie into an obedience team—and it looks as though she's succeeding.

Right from the start, Lesley, from Brompton in North Yorkshire, had faith in Kellie, despite the so-called experts in dog training telling her that she would never make anything of her dog. She recalls, 'Some top trainers told me to put her to sleep. I couldn't even bear to think about doing that, so I decided to prove everybody wrong. It's something I have never regretted.'

Through a long process of trial and error, Lesley translated conventional dog commands into sign language. She also voices the commands, even though she knows Kellie can't hear her, so she can pick up her facial expressions as well. Lesley adds, 'Having a deaf dog is similar to having a handicapped child—they need extra care and attention. You have got to give them so much more time and stimulation, but Kellie has repaid me more than anyone could imagine.'

As Kellie became more and more adept, Lesley entered her into competitions, many of which she won. She also takes the dog to visit deaf children and to the occupational therapy unit of a local hospital to cheer up patients.

Lesley is now in remission from her illness and, last year, did take part at Cruft's with her much-loved Kellie.

Elephants are undoubtedly some of the most sensitive animals in the world. They are known to form strong bonds of friendship and cry real tears of grief. Just how strong their emotions can be was demonstrated by a cow Indian elephant named Damini who lived in the Prince of Wales Zoo in Lucknow, northern India.

Damini first came to the zoo in 1998 after being rescued from smugglers. She was alone at the zoo for five months until a younger, pregnant elephant named Champakali arrived from a national park. The two elephants quickly became the best of friends. Among elephants, it's common for older females to look after younger pregnant elephants and help them through maternity. Then tragedy struck. The calf was stillborn, and Champakali died too from complications. The older elephant was devastated. Her keepers reported that she wept thick salt tears and refused to move, as if she had given up the will to live. For days she just stood on the same spot, ignoring the sugar cane and bananas provided by her desperate keepers. Eventually, she collapsed on the spot and lay on the ground, a truly pathetic sight with tears still rolling down her cheeks. Her keepers tried to feed her, but she refused to cooperate. They erected a tent around her, sprayed her with cool water and set up fans to protect her from the fierce sun, but she showed no interest in what they were doing for her. She was determined to die, and, after twenty-four days, on 5 May 1999, she passed away in her enclosure.

The nursery rhyme 'Mary had a Little Lamb' is based on real life. Mary was Mary Sawyer, and she really did have a little lamb. In 1814, when she was eight years old, she saw a sickly and weakened lamb in her father's sheep pen in Sterling, Massachusetts. It would very probably have died had not Mary insisted on bringing it indoors with her. She stayed up all night cuddling it in front of the fire and teaching it to drink milk. Gradually, the lamb's health returned and it became a much-loved family pet. On schooldays, the lamb really would go with Mary and her brother to school and sit in the classroom. A visitor to the school, John Roulstone, was charmed by this, and the very next day he gave Mary a three-verse poem he had composed. Apparently the animal's fleece really was 'as white as snow', and Mary later donated the fleece to help raise funds to preserve Boston's Old South Church. The little poem kept on growing in popularity and was first published in 1829 in a book of children's poetry by Sarah Hale, who had added three verses of her own to the poem.

Did you know . . .
just like humans, gorillas and chimps have sweat glands under their arms and suffer from smelly armpits.

The police used all their resources when Humphrey the tortoise was—well, tortoise-napped. He was snatched by a bogus caller at pensioner Alice Ward's home in Oundle, Northamptonshire. After an intensive week-long search through two counties, the police finally tracked the culprit to Nottinghamshire and caught him red-handed. Humphrey was found fast asleep in the bottom of the man's bag and was soon returned to Alice, who had owned the tortoise for twenty-two years.

'I've got nothing but praise for the police,' said a grateful Alice later. 'They moved heaven and earth to get Humphrey back. You hear stories about them not bothering with petty crimes. I don't believe a word of it.'

A driver was just about to start his JCB bulldozer up when he noticed a new bird's nest in its engine. He called the site foreman, who identified the eggs as belonging to a rare wagtail. Bird lovers quickly responded by paying for another digger so that the original one could be laid up for the week until the birds were born. As soon as the original digger was left alone, the two parent birds were seen flying back to it, and a few days later five baby wagtails were successfully hatched.

Stories about mongooses are few and far between, but I found this one which I think is really interesting. The creatures are very small and fall easy prey to predators. The way they survive is by climbing as high as they can and moving rapidly.

Naturalist Ann Rasa was observing a group of wild mongooses. One of them, whom she named Tatu, became wounded, but rather than give up on her, the other mongooses in the pack would slow down their search for food so that she could catch up, even though this put them in more danger. Tatu was even allowed to share the prey that another mongoose had caught—a practice which is usually strictly forbidden in mongoose society. When Tatu became unable to groom herself, the other mongooses did it for her.

As Tatu grew weaker it was obvious she was going to die. Again, against all their natural instincts, the whole clan stayed with her to the end, choosing to go hungry and risking danger from predators rather than abandon their friend.

Grey Owl was a Canadian Ojibway Indian who dedicated his life to preserving Canada's wilderness areas and who became known as the father of the modern conservation movement. However, it wasn't until his death in 1936 that Grey Owl's secret came out. He was no Indian, but an ordinary Englishman, Archibald Belaney, born in Hastings in 1888.

Despite his background, Grey Owl became an expert trapper and guide. He lived among the Indians and married an Indian girl named Anahareo.

One day he found two tiny abandoned beavers and took them home to his log cabin to raise them. He observed them closely and saw that they were full of life and mischief, and this convinced him that trapping was wrong and that from then on, he would give it up.

The two beavers were named McGinnis and McGinty, and they quickly grew used to their home. One day Grey Owl brought a large pile of moss home with him, which he planned to stuff in the cracks between the logs of his cabin to keep the draughts out and provide insulation.

That night Grey Owl and Anahareo went to sleep, and when they woke up they found that the job had been done by the beavers, as high as they could reach. What's more, it had been done far more expertly than the humans could ever have managed.

Grey Owl and his wife used to keep their food on a tall table, out of reach of the hungry beavers. On another occasion, they came back into the cabin to see that the crafty animals had gnawed the legs of the table right down, so that the table top was now just a few inches off the floor and they could tuck in to everything they'd been missing!

Grey Owl's epitaph reads: 'Say a silent thank you for the preservation of wilderness areas, for the lives of the creatures who live there and for people with the foresight to realise this heritage, no matter how.'

Rough the terrier lived on a farm and every morning would sit and wait expectantly while his owner made breakfast. His treat was to eat a slice of toast, which his owner cut into four pieces. Rough would munch down three of them, but being a very generous dog, he would carry the fourth in his mouth all the way over to the hen house to a particular hen he'd struck up a friendship with. While the hen pecked at the toast, Rough would stand guard, barking at any other hen audacious enough to try to steal it.

Baggy the collie was a flop at herding sheep—but makes a great surrogate mum. 'I bought him to herd the flock,' said his owner, Chris Brake, at the Blackdown Hills Welcome Centre in Devon, 'but he is too passive and just used to sit in the field watching them!'

Determined that Baggy would still earn his keep, Chris then hit on an unusual idea. He strapped two baby's milk bottles to Baggy's collar for newborn lambs to suckle on. The daft dog now wanders around the field with a flock of lambs padding behind, waiting their turn for a drink!

The prophet Mohammed thought that dogs were rather vile and wretched, but he had a soft spot in his heart for cats. Legend has it that one day the Prophet's pet cat Meuzza was sleeping soundly on Mohammed's robe when the call came to go to prayers. Rather than disturb Meuzza, Mohammed cut off one of his sleeves so that the cat could sleep on, uninterrupted. When the cat woke he was so thankful for his master's kind gesture that he bowed to the Prophet, and Mohammed stroked him three times in turn, blessing both him and other cats with something they'll be forever grateful for—the ability always to land on their feet.

While working as a missionary in Africa, Albert Schweitzer had a pet called Sizi—and he displayed the same consideration to it as Mohammed did to Meuzza. Visitors to his clinic at Lambarene often found it difficult to read the prescriptions Schweitzer had given them. Doctors are renowned for their bad handwriting, but in this case it was due to the left-handed Schweitzer writing with his right hand. The reason? Sizi would often fall asleep on his left arm—and he didn't want to disturb her.

Similarly, the Irish poet W. B. Yeats was about to leave the Abbey Theatre in Dublin when he noticed the theatre cat fast asleep on his coat. Rather than disturb her sleep, he carefully cut around the piece of cloth she was lying on so she could continue her rest. He then put on his coat, complete with cat-shaped hole, and went on his way.

Did you know . . .
lions go silly on catnip just like their smaller relatives.

Topa the hedgehog never forgot the kindly vet who helped fix her broken paw. The hedgehog was lucky enough to have been discovered lying injured on a desolate country road in the then Soviet Union in 1979 by a vet named Nadezhda Ushakova. The vet fixed her paw and then gave the hedgehog to her granddaughter to keep as a pet. Topa didn't settle in well, though. She refused to eat and moped around the house, so the granddaughter thought the kindest thing would be to free her in some woods. Two months later, Dr Ushakova returned home from work to see Topa sitting on her front doorstep. Somehow the hedgehog had tracked her down despite the fact that she was freed nearly fifty miles away from where the doctor lived.

Minnie the pony was born on the battlefield. The veterinary corps hadn't noticed her mother was pregnant when they shipped her and two thousand other mules, donkeys and ponies to Burma to help in the conflict against the Japanese in the Second World War. Minnie came into the world on the White City base at Henu as Japanese mortar shells rained all around. The tough Chindit fighters manning the base took to her immediately, although she was a sickly and frail little thing. She proved a welcome distraction for the war-weary men in the jungle, frolicking with them and stealing their tea straight from the teapot. They admired her bravery too. She wasn't frightened of shell fire.

Unfortunately, other animals weren't so calm, and one day Minnie received a terrible kick in the head from a donkey spooked by an exploding shell. She was knocked unconscious and seriously hurt. The Chindits were devastated. Even columns deep out in the jungle on raids would radio back asking about Minnie's condition. Commander 'Mad Mike' Calvert personally ordered that every unit be kept informed of Minnie's progress, and when the plucky little horse pulled through, 'the news was almost as welcome as a major victory', as one historian put it.

When the troops were finally ordered to head north for a major new offensive, Minnie was still too weak to go with them. Orders were given to abandon her in the jungle—but the Chindits weren't prepared to do anything of the sort—even if it meant breaking every rule in the book! The 14th Brigade and the Nigerian army launched a special assault on a nearby jungle runway, risking their lives to drive out the Japanese troops there. Then officers of all ranks turned a blind eye as a transport aircraft was called in just for Minnie. She was led aboard and swiftly flown to safety in India, where she was treated as a hero on her arrival.

By all accounts Minnie desperately missed the men she had played with as a foal, and was delighted when, a few months later, they came back out of the jungle and were reunited with her on the Indian base at Dehra Du. The soldiers were equally pleased to see her and she was given the freedom of the base, where she regularly caused an uproar. Her favourite trick was to wander into the sergeants' mess and eat the food off the soldiers' plates before trying to eat the tablecloths as well. Minnie also wrecked more than one parade by trying to insinuate herself into the ranks, but no one minded. When her regiment left India in 1947, Minnie travelled home with them on a troop ship and spent the rest of her days as the official regimental mascot of the 20th Lancashire Fusiliers.

In 1971, *African Wildlife* magazine carried a very strange report by a wildlife photographer named Reucassel. He had set up his camera near a water hole in the Kruger National Park, intent on filming a crocodile known to lurk in the muddy brown waters. One evening, a herd of impala came down to the water hole to drink. As Reucassel watched through the camera viewfinder, the crocodile erupted out of the water with terrifying speed, jaws closing on one ewe and dragging her down into the water. Crocodiles drown their prey, and the struggle went on for what seemed like forever—until help suddenly arrived from a most unexpected quarter. A hippopotamus appeared as if from nowhere in Reucassel's viewfinder, deliberately charging the crocodile. The incredible impact freed the impala—and sent the crocodile reeling away back into the water. Then, as the photographer looked on in utter disbelief, the hippo scooped the gravely wounded impala out of the water in its gaping jaws with incredible tenderness—and helped to put it back upright on its feet again! 'In the burning heat the animals looked at each other,' Reucassel wrote, 'the rescuer who seemed to sense that its intervention had come too late, and the rescued who realised, perhaps, that this was its last African sun.' Sadly, the impala was too badly hurt to go on, and collapsed shortly afterwards. Obviously concerned, the hippo walked to where it lay and gently lifted the impala's head up on to its own snout, pressed against it and then opened its mouth and, Reucassel says, seemed to be trying to breathe life back into the impala. When it realised the impala was gone, it lay beside it for some fifteen minutes before finally returning to the water. In all his thirty years of being a wildlife photographer, Reucassel confessed he had never witnessed a scene like it.

When tiny tawny owl chicks Little and Large lost their mum, things didn't look good. A tree surgeon had chopped down the tree with their nest in and Mum flew away, leaving the week-old chicks to fend for themselves.

Luckily they were found and brought to Hydestile Wildlife Hospital in Surrey, where they were quickly adopted by foster mum Josie, a fully grown tawny owl who lives at the hospital because her eyesight is poor. Josie took to the chicks immediately and refused to leave them until they were old enough to be released into the wild.

It was Kuni the bonobo chimp to the rescue when an injured starling landed in her enclosure at Twycross Zoo. At first her keeper was frightened she'd harm the bird, but nothing was further from the seven-year-old ape's mind. She delicately picked up the bird, unfolded its wings and tried to launch it back into the sky! When the bird failed to fly away, Kuni sat a stern guard duty to keep the other curious bonobos away until it had recovered enough to fly off again under its own power.

Did you know . . .
the average kangaroo can leap
about twenty-five feet in a single
bound—and more than eight feet in
the air. Leaps of over forty feet by
more athletic specimens have been
reliably reported.

One afternoon in October 1990, a four-year-old Jack Russell terrier called Mugsy was hit by a car outside the house of his owner, Viola Tiszl, of Severna Park, Maryland.

Viola was out at the time, but her boyfriend Glenn Maloney heard the screech of tyres and rushed out to investigate. He saw Mugsy lying in the road and picked him up, but the last signs of life flickering in the dog's eyes faded and he went limp. He carried the body into the backyard and buried it in a three-foot-deep hole. He told reporters afterwards, 'I know a dead dog when I see one. This one was real dead. He was not breathing. He had no heartbeat.'

That evening, when Viola came home from work, she took a look at the grave and prayers for dear Mugsy were said. But at 5.30 the next morning, fourteen hours after Mugsy had been buried, Viola and Glenn were woken by a scratching at their back door. Glenn recalled, 'I went to the back door and I couldn't believe it. There was Mugsy with his little tail wagging ninety miles an hour!' The little pooch was covered in dirt and his eyes were bloodshot, but otherwise he acted as if nothing had happened.

Viola felt that Mugsy's miraculous recovery was down to his breeding, claiming, 'Jack Russells are bred to burrow after foxes. I guess when he woke up, he just thought it was another old hole and dug his way out, not knowing it was supposed to be his grave.'

Bamse was probably not the most suitable mascot to have on board ship. For one thing he was the biggest St Bernard imaginable, and second, he was often violently seasick. But to the crew of the Norwegian minesweeper *Throdd*, Bamse meant everything. When the Germans invaded Norway during the Second World War, the *Throdd* sailed for Scotland and fought alongside the Royal Navy. The ship helped evacuate British troops from the beaches at Dunkirk and played an important role in keeping the shipping lanes free of mines for the convoys. Between voyages, the ship was berthed near Dundee, and Bamse became a regular sight around town. There was no mistaking him. When he stood on his hind legs he was six feet tall—and he weighed at least fourteen stone. Added to that, he wore his own Norwegian sailor's cap proudly wherever he went. Strangely, Bamse decided that his official job was to look after sailors on shore leave. He knew which bus to take into town from the docks and would head out of a night to search the pubs and cinemas for his shipmates. When he found one much the worse for wear, he would grip the sailor by his coat and tug him out of the pub and all the way to the bus stop. The locals were amazed, and started a fund to buy Bamse his very own bus pass, which he wore proudly in a transparent pouch draped around his neck.

The St Bernard had another skill too— breaking up drunken pub fights. He would bound between the men who were fighting, then jump up at them and stare straight into their eyes. No one resisted. One day, the second-in-command of the *Throdd* was walking in the dockyard when he was attacked by a man with a knife. Bamse leapt at the attacker, grabbed him by his clothes and then dragged him kicking and shouting to the quayside, before unceremoniously dumping him in the sea!

Although he was undoubtedly tough, Bamse was also as gentle as a lamb. He was a regular sight at the football matches played between ships' teams, howling with delight when his side scored. Children would come from all over Dundee and Montrose to play with him or to go for rides on his back. Everyone— locals and sailors alike—loved Bamse.

Sadly, his huge heart finally gave out on

22 July 1944 and he died quietly on board the ship he loved so much. At his funeral two days later, his coffin was draped with the Norwegian flag with his sailor's cap resting on top. Eight hundred Scottish schoolchildren lined the funeral route and all schools were closed for the day as a mark of respect. Local dignitaries attended in all their finery and the crews of six Norwegian navy vessels formed a guard of honour. Bamse was laid to rest in the dunes near the banks of the South Esk River, his head facing north-east towards his Norwegian home. Even today, crew members from Norwegian naval vessels putting into port still make a point of visiting his grave as a mark of respect for a big dog with an even bigger heart.

In 1994, Rome's mayor, Francesco Rutelli, set aside money to create an 'office for animal rights' which handles complaints and concerns on all aspects of animal welfare. The office is manned seven days a week and provides practical advice as well as liaising with the police, fire brigade and Italy's national animal charities. Every local authority should have one.

The stresses and strains of running his own successful Volkswagen body-shop in Florida caused Richie Moretti to sell up and retire to Marathon Keys in Florida Keys, where he bought the Hidden Harbor Motel.

While he was there he got interested in the wildlife and, in particular, in turtles. Once his interest was known, people finding injured turtles would take them to him. Some had had their shells damaged by propeller blades. Others had been caught in discarded fishing lines. Although he had no medical training, Richie established his own turtle hospital where he was able to care for injured turtles before releasing them back to sea. He even used his body-shop skills to develop a way of patching up damaged shells with fibreglass.

But Richie really got hooked on helping the turtles when he saw more and more of them suffering from unsightly growths on their flippers, faces and especially around their eyes. He consulted experts from the University of Florida, who eventually diagnosed the condition as a type of tumour peculiar to turtles which, unless quickly treated, can result in death.

Today Richie is one of the leading authorities on this condition. The turtle hospital now has a fully equipped operating theatre, and while vets remove the tumours, Richie assists. The turtles are kept under observation and then, when given the all-clear, are released back into the warm Florida seas. Richie has devoted his retirement to saving the turtles—the hospital and its work are financed by a combination of his savings, income from his motel and voluntary donations.

Richie can see similarities between his job at the VW garage and saving the lives of turtles. 'They come in broken and we fix them up,' he says.

Did you know . . .
the blue marlin can reach speeds in
the water of over 40 mph.

In 1990, Smajo Malkoc was a migrant worker in Austria, sending money back home every month to his family in the little Islamic village of Jezero in Bosnia. When he finally made it home again, he made sure he had a very special present for his two boys Dzevad and Catib—two goldfish in a little aquarium. They were good times, and no one had any idea that a terrible war was just around the corner. Two years later, the Serbs invaded Jezero. Smajo Malkoc and other men from the village fought a desperate holding action while the women and children fled to safety. Many of them, including Smajo, died in the battle and the Serbs put the village to the torch. After they had moved on, Smajo's wife Fehima came back down from the hills to bury her husband and to see what she could salvage of the family's possessions. The aquarium and her children's two fish were about the only things not looted or smashed by the Serbs. Fehima took the goldfish and freed them into the lake. 'This way they might be more fortunate than us,' she thought. The family lived as refugees for three years, before finally being able to return to their village, penniless and with only the clothes they were wearing. When they arrived, they couldn't believe their eyes. 'The whole lake was shining from the myriad golden fish in it,' Fehima recalls. 'I had to think of my husband. It was something he left me that I never hoped for.' The family started selling the fish as a way of earning a living, and their business thrived. Today, Fehima and her sons have one of the biggest houses in Jezero and can live in comfort. Their neighbours can catch and sell the fish to make money as well if they want to—but most don't. 'They threw the fish into the lake,' says one of the neighbours. 'It's their miracle.'

Partner the golden retriever is one of the unsung heroes of the Oklahoma bomb blast that left hundreds dead and injured in April 1995. He wasn't used to search for victims buried beneath the wreckage and rubble, but instead played an important role in the therapy that many traumatised rescuers, survivors and relatives underwent after the tragedy—showing them love and helping them to come to terms with the disaster.

Partner is so affectionate that even just spending a short time with him has enabled people to overcome a lot of their initial grief. He was introduced to them by Kris and Amanda Butler, who work alongside health-care professionals at the Jim Thorpe Rehabilitation Hospital in Oklahoma City, and for his help was awarded the American Delta Society's 1995 Family Service Award.

On Alan Kirby's dairy farm near Brompton, Northallerton, North Yorkshire, they're known as the Odd Couple. An orphaned foal named Lucy and Poppet, a Friesian cow.

Alan had planned to settle Lucy with his four adult shire-horses he parades at local shows, but unfortunately they rejected her. Poppet was the only other mum on the farm. Alan introduced them and now Lucy is thriving. 'Lucy was fading fast,' Alan said. 'She was in dire need of a mother figure to give her the will to live. Poppet had just calved and I thought I could appeal to her mothering instincts. It worked better than we could have hoped.'

In just a few hours Lucy and Poppet were running side by side in the fields, and Lucy had started eating properly. Alan's only worry now is if the bond between the two animals becomes too strong, adding, 'I'm afraid Lucy will really start to think she is a cow!'

A dog is a man's best friend, but Aaron Gonzalez proved that man can be dog's best friend by voluntarily flooding his house with raw sewage trying to rescue his dog's puppies!

It happened in 1992 when Girl, his Huskie/Chow mix, accidentally knocked away the inspection cover to the drainage pipe in the backyard. Aaron heard her yelping and whimpering, and went to investigate. There, trapped inside the sewer, were Girl's seven two-week-old puppies. Aaron's wife Sharon managed to pull two of them to safety but the others were just too far out of reach.

Fearing that they would drown, Aaron immediately started digging downwards to where the sewer pipe ran. In cracking it open he flooded his bathroom with sewage and also cut off the water supply to his house—but he still couldn't reach the puppies, who were too terrified to move. He rang the council, but since the incident was on his own property they wouldn't help. It was now getting late, so Aaron tried a desperate measure; he borrowed an industrial vacuum cleaner and miraculously managed safely to suck up three more of the puppies, leaving two still trapped.

It was now the early hours of the morning and Aaron decided to wait for daylight to begin the rescue attempt again. All night, Girl stood vigil over the drain, refusing to leave the last two puppies.

In the morning Aaron called the council again. Their advice was to let the puppies die and flush them out. Horrified, he enlisted the help of his neighbour, who knew one of the councillors. Using his clout, he persuaded two teams of city workers to turn up with pneumatic drills and start digging a trench down to the sewer pipe. By the time they'd done this one of the puppies had died, but the other was rescued, barely alive and completely covered in sewage. This puppy was instantly given a name—Stinky.

Six out of the seven puppies had been saved, but damage to the property was extensive and Aaron didn't have any savings to begin repairs. However, when the story was reported on the local news, friends and other animal lovers donated cash and supplies to help get Aaron and Sharon back on their feet. One of the benefactors was Kirstie Alley, star of *Cheers*, who gave them a large cheque to pay for the balance of the repairs.

Dolphins came to the rescue of a pod of eighty

pilot whales stranded on Tokerau Beach in New Zealand in September 1983. All human efforts had failed. Rescuers had tried to soothe the whales by talking to them and stroking them, keeping them wet as the tide rolled out. As the tide returned, they turned the whales seaward and waved them off—only to have all eighty turn around and beach themselves again. That's where the school of dolphins came in. They were fishing nearby and seemed to understand the whales' plight. Swimming into the shallows, they mingled with the whales and somehow got them to follow them back out to sea again.

Farmer Ron Hunt was walking around his fields near Portsmouth in 1989 when he thought he saw a fox cub dash down a fox hole. Nothing unusual about that, you might think, except that this 'fox' looked like no other fox that Ron had ever seen.

He waited patiently for it to make a reappearance and, when it did, he was astonished to find that it was actually a collie puppy. It turned out that the dog had been brought up by the vixen, living life just like a fox, and was remarkably fit and healthy.

An express train was delayed leaving Rome's main-line station, but this time the railway didn't blame leaves on the line or the wrong kind of snow; a cat was lying between the rails having kittens—literally.

A sharp-eyed guard had noticed her just before the train was about to depart and held the train there until four kittens were safely delivered and escorted to safer surroundings.

The floods in Venezuela totally devastated the country in December 1999. In the desperate attempts to find survivors, little thought was given to their pets and livestock. As the last survivors were located and the rescue ended, one rescue volunteer in a coastal town decided he still had a vital job to do. Ricardo Rodriguez wanted to do everything he could to ease the terrible animal suffering too. 'As there weren't any people left I decided I would dedicate myself to the animals,' he said, seeing cats, dogs, parrots and rabbits wandering aimlessly in the ruins, waiting for masters who might never return. His story attracted news reporters on Christmas Eve and he told them, 'So far, I've rescued about eighty dogs. I've also set free parrots and monkeys from their cages.' On finding lost or trapped animals, he gave them food and fresh water from a store he had hoarded in an abandoned house, and then rehoused them with soldiers or volunteers involved in the relief effort as they left the area. However, two dogs quickly adopted Rodriguez and were to be seen following him on all his rescues. One was a grey Great Dane and the other a red cocker spaniel he had found buried up to her neck in liquid mud and rescued from certain death. Rodriguez told reporters he knew he couldn't keep the one-man rescue effort up for ever but was philosophical about it. 'At least when I leave here I know that I'll have done something good,' he said. 'Animals have a right to life too.'

Did you know . . .
in the wild a contended elephant
will make a tummy-rumbling sound
like a cat's purr. It can be heard
over half a mile away!

An important rugby match between Clifton and Warminster was delayed for two minutes' silence in March 1984. Full-back John Hickey had arrived late at the ground, explaining that there'd been a sudden death in the family. Before he knew it, the captain had spoken to the officials, who agreed that the silence was the least they could do in his moment of grief—they were grateful that he'd put the club before his personal feelings and had shown up for the game. Word soon got round the ground and there was a unanimous show of respect and sympathy for John's loss.

It was only after the match that John could bring himself to tell his team mates that it was his pet cat that had passed away.

Spot, an eleven-year-old Border collie, arrived at Chris Murray's Pennywell Farm in Devon three years ago after retiring from sheepdog trialling. Any thoughts he might have had about settling down to a nice quiet life were shattered when he became a surrogate father to three orphaned lambs.

Spot started to take care of them when they were just three days old. Chris Murray said, 'When our first white-face Dartmoor lambs arrived we had to take in three to be bottle-fed. Spot cleans up their faces, which get covered in milk when they feed, and he keeps them warm. He also protects them if he sees any foxes on the farm.'

Proof indeed that man's best friend is also the baby lamb's best friend.

It's quite common to hear about dogs raising kittens—or cats raising puppies—after they've been abandoned by their mothers, but nothing compares to Kali, a mongrel dog who lived at

Gilsborough Grange bird and pet park near Northampton. In her time there Kali weaned and raised two baby pumas, a lion cub, a leopard and an Arctic fox.

Life seemed destined to be quite short for Derby the ram. He was intended as food for the rebels holding the city of Kotah during the Indian Mutiny in 1858. Worse still, when the British Army attacked, he found himself caught in the crossfire, tethered to a stake in a temple compound. Things certainly didn't look good, but Derby hadn't counted on the kindness of the commanding officer of the Sherwood Foresters or the bravery of one of his soldiers. During the battle, the British CO spotted the hapless ram looking distressed and hungry and asked one of his men if he could possibly rescue him. The soldier laid down his rifle and backpack and went forward, climbing over a number of low walls and crawling across open spaces. A sniper opened up on him, but he kept going and reached Derby. Naturally, the ram was frightened, but rather than just grabbing him, the soldier took time to calm him and fuss over him before picking him up and racing back to safe ground, manhandling the ram over the walls as best he could. After the battle was over, Derby became the official regimental mascot, and was awarded the

Indian Mutiny Medal, which has been passed down to successive regimental mascots ever since.

Maizie was a black-and-white ship's cat who lived on a US destroyer during the Second World War. When it was torpedoed by the Japanese, Maizie and six crewmen managed to scramble on to a life raft but found themselves helplessly adrift in the Pacific for days. Maizie stayed alive by eating malted milk tablets and a little water, and would comfort each one of the sailors in turn by curling up in their laps. This kept their spirits up and helped them all to find the strength needed to survive their ordeal. Eventually the drifting sailors were spotted by a sea plane and rescued. All had survived—thanks to Maizie. As one crewman later said, 'Without Maizie we would have gone nuts.'

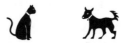

Only one Pope has been known to own a pet elephant, and that was Pope Leone I. The beast, an Indian elephant called Annone, was a gift from the King of Portugal and was delivered to the Vatican by the explorer Tristan de Cunha in March 1513. His boat docked in Italy at Porto Ercole, and Annone and his handlers made the journey by road to Rome. Soon hordes of people lined the streets to catch a glimpse of the strange procession. De Cunha, Annone and the handlers stayed at a villa for the night, where they washed and cleaned themselves up for the big day. The next morning they made their way through the streets of Rome and even more spectators lined the route to catch a glimpse of this peculiar-looking beast.

Annone was covered in silks and carried on his back a chest of gold and jewels as a gift for the Pope. Eventually they arrived at the Vatican. The Pope looked down from the Borgia tower to view his guests. Annone raised his head towards him, then trumpeted three times before kneeling in reverence.

The Pope took to Annone immediately and he moved into the Vatican. Every Sunday the public were allowed to visit him. On these occasions Annone would 'dance' and perform tricks for them. He lived happily in the Vatican for three years but fell ill with a chest complaint in 1516. The Pope's own physicians administered their special cure: a laxative potion mixed with gold dust. This didn't seem to work, and in June that year Annone passed away peacefully.

Pope Leone grieved for a long time. He wrote Annone's epitaph and commissioned the artist Raphael to paint a life-sized portrait of the great elephant, a fitting memorial to a truly noble beast.

When the Second World War broke out, Tot the Pyrenean wolfhound definitely knew whose side she was on! She lived in Amiens in France, in a convent boarding school where she was a particular favourite of the nuns. Soon after war was declared, soldiers from the British Expeditionary Force arrived in the town and were billeted at the school. Tot took an instant liking to them—possibly because they stuffed her full of cream buns and chocolate eclairs whenever the nuns weren't looking—and when they marched off to face the Germans, Tot even ran away with them. The soldiers reluctantly decided she'd be safer back at the convent and sent her home again.

In 1940, the German *blitzkrieg* swept through Amiens and the town fell to the invaders. In contrast, Tot now took an instant dislike to everyone and everything German. She only had to hear them speaking or singing in German—or catch a glimpse of a jackboot—and her hackles would go up and she'd start growling and barking at the invaders. One German soldier who went to retrieve a football which had landed in the convent-school garden had to flee for his life and scramble back over the wall as Tot spied him and decided to give him a piece of her mind. Another time, a German officer turned up on the doorstep and was immediately set upon by Tot. The nuns had to do everything in their power to stop him shooting the furious dog.

Tot's opposition to the Germans became a local legend, and she was an inspiration to the occupied people. The nuns even swore that Tot could tell the difference between Allied and German aircraft as they flew overhead, leaping for joy when Allied planes came over, and snarling and snapping at the Luftwaffe!

Despite her open defiance of the Nazis, Tot managed to live out the war and see her country freed once again.

Harry de Leyer was a man who knew something about horses, and when he spotted a white horse being loaded on to a van to meet an ignoble end at a local pet-food factory, something about the horse made him act. He approached the van driver and gave the horse the once-over. He was a mess, chafed raw by a heavy collar, covered in dirt and minus one shoe. Still, there was something—so Harry gave the driver $70 and the horse was spared. Harry took him home and named him Snow Man. After nursing him back to health, Harry then sold the horse for a tidy profit to a local doctor. However, Snow Man had taken quite a shine to Harry and jumped his new paddock fence to return to him. The doctor built a higher fence. Snow Man easily jumped that too. At this point Harry got the message. He gave the doctor his money back, took Snow Man home and started training him to be a show-ring jumper.

At his first big show, Snow Man went up against the open champion Andante. And beat him. In his next major competition he took on Diamante—one of the truly great international jumpers—and beat him too. Then, to cap it all, at Madison Square Garden he easily defeated First Chance, the reigning world champion.

In just six months, the horse destined for the dog-food factory had risen to capture the triple crown in show-ring jumping.

Did you know . . .
the Emperor Nero was such a huge
fan of the chariot races, he had a
flock of homing pigeons trained to
bring him the results fresh from the
arena!

One cat became the unwitting subject in a game of international tug-of-war. It started in 1987 when the cat, a one-year-old, stowed away in the back of a lorry travelling from Paris to Welwyn Garden City in Hertfordshire. MSAS Cargo, the transport company in whose

278

lorry the cat had hidden, named him Top Cat and took him in. Meanwhile, in France, *Le Parisien* newspaper named him Napoleon, claiming that he'd been 'cat-napped', and started a campaign to have him returned to his place of birth.

Allegations and counter-allegations, threats and counter-threats flew, but MSAS resisted pressure, and in the end the French capitulated. MSAS paid for Top Cat's quarantine and gave him a comfortable home in their headquarters in Bracknell.

During the Second World War, an RSPCA inspector searching a bombed-out house for trapped animals found a cat pinned in a narrow gap in the rubble. He freed her, gave her a saucer of milk to drink and then tried to coax her into a basket. The cat refused to go and repeatedly tried to climb back into the hole she had been rescued from. Thinking that her owner might be trapped down below, the inspector kept digging—and eventually found the family dog, injured but alive, deeper inside the ruins. Now that the dog was safe, the cat was quite happy to leave the scene.

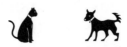

Rusty the Irish setter was a familiar sight at the

town butcher's shop. Every day he'd trot in and sit patiently by the counter until the butcher threw him a big juicy bone. With a wag of his tail he'd be gone—only to return a few minutes later and go through the same procedure again, returning home with a second bone. Customers began to ask what was going on, and the butcher explained that Rusty lived with another Irish setter called Red. Sadly, Red had been injured by a car and couldn't get about very well. So every day Rusty went to the butcher's to collect a bone to take home to his friend—and then went back to receive his own bone. How could he refuse such a kind-hearted dog? said the butcher.

I know they say that opposites attract, and that love is blind—but the most extraordinary romance I've ever heard about was between a dog and a beluga whale! In 1993, Rocky the husky dog was out sailing on his owner Jim Johnson's boat in Chedabucto Bay, Nova Scotia, when he attracted an admirer. Wilma the beluga whale was a regular sight around the bay. She had been orphaned at sea and now enjoyed swimming up to boats and meeting the humans. The moment she set eyes on Rocky the husky, though, her whole behaviour changed. First she swam round and round the boat, then she stood up on her tail and just stared and stared at the dog. Amazed onlookers swore that she was even acting a little coy, turning her head bashfully from side to side. Rocky stared back in amazement and Wilma tried to break the ice with a little light conversation, making clicking and whistling noises with her blow-hole. Whatever she said, it seemed to do the trick. Rocky suddenly leaned right out of the boat and rubbed noses with the whale! After that, Wilma sought Rocky out whenever he put to sea. On one occasion, Rocky couldn't resist jumping into the water to join her, and the two romped happily in the water together 'like two little puppies', according to witnesses. Of course, there could be no future for a husky-whale romance, and in time Wilma set out to sea again to find other whales—but for the time it lasted, their love touched the hearts of everyone in Chedabucto Bay.

Lucky the puppy owes her life to two big-hearted police officers who went well beyond the call of duty to help her. On the night of 25 February 1999, police officers Patrick Brown and John Romoga were on patrol in their squad car in Cleveland, Ohio, when they spotted the tiny light-tan mongrel puppy pathetically dragging herself along the road. She had been struck by a car and received terrible injuries to her back legs and hips. It was night, the temperature was almost freezing and the puppy was obviously in a great deal of distress. The police officers stopped, scooped her up and then raced her to an overnight veterinary clinic—where they got a shock. The vet refused to help the puppy without being paid.

'We were told either to have the dog put down or come up with the money. It wasn't even going to get a painkiller until the money came in the door,' Officer Brown recalls. Both officers turned out their wallets and gave the vet $150, all they had on them. 'I'm an animal lover. I knew that this dog was in a lot of pain,' Brown explains. The vet then agreed to treat Lucky—but warned that the total bill could exceed $1,500.

As soon as they got off duty, Brown and Romoga toured their precinct house collecting money for Lucky's operation, and then did the same at a local cops' bar. To top up the donations, Officer Brown put in another $400 of his own personal savings, and his partner gave another $250. The next day, Lucky had the operation she desperately needed and made astonishingly good progress. At first she went to live with Officer Brown, but he knew that he couldn't look after her properly because of his shift work and gave her to an animal foster home where she could receive constant care.

The police officers' kindness and generosity became headline news in Ohio. Three television stations and a local newspaper ran reports, and the policemen found themselves deluged with cheques and offers of money to help pay for Lucky's treatment. 'We saved the dog's life. I don't expect to be reimbursed for doing that,' Brown says, and all the money donated was given straight to animal charities. At the same time, over 200 people called to offer Lucky a loving home, and a dog-food company promised to feed the puppy for a year. It was agreed that the two officers could help choose Lucky's new home. 'I want Lucky to go to someone who has a real nice, big, fenced-in yard with a lot of kids and someone that can keep her company twenty-four hours a day,' Brown says. 'I'm glad people appreciate what we did, but that's not the reason we did it,' his partner adds. 'I would hope that most people would do what we did.'

Susan Hoicowitz, who runs an animal foster programme says, 'You'll be surprised how many police officers don't want it known that they carry biscuits and leashes in the trunk of their car. They like to pretend and keep up their tough-guy image.'

Did you know . . .
armadillos always produce identical
twins.

CHAPTER EIGHT

NAUGHTY BY NATURE

Computer owners should stick to having mice on their desks—not cats. A bank worker in San Francisco decided to take his Siamese cat, Morris, into work with him one day. While walking across the keyboard of his owner's computer, Morris accidentally keyed in a secret five-letter code that erased $100,000 worth of clients' account files. As you can imagine, his employers were not amused.

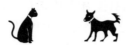

The staff at the village store in Upper Heyford, Oxfordshire, had never seen anything like it before. A shoplifter who was so brazen he calmly picked up what he wanted and walked straight past the till to the door. They would probably have called the police if the shoplifter hadn't been a ten-year-old Labrador!

He's called Benson and belongs to Mrs Win Huddle, who recently moved to the village with her husband David and fifteen-year-old daughter Julia.

The whole thing started one day when the shop was very busy. 'The shop's owner called me over and pointed to Benson. He had taken a tin in his mouth and was skulking out of the door with it,' says Win. 'It was a bit of a shock, but luckily I know the shopkeeper very well and she saw the funny side of it or it could have been very embarrassing.'

People have asked Win how she trained her dog to shoplift, but it's something he picked up himself. 'Now Benson helps himself to a tin every time I go to the shop, which is about twice a week,' she says. 'Labradors by nature like picking things up and putting them in their mouths. Benson just takes it a bit far.'

It's just as well that Benson doesn't know about Tommy the cat burglar, otherwise they'd end up as the Bonnie and Clyde of the animal world.

Tommy belongs to Ali Daffin and lives with her and her partner Paul Blake in Taunton, Somerset. Almost every night for three years Tommy has stolen a variety of objects, dragging them back to his home through the cat-flap. Her booty has included designer clothes, trainers, socks, jumpers, a Manchester United hat and several pairs of knickers.

Ali said, 'It was funny at first, but his haul just got more and more adventurous. Once he brought home a matching pair of expensive trainers. He brought the left one home one morning and then two days later I got the right one. She added, 'It looks like I've trained him. I reckon he's slipping in other people's cat-flaps.' She spoke to a newspaper in the hope that people will recognise the hoard and come to claim it.

But Tommy's behaviour is not that unusual, according to vet Paul Mitchell. He says that Tommy is trying to fit in with the family. 'Cats do it to ingratiate themselves as part of a group.'

Detectives at Brixton police station were puzzled (and more than a little embarrassed) when items started going missing from the handbags of staff working in the typing pool.

They were even more red-faced when it was discovered that the thief was actually on their payroll. It was Duke—one of their own police dogs.

Gangs of wild macaque monkeys were reported to be infiltrating apple orchards in the western suburbs of Tokyo, eating fruit there and then, but also carrying apples away with them. Reports state that some of the monkeys were even seen carrying the fruit away in plastic carrier bags.

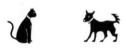

Grip was a retriever with a difference. He would retrieve wallets after being trained by his owner Tom Gerrard, a famous eighteenth-century London thief.

The dog used to trot up to well-dressed men in the street, wagging his tail and looking eager for them to pat him. The stranger would usually take to Grip right away and would bend down to stroke the dog. Grip had been trained to smell leather and could quickly locate the victim's wallet. With a quick snap of his head, Grip would seize the wallet in his teeth and would then run all the way home, where he delivered the wallet to Tom in return for a treat!

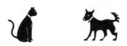

Percy the parrot blew his big chance in show business when he decided to do some improvising during a children's pantomime called *Pirates on Treasure Island* in 1999. The children's show, being staged in Blandford, Dorset, was going perfectly, until the seventeen-month-old Amazon parrot decided that 'Pieces of eight!' was a dull line and the play should really be spiced up with some salty four-letter words! Needless to say, he did not get an opportunity for an encore.

Art Peltz ran an exclusive jewellery shop in Laguna Beach, California, and always at his side was his 60-pound mixed-breed, Duque, his companion-cum-guard-dog.

In 1991 Carolyn Solomon visited the shop to get her $15,000 diamond ring cleaned.

Duque loved it when Art cleaned jewellery, and would jump up at the steam that sprayed out of the ring-cleaning machine. Some people even came into the shop just to see him do this, irrespective of whether they were interested in buying jewellery or not.

On this particular day, though, Duque got overexcited, and as Art held Carolyn's ring in the steam, the dog leapt up and swallowed it.

Art recalled the event: 'I was cleaning Carolyn's ring when I told her, "One day he's going to eat a ring . . . Oh, oh, I think he just did." I couldn't believe my eyes when the ring disappeared.'

Carolyn added, 'I always thought it was so cute the way the dog reacted to the steam. But when he swallowed my diamond, I didn't think it was so funny.'

Carolyn immediately took Art's dog to an animal hospital, refusing to let the dog out of her sight. There, an X-ray showed that the ring was in Duque's stomach, and the vet, Dr James Levin, gave the dog a drink that made him bring the ring up.

Carolyn then drove Duque and her ring back to Art's shop, where he gave the diamond an extra-special clean, considering where it had been. This time, though, Duque stayed in the front of the shop.

Rolo the black-and-white cat thinks he's a retriever. Jennifer Stallwood, his owner, says she never knows what he's going to fetch in next. Among the items he's retrieved are a Liverpool supporter's hat, a pair of gloves, bin liners, a windscreen wiper, empty milk cartons and a large number of banana skins!

It was 4.30 in the morning when mother-of-five Linda Perrott was woken by the sound of what she thought was someone clambering over the roof of her house in Melton Constable, near Holt in Norfolk. Fearing burglars, she persuaded her husband Leonard to investigate. Combing the house carefully, he couldn't find any evidence of entry—and certainly no intruders. The noise, however, continued as the couple tried to get back to sleep.

All was revealed, however, in the morning, when Mrs Perrott caught sight of the source of the racket: a tabby cat on her roof with its head firmly jammed in a tin can.

The stray must have found the can among

the rubbish and, in its eagerness to get something to eat, got its head stuck. It's thought that it chose to climb on the roof, blindfolded as it were, so it could shake the can off by banging it against the roof tiles.

Mr Perrott tried to coax the cat down to the ground but it refused. The RSPCA were equally unsuccessful, and it was a fireman who eventually saved the day. Once down on the ground the can was carefully prised off and the cat taken to a local vet's to recover while his owners were traced.

Inspector John Bowe of the RSPCA said, 'I've had to help cats stuck on roofs before and cats with their heads stuck in tins—but never both at once.'

Did you know...
racing pigeons can reach speeds of
up to 90 mph.

To stop his two cats scratching his furniture while he was out at work, Roger Sjoberg of Stockholm locked them in the bathroom. He came home to find that the mischievous moggies had jammed the shower taps on and flooded his flat. The bill came to over $60,000!

It was probably a mistake to keep a pet goat in the White House. It was certainly a mistake to keep a goat as frisky and bad-tempered as Whiskers—but when President Benjamin Harrison moved in with his family, his son Russell was so attached to the goat that he refused to leave it behind. Whiskers became a regular sight grazing on the White House lawns, until one day he took it into his head to escape. Passers-by on Pennsylvania Avenue were astonished to see a goat skittering down the road, with the President of the United States in hot pursuit, puffing, red-faced and swearing his head off. Happily, more recent presidents have helped to restore fully the dignity of the presidency.

Billy, a goat in Brazil, was very happy on his farm. Until the day, that is, when his owner sold fifteen nanny goats to another farmer. Seeking revenge, Billy got into the farmhouse and ate all twenty-four of the hundred-cruzeiro notes received in payment.

In 1983, Clinker the koala was guest of honour at a special ceremony at Sydney's Royal Botanic Gardens. The occasion was the presentation to the park of a generous donation of $50,000 by the Kimberly Clark Industrial Group. Unfortunately some bright spark from the company's PR department had the idea of printing the cheque on a eucalyptus leaf. Clinker the koala took one look at it, snatched it out of the dignitary's hand and proceeded to eat it.

Samantha was a tidy puss. Whenever she saw someone drop litter in the street she would run after it and pick up the discarded wrapper or bag, taking it back home to bury in the garden. She even followed schoolchildren, knowing they were likely to drop sweet and crisp packets.

One day, though, her habit for cleanliness got her into trouble. Samantha had entered a neighbour's house through an open window, and seeing some litter on a table, picked it up in her mouth and buried it in her garden. The only problem was that the 'litter' was actually banknotes. Oh yes, and Samantha's owner was a policeman!

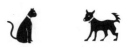

Delinquent monkeys going on the rampage in the northern Indian State of Punjab have forced the authorities there to take desperate measures. Gangs of monkeys have been reported mugging passers-by for their handbags, and a troop of monkey squatters have taken over two whole blocks of the regional government buildings and enjoy chasing civil servants. Monkeys are protected in India because of their association with the Hindu god Hanuman, so there is no question of sending the offenders to that great banana tree in the sky. Instead, the authorities have set up a special jail for monkey criminals. Any monkeys captured while committing crimes are incarcerated here and kept locked up until someone decides they've learned their lesson and are no longer a threat to society. Just how you can tell if a monkey has learned its lesson I'm not sure, but the system is said to be working extremely well.

Every day for ten days, the milk went missing from the doorstep of the McLoughlin family in Belfast. Determined to discover who was pinching their pinta, Colum McLoughlin set up a video surveillance camera—and was astonished to find that the culprit was their neighbour's collie, Poppins, who was making off with the bottles and burying them in her own garden next to her prized bones. Poppins's baffled owner said, 'The only way we can explain it is that it started shortly after our cat Frisky passed on. Poppins used to drink milk from her saucer.'

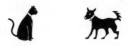

Friedrich Baier from Cologne specialised in posing as a doctor to make nuisance phone calls to women. He was eventually shopped to police—by his own pet mynah bird! One of his victims heard the bird shouting out Friedrich's name. 'During the call I could hear this cheeping and squawking in the background and then I clearly heard a man's name,' she said.

Another bird who turned stool pigeon to shop his master was the parrot belonging to a counterfeiter in Mountain Ash, South Wales. When trading standards officers raided his home looking for pirate computer software they were unable to locate the master disks—until the helpful parrot started squawking, 'Under the mattress! Under the mattress!' He was right as well, and officers seized goods worth nearly £10,000.

When the Webb family came to fill in their insurance claim for the £1,500 worth of damage to their car, they wondered what the insurance company would make of 'Act of Rhino' as the reason—especially since they lived in tranquil Worcestershire rather than the African veldt! The family had been on an outing to the West Midlands Safari Park near Kidderminster when a five-year-old white rhinoceros took rather a liking to their bright red Volvo estate. The rhino, named Tutsu, decided she would rather like to climb on the bonnet. Bill Webb remembers, 'I tried to reverse but nothing happened—which is not surprising when you've got a two-tonne rhino on the bonnet. The engine stalled. The rhino scrambled forward and tried to put its right foot through the windscreen, which bowed inwards and started to splinter.' Fortunately, park wardens were quickly on the scene and nudged the rhino away with their own vehicle.

In 1991 the first sighting was made of a rare American buff-breasted sandpiper at Pennington Marshes in Hampshire. Before dawn the next day, hundreds of birdwatchers arrived armed with powerful binoculars, camera lenses, video cameras and sound-recording equipment to 'capture' this new species.

The sandpiper arrived on the scene at first light and began to feed. But then so did a local sparrowhawk, which swooped down on the visitor and carried it off.

The birds that pecked the milk bottles belonging to Dr Jack Crosby were definitely not bird-brained. They knew quite well that the silver-topped milk was creamy, while the blue and red tops were skimmed. Over eight consecutive days nine out of sixteen silver tops were pierced, but no blue or red bottles were touched. The odds against this being pure chance were put at a thousand to one.

Did you know . . .
in 1966, a type of possum thought
to have been extinct for 15,000
years was found behind a rubbish
bin in a ski lodge in the Australian
Alps.

The mice in Doncaster apparently have excellent taste. As soon as they saw the bright red Ferrari convertible belonging to Robin Goforth, they decided it would make a rather upmarket winter home. They moved en masse into the car, which Mr Goforth had put away in his garage for the winter, and decided to make a nest in the engine, filling the space under the bonnet with scraps of bird feathers. When they got a bit peckish, they didn't have far to go to dine out in five-star luxury—just as far as the soft-top roof, in fact. By the time Mr Goforth discovered them, they had run up a restaurant bill in the region of £3,000.

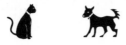

Joseph Vellone was out driving with Ebony, his Alsatian, around Norwalk, Connecticut. They'd stopped at traffic lights when Joseph decided to open the door and clear his throat. Whether she was just being playful or because she wanted to drive we'll never know, but Ebony pushed her owner out of the car, into the street.

She then moved over to the driver's seat while the car rolled across the junction, coming to a halt when it mounted the pavement and crashed into a building on the opposite side of the street. At which point Ebony jumped out and joined her stunned owner still lying dazed in the street.

Chips, a collie/husky mix, served in North Africa during the Second World War as a US Army battalion guard. He participated in the invasion of Sicily and won the Silver Star for capturing a machine-gun nest during the engagement. Although he was slightly wounded in the battle, he was refused the Purple Heart. On a later occasion, Chips bit President Dwight D. Eisenhower as he was inspecting the troops. (The US Defense Department denied that the incident was in any way related to the President's refusal to honour the dog.)

Chef Steve Lewis from Newcastle under Lyme now removes his hamster Cassie's exercise wheel before he and his wife go to bed. Don't worry, though. He's not being a killjoy—he's just taking precautions.

One day Cassie was a little too enthusiastic in her workout and the friction from the wheel caused a spark which set fire to her sawdust, the fire in turn spreading to some nearby curtains.

Cassie herself was uninjured and it was the insurers who pinpointed the exact cause of the fire. Although it was very unusual circumstances, they agreed to settle Steve's £386 damage claim.

In June 1997, two women were driving along in East Sussex when they spotted a dog running loose back and forth across the busy main road. They quickly pulled their car over and went to help before there was a terrible accident. In a great act of ingratitude the dog—a fourteen-stone Pyrenean mountain dog—jumped straight into their car via the open passenger door and then refused to let them back in, growling menacingly whenever they approached. A dog warden had to be called to evict the unwanted hitch-hiker.

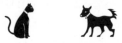

Some dogs aren't fussy when it comes to what they eat—their hunger (or just plain curiosity) gets the better of them—and a certain German shepherd called Nike was no exception.

His owner, Robert Hoffman, was a keen golfer who frequently went to a practice tee near where he lived in New York. For company (and to give him exercise), Robert started taking Nike with him, but after a while he noticed that his dog wasn't well.

He took him to the vet, where it didn't take long to discover that Nike had a severe stomach complaint; he'd eaten something he shouldn't—twenty-four golf balls to be precise!

The operation to remove them went smoothly enough, but to make sure Nike doesn't get the urge again, Robert now sprays his golf balls with dog repellent!

On Britain's motorways the greatest dangers you face are from speeding cars, fog or dodgy food at the service stations. In South Africa, it's a little different. Drivers on some of their busiest motorways face the added danger of delinquent baboons! In January 1997, the main highway between Cape Town and Johannesburg was almost closed because a troop of baboons were ambushing cars and pelting them with rocks. After numerous complaints from motorists, South African police moved in to clear the baboons—and had to retreat under a furious hail of rocks and stones! The police officers took cover, armed themselves with rocks and started retaliating, pelting the baboons back in a tit-for-tat fight that lasted for several hours! The battle ended in victory for the police, with the baboons running off.

Admiral George Dundas once bet his fellow naval officers that he and 'one other' could eat 16 pounds of tripe in a single session. The officers thought it was completely impossible and eagerly took his bet. Dundas sat down, ate about 2 pounds of the tripe and declared it was time for the 'one other' to eat his share. He then reappeared with a large bear! The bear scoffed the remaining tripe in a matter of seconds. The officers formed a council to discuss if Dundas had cheated or not, but were forced to conclude that the bear did indeed count as 'one other—' and the Admiral made himself a very tidy sum of money.

The Society for Indecency to Naked Animals started out as a joke, but then many of its members started to take it seriously. Their finest hour came in 1963 when they picketed the White House demanding that Jackie Kennedy put trousers on her horse. A spokesperson for the movement claimed at the time that by the end of the decade, all dogs would be wearing boxer shorts (especially boxer dogs).

Most times you see a horse on stage it's a panto horse, but in a rehearsal of Wagner's *Götterdämmerung* at London's Covent Garden Opera House, a real animal appeared as Brünnhilde's horse.

The conductor, Sir Thomas Beecham, was frustrated by the playing of one member of the orchestra, so he didn't mind too much when the horse wandered over to the edge of the stage and relieved himself all over the unfortunate musician. Beecham put down his baton and commented, 'The spectacle may be distressing, gentlemen, but that horse is a damn fine critic!'

Did you know . . .

young deer enjoy playing
hide-and-seek.

We've all heard of 'eagles' and 'birdies' in golf, but now it seems that other animals are getting in on the action too, on golf courses in the more exotic parts of the world at least. Golfers on the public courses in Darwin, in Australia's Northern Territory, regularly have to contend with play interrupted by crocodiles, wallabies, monitor lizards and snakes mistaking the ball for a nice juicy egg and swallowing it whole! It's a common enough mistake. Birds of prey regularly spot a golf ball, think it's an egg and then swoop down and carry it away in their talons.

In 1961, players on the links at the Ocean Shores Golf Course near Aberdeen, Washington State, fled in terror as a large black bear strolled on to the fourth fairway. It was chased away by a helicopter, but not before stealing a golf ball. Club officials had to be consulted on how the next shot should be taken. They concluded, 'If a ball is picked up by a bear, players may replace and take one penalty stroke. If a player manages to get his ball back from the bear, he may take an automatic par for the hole!'

When teddy bears and other fluffy children's

302

toys went missing from a neighbourhood in Oxfordshire, police were puzzled. There were no reports of break-ins—whoever stole them could have only slipped in through partially open windows and must have had the agility of a cat. It turned out they were right. The thief *was* a cat—called Elija—who belonged to a young girl, Tamara Oppenheimer. She discovered by accident a whole stash of soft toys that Elija had hidden in their house, and all the neighbours were invited in to reclaim their possessions, including several pairs of fluffy slippers.

Airports the world over are on high-security alert in case of terrorist attacks—but few are prepared for attacks by moose! Anchorage International Airport certainly is now, after two juvenile-delinquent moose broke through the perimeter fencing and started banging their antlers furiously against the parked airliners on the tarmac. They caused over £14,000 worth of damage before they were finally shooed away. Apparently the young moose had been trying to shed their antlers.

You wouldn't expect BT engineer Ryan Hoare to have a particularly dangerous job—but he has, because he's called upon to visit the Copthorne telephone exchange in Sussex. There, in a pen next to the exchange, is a llama. He's normally a docile creature, but the sight of a BT uniform to this llama is like, well, a red rag to a bull. At the first sight of Ryan approaching the exchange the llama makes a dash for the fence, rears up on his back legs and lunges at the engineer. Unless he's nimble, Ryan (or his colleagues) is grabbed by the scruff of the neck and held captive.

Those engineers who are nimble on their feet or who keep their distance suffer an arguably worse fate than being bitten. Llamas are famed for their copious and accurate long-range spitting—and this one is no exception.

BT field engineer Jamie Knight commented that: 'We have to test the exchange's equipment each day but every time an engineer approaches, the llama is at the fence in a flash. He acts as if he's a watchdog. It's impossible to slip in and out without him spotting you. He seems to have claimed the exchange as part of his territory and guards it jealously.'

But BT's boffins have come up with a secret weapon to counter the attacks. To cause a diversion so that they can enter the exchange safely, engineers are now issued with apples in their toolbags.

Inhabitants of the Indian state of Bihar keep their eyes open for a particular elephant who's developed an addiction to alcohol, and who gets particularly violent when drunk.

When the elephant in question wants a drink, literally nothing will get in its way. It's been known to knock down villagers' illegal breweries, as well as break into stores containing rice beer.

Once drunk, the elephant will then go on a rampage looking for more.

This particular creature doesn't have a name, but is known by the locals as 'The Excise Commissioner'.

African elephants in the Kruger National Park are cleverer. They don't go round looking for beer. They make their own. Keepers at the wildlife reserve have observed elephants gobbling down lots of fruit from the marula tree, drinking equally large volumes of water, then running around to start off the natural fermentation process.

After a short while the mixture turns to alcohol—and the park becomes full of staggering elephants.

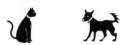

Police were called to the Earl of Iddesleigh's

country home near Exeter in 1981 to investigate an attempted break-in. French windows were found smashed and police spent hours searching the premises and making door-to-door enquiries. The case was solved when they discovered the culprit—a neighbour's goat who'd been head-butting the windows.

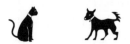

Terrified by the prospect of vandals damaging their courts on the eve of an important tournament, a certain Australian tennis club employed an Alsatian guard dog to deter trespassers. The next morning, staff discovered that no less than nine square yards of the centre court had been ripped up. The guard dog had become bored during the night and gone on a hunt for buried bones!

Fiest the pub guard dog decided to take extreme measures to stop thieves making off with the pub's takings. As landlady Diane Watkins was counting the cash at her pub in Driffield, north Humberside, the security-conscious Alsatian decided that the piles of banknotes were just too vulnerable there on the worktop—and decided it would be best to shred them. Diane and her husband Andrew watched in horror as Fiest grabbed a thousand pounds' worth of tenners and chewed them into tiny pieces before their eyes. 'We tried to salvage what we could,' Mr Watkins recalls, 'but Fiest had done a very good shredding job and the bank would only accept eight of the notes.' The Watkinses' insurance company listened sympathetically, agreed it was a very funny story—and then refused to pay out.

In 1994, villagers in Lepton near Huddersfield were plagued by mysterious power cuts. The local electricity board were completely in the dark as well, until they discovered that three shire-horses—Dolly Blue, Billy Whizz and Tommy Sausage—were to blame. They lived in a field underneath the village's power lines and loved nothing more than to scratch their itchy backsides on a pole supporting the electricity cables. When they really got into it, the pole started to sway and the power lines touched each other and shorted out!

Did you know . . .
that David Niven once performed a
marriage ceremony for two gorillas,
and later became their son's
godfather!

Do horses find racing as exciting and dramatic

as racegoers do? Well, Lost Link certainly doesn't. In a race at Saratoga Park in July 1991, to the annoyance of its owner, trainer, rider—and the punters—it fell fast asleep in the starting gate.

His official name was Pride of Rondebosch— but everyone knew the lanky Great Dane as Nuisance because of his uncanny ability to get in everyone's way! In August 1939, Nuisance was enlisted into the Royal Navy as a mascot with the rank of Able Seaman. His official occupation was given as 'Bonecrusher First Class'. His naval conduct reports showed that he wasn't exactly the pride of the navy. His character was described as 'very good' but his efficiency could only be rated 'moderate' and his discipline was frankly rated 'poor'. He liked to hang out in pubs with his comrades and was just a little too fond of lager. He had a tendency to go absent without leave whenever the mood took him, and he could certainly be relied upon to get in the way. However, he did have some redeeming qualities. He would stand rigidly to attention whenever he heard the National Anthem, he broke up bar fights and on one occasion at least he saved a fellow crew member's life when he found him collapsed with malaria in a rarely visited part of a shore base.

Sadly, Nuisance became ill and died in April 1944. He was buried with full military honours in Simonstown in South Africa. Today, his statue still stands in Simonstown, and South African animal charities often collect money at the site.

A certain Jack Russell is currently in the dog house. While his owners were out, he accidentally pressed the redial button on their telephone and then spent thirty minutes barking a message on to a family friend's answering machine. Unfortunately, the Jack Russell lives in Canada and the family friend, Joanne Collingwood, lives in Tadworth in Surrey!

Kevin and Gillian Hewitt from Redcar, Teesside, were convinced they'd hidden their spare cash where no burglar would ever find it. Unfortunately, they hadn't counted on the keen senses of Ben, their Border collie. When no one was looking, he nosed into the gap behind the kitchen wall, pulled out a roll of banknotes amounting to £120—and promptly scoffed them all down! Amazingly, the couple managed to retrieve £110 of the money by following Ben everywhere and then checking his unmentionables for scraps containing the banknotes' serial numbers. The Bank of England then credited them for the lost notes—and replaced them with nice clean new ones.

The sight of a hairy Boy Scout walking into a bar so shocked customer Joan Hemmer that she dropped her drink, fell back against a wall and injured her shoulder.

The Boy Scout in question was actually a chimpanzee called Mr Jiggs, dressed up. He and his owner, Ronald Winters, had stopped at Fricke's Old Hook Inn in Freehold, New Jersey, on their way to entertain at a local Scout jamboree. Joan sued Ronald for her injuries but lost. The court heard that Mr Jiggs had lived with his owner since he was a baby and was very tranquil and domesticated. Ronald told the court that he had certainly had no intention of scaring Mrs Hemmer— and that was Scout's honour.

CHAPTER NINE

WELL I'LL BE A MONKEY'S UNCLE!

An animal shelter in the American Midwest has come up with an ingenious fund-raising idea. It's called 'Cow Chip Bingo' (here it would be called 'Cow Pat Bingo'). Basically, a football field is divided into squares, each with a number on it. The area around the outside is reserved for a huge family picnic, with participants buying any amount of numbers, as they would lottery tickets, for the chance to win a cash prize.

How do they win? Well, a very well-fed cow is led on to the football field, and whichever square she deposits her droppings on is the winner.

It worked very well for the animal shelter in question. I just wonder how the participants felt as they were trying to have their lunch . . .

A few years ago a very active senior citizen, a blind lady in Australia, used to fly all round the country, using a small internal airline. She always travelled with her guide dog, a beautiful golden Labrador, whom the flight crew used to spoil something rotten. The dog always had a seat next to her, where he'd sit contentedly for the duration of the flight.

One day, however, the plane had to wait on the tarmac to collect passengers from an interconnecting flight. During this delay, the dog became restless and the old lady summoned a stewardess to ask if she could take him for a walk on the apron.

The captain overheard the conversation and volunteered to take her dog for a short walk himself, just to pass the time.

The sun was beating down, so he put on his sunglasses, took the dog's lead and walked proudly down the steps in his four-stripe pilot's uniform.

Just then, the bus with the transfer passengers turned up—only to see their pilot with dark glasses, apparently being led by a guide dog.

Many of them refused to take off . . .

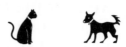

The authorities in Florida have strict regulations as to how many domestic pets may be kept in a single house. These rules were devised to ensure that the pets are well looked after and have enough space. Great idea in principle, it's just that the rules are a little confusing.

Basically, Florida residents can keep up to four pets, or five if one of them is a fish. If none of the five pets are fish, then each pet must be under 10 pounds in weight. Ten pets are permissible, but only if none of them weighs more than a pound, but you're allowed up to twenty-five pets—providing they are all fish. Got that?

If you go up before a judge, it pays not to antagonise him—but that's exactly what David Ashley of Senaca Falls, New York State, did. He was up before Judge Gordon Tetor on a charge of raising poultry without a licence but appeared holding a rooster under his arm.

When the judge ordered the bird to be removed from the courtroom, Ashley protested, saying that the bird was his attorney and explaining, 'It was the only legal counsel I could afford.'

In the early 1960s, stockyard owners in America's Midwest were puzzled to find that their cows smelled nice. Well, maybe not actually nice, but a lot better than they normally did. They couldn't figure out what had happened to them—and wouldn't until thirty years later.

The answer was revealed under the Freedom of Information Act. The cows smelled nice because they had been sprayed with deodorant. It was all an exercise carried out under enormous secrecy by the military at the height of the Cold War. Crack teams of Green Beret marines infiltrated the stockyards undercover and sprayed as many of the herd as they could before making their escape. And the purpose of this mission? It was to demonstrate just how easy it would be for Communist agents to enter the cattle pens and spread a deadly virus in the same way.

I'm not a gambling man, but I love this tale about a bet. It concerns Charles James Fox, the eighteenth-century statesman. One day he was walking through London with the then Prince of Wales, who later became George IV.

Fox surprised the Prince by betting that if they were each to choose a side of the street, then he would see more cats on his side than the Prince. The future King of England was taken aback but took up the bet, thinking that Fox was either stark staring mad or a compulsive gambler.

The Prince chose his side of the street and Fox crossed over to his. By the time they'd reached the end, not a single cat had been seen on the Prince's side, while no fewer than thirteen had been found on the side chosen by the statesman.

The Prince of Wales duly paid up but couldn't understand how his friend had been so convinced that he would win.

Fox explained, saying: 'Your Royal Highness took, of course, the shady side of the street as the most agreeable. I knew the sunny side would therefore be left to me, and cats always prefer the sunshine.'

It's easy when you know how!

Did you know . . .
the ancient Persians respected their
dogs so much that their wise men
were given the title 'Khan',
meaning dog.

The police force in Chaguanas, central Trinidad, were baffled. Somehow rustlers were spiriting away sheep and goats from local farms in the middle of the night and no one had seen anything, despite police surveillance on the roads. There were no trucks loaded with livestock to be seen, but animals were disappearing with frightening regularity. Obviously the criminals had hit upon a particularly ingenious scheme. The mysterious animal thefts continued until one night a patrol spotted a rental car cruising along with its lights off. The patrol car gave chase, and after a furious pursuit through the dark country lanes, the rental car suddenly pulled over and the driver fled into the fields. The police approached the car with great caution, seeing that there were still people inside. As they shone their torch into the abandoned car, an unbelievable sight met their eyes. Sitting in the back seat was a goat wearing a shirt and trousers and a hat. Next to him was a sheep—in a dress. Two more goats were found in the boot of the car, both wearing shirts and trousers. The rustlers had been disguising the animals as human passengers and driving them straight past the police patrols!

In Queensland, Australia, there are a lot of professional crocodile handlers employed in the state's many game parks and farms. To minimise the risk of injury, the state recently issued an official Workplace Health and Safety Guide giving employees helpful hints, tips and advice on the correct procedures to adopt when handling these dangerous reptiles.

Critics, however, thought the state was underestimating the intelligence of the readers, citing advice given in the manual such as 'Do not place any part of one's body in the mouth of a crocodile' and 'Do not sit on the back of a crocodile.'

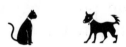

Tiddles was an aptly named cat, living as he

did in the ladies' lavatory at Paddington station for over fifteen years. He belonged to June Watson, the toilet attendant, but soon got to know his regular 'customers', who used to feed him treats when they paid a visit.

The small scraps Tiddles ate soon turned him from a sprightly kitten into a veritable fat cat. If he wasn't sleeping he was eating, and it wasn't long before Tiddles became one of the heaviest cats in the country, weighing in at a massive 30 pounds. In 1982, he was named 'London's Fat Cat Champion'.

As Tiddles got fatter, so did his appeal. His fame spread worldwide, with fans sending him letters addressed simply to 'Tiddles, Paddington Station, England'.

What was also funny about the situation was that many of the women using the toilets at Paddington station didn't realise they were sharing them with a man—Tiddles was a tom cat.

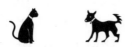

It's wrong to think that cats hate water—it's the unexpected wetness that frightens them. At Devil's Point naval base in Plymouth, a cat used to plunge into the sea every day and present her catch to the soldiers in the guardroom for inspection.

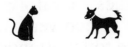

For years people tried to guess what had inspired Sir Edward Elgar's great 1899 composition the *Enigma* variations. Years later he admitted that it had nothing to do with cathedrals or organs, as had been thought. Instead it was inspired by Dan, the fat bulldog who belonged to his great friend George Sinclair. Apparently Sinclair had described how Dan had been walking along a steep bank of the River Wye when he fell in. He then paddled upstream until he reached a landing place, waddled out and rejoiced with a cheery bark. According to Elgar, 'Sinclair said, "Set that to music", so I did.'

Smokey is officially Britain's oldest living cat. Last year she celebrated her 32nd birthday. The previous year she had outlived her elderly owner and was taken in by a rescue centre before being found a new home. Sara Cox, a volunteer at the rescue centre, said, 'When we rescued Smokey she was in a terrible state and could not clean herself. But she is a tough old cookie and after some dental treatment Smokey really picked up. It is absolutely wonderful to see the change in her.'

Although partially deaf and blind in one

eye, Smokey can still get about and miaows loudly for her favourite tinned cat food at mealtimes. Not bad for a 32-year-old! (Incidentally, I worked out that in her life, she must have eaten over two tons of the stuff!)

Whether it's the solitary nature of the profession that leads writers to value the companionship of cats, or whether they find it gives them inspiration, is hard to tell. Whatever the reason, writers seem to adore them. The following authors all owned cats, and in some cases wrote about them: William Wordsworth, Charles Dickens, Ernest Hemingway, Sir Walter Scott, Edward Lear, Victor Hugo, W. B. Yeats, Samuel Johnson, Lord Byron, John Keats, Rudyard Kipling, Dorothy L. Sayers, T. S. Eliot, H. G. Wells, the Brontë sisters, Mark Twain, Jeremy Bentham, Horace Walpole, Paul Gallico, Truman Capote, Alexander Dumas, Raymond Chandler and Edgar Allen Poe. Aldous Huxley was asked for advice by an aspiring young author. His reply was, 'If you want to write, keep cats.'

In 1504, Conquistador Vasco Nuñez de Balboa managed to take Panama with his mastiff

Leoncico (Little Lion). The Indians were so scared of Leoncico that they threw down their weapons and fled at the first sight of him. Afterwards, the dog was given a solid-gold collar, promoted to the rank of lieutenant and drew a crossbowman's pay.

If you're one of the tens of thousands of people in this country who are violently allergic to cats, but would dearly love a mog of your own, you might want to consider owning a Devon Rex or a Cornish Rex. These lovely curly-coated cats don't seem to cause the allergic reactions experienced with other breeds of cat.

If you're a horse the last allergy you want is hay fever—but that's what Teddy, a five-year-old bay, suffers from. He belongs to Sandra Ashby of Exhall, near Coventry, and, what's worse, he's allergic to straw as well.

Before the allergy was diagnosed in March 1996, Teddy suffered from constant coughing and wheezing. To overcome these symptoms, Teddy was given a long course of animal antihistamines, but the only real long-term solution was to ban hay and straw entirely. As a result, his bed is now an expensive mixture of peat and wood shavings and his feed has to be thoroughly soaked before he can eat it.

The extra costs are well worth it. As Sandra says, when he's suffering from the allergy, 'he looks really sorry for himself, and is pitiful and very chesty'.

Did you know . . .
a boy hippo tells a girl hippo that
he's interested in her by yawning in
her face.

In an extraordinary safety drive, all the reindeer in Finland are now being fitted with special reflective collars so that drivers can see them at night. Many reindeer are involved in accidents at night on Finnish roads. When you consider that, in the northernmost extremes above the Arctic Circle, a night can last up to six months, it's a very sensible precaution for the government to take.

The Allied forces in Burma in the Second World War badly needed the help of locals to assist in building strategic roads to transport soldiers and vehicles. The Burmese, however, were reluctant to help because Japanese propaganda had persuaded them that the Allies were the enemy.

A British colonel, however, had excellent

knowledge of local customs, and was aware of the fact that white cats were a symbol of beauty and good luck to the Burmese. He ordered his troops to round up every white cat they could find and adopt them as pets. He also ordered that white cats be painted on the sides of military vehicles to give the impression that they were the emblem of the British Army. When the Burmese saw so many white cats with the British, they quickly changed sides.

The Dean of Worcester College in Oxford had a problem. He was about to take up his post when he learned that the college, like most others, did not admit dogs. He was worried that he'd have to leave his beloved pet Flint behind until some bright spark had an idea— and that was for the governing body of the college to declare Flint a cat. It did the trick!

St Bernards were only called that after a dog show in England in 1862. Up until then the breed was known as bear hounds—or barihunds—because they looked like bears. The name St Bernard comes from the saint who founded a hospice to help people crossing the Alps; the monks there would use their mastiffs to look for travellers lost in the snow.

What do you expect from two piglets raised on the Isle of Dogs? Porkers Percy and Patch think they're puppies. The two baby pigs had to be removed from their mum at the Mudchute urban farm after she kept threatening to roll over and squash them. Farm worker Ruth Mortimer took them home to her pet pooch Elsa, who immediately fostered them. Now the piglets think they're dogs, and while they don't actually bark, they have learned to sit up and beg!

Another piglet, called Mr Muscle, believes he's a cat. Mr Muscle, a Vietnamese pot-bellied pig, was rescued from a children's farm in Surrey by manager Jill Langrish after his brothers and sisters rejected him. Jill took him home with her, and was astonished to find that her black cat Tuppence immediately adopted the little porker, treating him just like a kitten. Mr Muscle by all accounts loved the affection and now sits on Jill's lap whenever he wants a stroke, just like a real cat.

When Lord Stodart of Leaston became a Member of Parliament in 1959, he practised his maiden speech by reciting it to the pelicans as he walked to the House of Commons through St James's Park. He said afterwards, 'Not a soul was looking and the pelicans seemed to be quite appreciative.' In any event, his speech went down well. The subject was the Mental Health Bill, under which the police were to be granted powers to detain for up to forty-eight hours any person deemed to be showing signs of eccentric behaviour.

Like talking to pelicans?

The smallest dog in the world is a tiny Yorkshire terrier pup called Posy. Posy, who lives in Greater Manchester with her master Kevin Horkin, weighs just six ounces and has to be groomed with a toothbrush!

Apparently, in America an increasing number of owners are calling their mongrel dogs Pizza. You know, 'a pizza this, a pizza that' . . . In Australia, mongrels are sometimes referred to as 'bitsers'—because they've got all kind of bits and pieces in them.

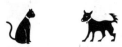

A cat may hold the secret to who really discovered America! The Maine coon is very similar to the Norwegian forest cat, and historians point to this as part of their evidence that cats came to America before Columbus—as pets of the Vikings.

Anglers should always pay close attention to the rules and regulations of their fishing permits, particularly in the United States. In Toltec, Colorado, fishermen are fined if they use their bare hands; in Washington State you can't shoot fish; in Santa Clara, California, you can't drug fish; while in Knoxville, Tennessee, it's illegal for anglers to use a lasso.

When it comes to *where* you can fish, the rules are even more bizarre. In Washington DC, for instance, it's against the law to fish for trout while horse-riding; while in Idaho you're not allowed to fish while seated on a giraffe.

A wealthy nineteenth-century Irish landowner named Adolphus Cooke believed that all animals were actually reincarnated people, and that the animals on his estate were really the great and good of centuries past. He insisted that one turkey in particular was a reincarnation of his own father and ordered—on pain of dismissal—that all estate workers should doff their caps to it and wish it a hearty good morning. Cooke himself believed that after his death he'd be reincarnated as a fox, so one of his last great projects was to have huge luxury fox dens built all over his land.

Did you know . . .
film star George Clooney has a pet
Vietnamese pot-bellied pig!

In March 1992, a gang of cat burglars broke into an electrical store in Miami. Although the shelves were lined with top-of-the-range hi-fis and TV sets, what they were really after was Bootsie, the black-and-white tom cat who lived there. They cat-napped him along with his favourite toys, litter box, food bowl and bed—then stole one of the store's delivery trucks to whisk him away. Police were completely baffled by the crime.

When the British Army burned Washington during the War of 1812, the wife of President Madison, Dolley, managed to escape from the White House with two of the country's most valuable items, the Declaration of Independence and her pet parrot. The parrot was given asylum in the Octagonal House, the French Ambassador's official residence, where he remained safe until the British were driven from the capital.

Can a dog give evidence in court? That was the question that baffled the finest legal minds in Britain in 1993. Defence barristers were arguing that evidence gathered by police dogs trained to sniff out drugs should be inadmissible in court because the defence could not cross-examine them. After much deliberation, Lord Chief Justice Taylor prepared a seventeen-page document on the issue. He judged that, as long as its handler could prove that the dog was reliable, and the jury were warned to view any evidence provided by a dog with care, then evidence given by a dog was admissible in law.

When Ursula Beckley of Long Island in America tried to make a three-egg omelette one day in 1989, she cracked an egg open—and a six-inch black snake slithered out. She sued her local supermarket for $3.6 million, claiming that she had been so deeply traumatised by the incident that she could never look at an egg again!

In 1859, Britain and America almost went to

war—over a pig! The provocative porcine in question belonged to an Englishman called Charles Griffin who lived on San Juan Island near Vancouver. The pig, whose name has been lost to the ages, used to stray on to a neighbour's potato patch. The neighbour, an American, didn't take too kindly to the pig's intrusions and started taking pot shots at it. Griffin complained and British troops arrived to back him up. Then the American called in the Marines. For thirteen years, the troops faced each other in an uneasy stand-off until the 'Pig War' was finally settled by arbitration.

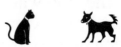

If you're having trouble sleeping, and your imagination doesn't stretch to visualising sheep, you can always buy a copy of a new American book called *Count Sheep*. Inside are literally hundreds of photographs of . . . you guessed it, sheep. The idea is to start counting them until you drift off. Should you have really chronic insomnia, you might discover that there are a total of 65,000 sheep in the book. An abridged 'travelling' version, featuring 28,000 sheep, is also available. Incidentally, if you prefer to count real sheep, by far the best place to go is the Falkland Islands, where there are around 350 sheep for every human being.

Rich eccentric Sir George Sitwell was a failed writer. He produced many works, including *The Origins of the Word Gentleman*, *Acorns as an Article of Medieval Diet* and *The History of the Fork*—but sadly, no one would publish them. It may have been his subject matter. It may have been his style. However, Sir George had an entirely different explanation. He blamed the local cows. Their huge white bodies were distracting him when he looked from his study window, he decided, thus preventing him from truly mastering his profession. His solution was—if you'll pardon the pun—novel. He employed leading artists to travel to his estate in Derbyshire and paint exquisite Chinese willow patterns on the sides of the cows to make them more inspirational.

The founder of the Heinz canned food empire, H. J. Heinz, had a gigantic pet alligator which he kept in a glass tank on the roof of his Pittsburgh factory. His official reason was that he thought his employees would enjoy seeing the 800-pound, fifteen-foot-long beast. It might just have been coincidence—but strikes at the factory were few and far between as well!

The film *Babe*, about the adorable talking piglet, had its title changed when it was shown in Hong Kong. Its new Cantonese title, translated, means 'The Happy Dumpling-To-Be Who Talks and Solves Agricultural Problems'!

When the Pope announced that he planned to visit Denver in 1993, local animal lovers became worried about the safety of their local prairie dogs. Prairie dogs are marmot-like rodents who live in elaborate underground 'villages'. The animal lovers were worried that 300,000 visitors to the area would cause the prairie-dog villages to collapse—and so they set off to relocate every prairie dog in the area. But prairie dogs are notoriously difficult to catch. They burrow deep and can give a nasty nip if frightened. The answer was at hand in the shape of a special $200,000 prairie-dog-friendly 'vacuum cleaner'. The animal lovers stuffed the nozzle into the burrows and sucked the elusive little rodents out one by one. Once captured, they were released a safe distance away from the Pope's planned visit.

The most unusual treasure in the vaults of the National Westminster Bank just has to be a five-and-a-half-inch-long butterfly fish. The fish apparently has some unusual markings on its tail which resemble Arabic and which devout Muslims have interpreted as reading: 'Divine universal. There none but God to be worshipped.' Originally discovered in a Dar-Es-Salaam market, the miracle fish is now under guard in the bank until a more permanent holy home can be found.

Did you know . . .
prairie dogs kiss as a form
of greeting.

Lionel Walter, the second Baron Rothschild, was obsessed with animals. This great Victorian eccentric loved nothing better than to ride around the lanes near his estate, Waddesdon Manor in Tring, Hertfordshire, in a trap pulled by a pony and three zebras. As a child, his pets included an opossum and a tame dingo. By the time he went to university in Cambridge, he had amassed a flock of several dozen kiwis and they all joined him at college. After graduating, Rothschild didn't go into finance like the rest of his illustrious family. With his fortune he started his own natural history museum. He would pay almost anything for a specimen he needed to complete a collection, and by 1920 he had amassed 2,000 complete mounted animals, 200 heads, 1,000 fish, 700 reptiles, 3,000 stuffed birds and 200,000 birds' eggs. He was completely obsessive about classifying animals and even had a sub-species of giraffe named after him.

In the 1890s Lord Salisbury was guest of honour at an important meeting of prominent politicians hosted by the Baron. As the guests took their places in the dining hall, they noticed there was an empty chair between each of them. Before they could work out who the additional guests were, servants opened the door at the other end of the room and in waddled twelve chimpanzees, all wearing dinner suits, who took their places at the table.

Jeremy Bentham, the eighteenth-century English philosopher and free thinker, valued his cat over most humans. He named him Sir John Langbourne and later promoted him to the Reverend Sir John Langbourne. If you think Bentham was a bit nutty, you're right. A condition of his will was that after his death he was to be stuffed and seated upright in his favourite chair.

The poet Samuel Taylor Coleridge once owned a cat who went by the grand name of the Most Noble the Archduke Rumpellstilzchen, Marcus MacBum, Earl Tomnefuagne, Baron Raticide, Waowhler and Scratch—but he called him Rumpel for short!

Wynard, a small town in Saskatchewan, Canada, has reinvented the Roman sport of chariot-racing—with a bit of a difference. Instead of the chariots being drawn by teams of horses, they're actually pulled by chickens. Granted, the chariots are much smaller, but these hand-built, scaled-down replicas are harnessed to teams of chickens who then race frantically around a purpose-built, fifty-foot track.

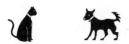

Don't rely on a dog's name to tell you where it originated from. Russian wolfhounds originally came from Arabia, while Great Danes first appeared in Germany. The English mastiff started out in Tibet of all places, and the Welsh terrier is an old English breed!

The Canadian Rhinoceros Party was once a political force to be reckoned with. It was formed by nationalist Quebecers and soon became the fifth largest political party in Canada. The leader was Cornelius, a rhino born in 1979 at the Granby Zoo in Montreal. In January 1980 the party (under Cornelius's leadership) declared war on Belgium after the character Tintin blew up a female rhino in one of his cartoon stories (the party claimed it was Cornelius's mother, Elizabeth). After much behind-the-scenes diplomacy, a peace treaty was signed on 30 January. As part of the war reparations, the Belgian Ambassador served lunch to members of the Rhinoceros Party. And guess who ate the leftovers?

More recently, from 1981 to 1989 the mayor of Sunol, a small town in California, was an 85-pound Labrador/Rottweiler cross called Basco. He led the town parade every year, wearing a red satin bow around his neck. His popularity among the 1,500 people of Sunol had grown every year since his campaign manager declared a three-point manifesto, 'a cat in every tree, a bone in every dish and a fire hydrant on every street corner'. That wasn't enough for one faction and they put up another candidate to stand against him . . . another dog. Needless to say, Basco won paws down.

At about the same time, Basco's feline equivalent was elected mayor of Guffey in Colorado. She went by the name of Sugar La Plume but her name is far grander than her office—a cardboard box at the back of a local store. Sugar retired in 1993 and her place was taken by a dog, Shanda. By this time the townsfolk thought that maybe the mayor should have a bodyguard, so they appointed one—another pooch, called Tojo.

Animals running for public office goes back a long way. Caligula, the Roman Emperor from AD 37–41, made his favourite horse, Incitatus, a senator (complete with its own house and servants). Nearer to home, in 1992, a cocker spaniel called Bob stood as the official candidate of the Monster Raving Looney Barking Mad Dog Party in a Swansea constituency. Sadly, he didn't win, losing his deposit—but leaving one of his own!

In San Francisco, in 1858, Thomas O'Brien was accused of grand larceny for stealing the valuable pure-bred dog belonging to James Donahue.

The judge dismissed the case, stating that under California laws, dogs were not classed as property. Failing on this count, Donahue then went back to court accusing O'Brien of petty larceny—for stealing his dog's collar and muzzle.

This time, he won.

Being mayor isn't enough for some ambitious canines. They want to be top dog, literally—and run for president. This happened twice in the 1980s, first in the 1984 election, when a black Labrador named Windy April Reedy registered with the Federal Election Committee to run for the presidency. All the necessary forms were accepted, including her paw-print as signature. Unfortunately she failed to secure many votes and the White House became just an unfulfilled dream.

Four years later, Punch Burger, an eight-year-old German shepherd cross stood for election, running on a platform of fewer import restrictions on beef. At the time, scandal erupted about one of his two-legged rivals; however, Punch's owner, Laura Van Sant of North Carolina, declared her dog free from any smut, telling reporters, 'Punch is no Gary Hart. He was neutered at six months.'

Morris, America's answer to our very own Arthur, ran for the Democratic nomination for president of the United States in 1988. His spin doctor said, 'The world is going to the dogs! America needs a president with courage, but one who won't pussyfoot around with issues of peace—a president who, when adversity arises, will always land on his feet. Morris is jumping into this candidacy with all four paws!'

To give credibility to his campaign, Morris was endorsed by Eleanor Mondale, daughter of the former vice-president, Walter. She said at the time, 'Morris realises that prejudices exist, but he believes that, like records, they are meant to be broken. Morris gives the examples of Harry S. Truman, who became the first haberdasher to inhabit the Oval Office, and John Kennedy, who became the first Catholic.'

I suppose they thought that after Ronald Reagan, any actor had a good chance, even an animal one.

A five-week-old seal pup called Marge has a bit of a problem which is baffling staff at the Sea Life Centre in Scarborough—she's terrified of water! The little pup was found lying injured on a beach in South Shields and was taken to the centre for treatment. She made excellent progress recovering from her injuries, but then staff discovered her strange phobia. 'She just hated the water when we tried to get her to go in,' says the Centre's assistant manager Ian Hawkins. 'You could tell she was really stressed. She doesn't even like being sprayed with water or washed. We have a bizarre problem. She could have been separated from her mother during a storm and her injuries caused by hitting the beach or rocks. She may have nearly drowned and that could be why she's now afraid of the water.'

The Centre is now feeding Marge with forty fresh herrings and mackerel every day, building up her strength and hoping to release her back into the sea when she's fully grown— if she'll let them, that is. The Centre has pledged that if Marge never recovers from her phobia, they won't force her to go.

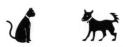

In the eighteenth century, men were employed as 'gull yellers' by local fishermen. Their job was to shout so loudly that it frightened off marauding seagulls. Apparently, some gull yellers could be heard over eight and a half miles away when plying their trade. Sounds like a good job for me!

It looked like the end of the trail for April. After a glittering career in cross-country competitions, the twenty-five-year-old mare suffered a bad fall and then developed terrible arthritis. The horse went into decline and had been given only days to live when a friend of

338

her owner, Gail Rawlings, offered to lend her a set of Bioflow boots. Each of the boots has a magnet which wraps around the leg and is supposed to create a negative charge in the blood to increase circulation. Even the distributors admit that there's no scientific evidence behind the claim—but it seemed to do wonders for April. She started a new show-jumping career, qualified for the 1999 National Veteran of the Year finals and even gave birth to a foal—not bad for a horse given just days to live! Her owner says, 'I don't believe in miracles or magical healing powers, but how else can you explain this? I really never thought the boots were going to work, but I had no choice. They have taken twenty years off her!'

Did you know . . .
the word 'moggy' comes from Old
English and originally meant a
dishevelled old woman.

A striped tabby cat with the memorable name of Bud D. Holly lives with Sharon Flood at her art gallery in Medocino in the US. Living at the gallery must have inspired him, because in 1992 Sharon held a one-cat show of his works, painted with just his paws and watercolours. Twenty of his paintings were sold, some fetching over $100 each.

Officials at the Malaysian resort of Pulau Langkawi came up with a novel way of protecting wild cattle from being hurt in road accidents, particularly in the light of their habit of sitting down in the middle of the road at night.

The cows had their ears pierced and fitted with red plastic reflectors like the ones you find on bicycles. It seems to have done the trick.

Once you've seen one penguin, you've seen them all. Well, at least that's what it seems like to scientists working for the British Antarctic Survey, who have the unenviable task of identifying different penguins as part of the various migration studies they carry out.

Then one biologist had a bright idea that's still being considered—gluing small barcodes to the birds' beaks and then using strategically placed scanners along their most popular routes.

Fat cats of the world look out! Pedigree pet foods in Britain have launched a campaign to get felines fighting fit, and the vet in charge has prepared a tip sheet on diet and exercise for anxious owners. Among the exercises suggested are 'Fishing-rod Pouncing Practice', where you dangle a toy on the end of a rod and line for your cat to chase, and 'Silver Foil Stair Aerobics', which involves dragging a piece of silver foil on a string up and down the stairs with your fat cat in hot pursuit!

Scientists in Japan have built the world's first robot dog. Why you'd want one when you can have the real thing baffles me, but manufacturers Sony believe that people will be willing to pay up to £1,500 for one! The robot dog, named Aibo (Japanese for 'Pal'), has four instincts and six emotions, including love, anger, search and movement. These are triggered by an internal video camera, infra-red distance sensors and special touch sensors which tell the robot dog when it's being stroked. Ingenious voice-recognition computer software allows the dog to learn the sound of his mistress's or master's voice and to respond to it. If you shout at it, it runs away. If you speak nicely to it, it will come over for a cuddle. It communicates back by barking, but can also sing you songs in English or Japanese. Oh yes, and its eyes light up and flash in the dark.

341

Personally, I think I'll stick to the flesh-and-blood variety. They don't need recharging . . .

An article which appeared in the medical journal *The Lancet* gave the latest news on a spinal condition which makes sufferers adopt an ape-like slouch. Two photographs were used—one of a sufferer and one of an ape—to show the similarity in posture. For reasons of confidentiality, the human had a black band obscuring his eyes—but there was also one over the ape's eyes!

I shouldn't really tell this story, but I thought it was funny. According to *New Scientist* magazine, the Washington Biological Survey have been fitting metal tags to migrating birds. The tags have been inscribed with an abbreviated version of the Survey's name— 'Wash. Biol. Surv.' In 1998, the Survey got a letter from a camper in Arkansas. It read, 'Dear Sirs, While camping last week I shot one of your birds. I think it was a crow. I followed the cooking instructions on the leg tail and I want to tell you it was horrible.' No one at the Survey could be sure if it was a joke or not, but just in case, they've now changed the inscription to 'Fish and Wildlife Service'!

In January 1999, Liliana Artega of San Juan de Acosta in Colombia found a strange bullfrog in her garden. She called her son Carlos over to see it, and he noticed there were purple markings on its leg that resembled numbers: 8794. On a whim, Mrs Artega chose those numbers in the next local lottery draw—and won £50,000! This was great news for Mrs Artega—but not such great news for the local bullfrog population, who were relentlessly hounded and chased by townspeople wanting to examine them for lucky numbers for at least the next six months!

In 1995, a sea bass brought ashore by fishermen at the banana port of Turbo appeared to have the numbers 1124 under its scales. Three hundred residents bet on that number in the local lottery and it came up, paying out £300,000—and bankrupting the lottery in the process!

Francisco Gibert was acting very nervously when he checked in at Madrid–Barajas airport in Spain, and a security guard's suspicions turned out to be correct when Gibert was stopped and searched. Hidden in the lining of his jacket was a live baby crocodile!

York magistrates fined Lawrence O'Dowd £100 in November 1984 for using 'threatening and abusive language and behaviour likely to occasion a breach of the peace'. His crime? To shout 'Miaow!' at a police dog.

Did you know . . .
almost all mammals dream?

America has some very strange animal-related laws. In Hartford, Connecticut, it's illegal to teach or educate a dog. In Oklahoma it's illegal to get a fish drunk. It's also against the law there to pull faces at a dog or to catch whales—a strange law to have on the statutes, since Oklahoma is about as far from the sea as you can get in the United States! According to the local laws in International Falls, Minnesota, dogs are expressly forbidden to chase cats up telegraph poles, and in Kirkland, Illinois, bees are not allowed to fly over the town, while in the town of Wilbur in Washington, you're not allowed to ride an ugly horse. In Alaska, it's illegal to look at a moose from an aeroplane, and in Milwaukee, elephant owners must keep their pets on a leash in public areas. Virtually every pet owner in Ohio must be a lawbreaker. There's a law there that states that all animals must carry a light on their tail at night! In California, it's illegal to drug a freshwater fish but not a salt-water one, while it's illegal to hunt camels in the state of Arizona. You will be in deep trouble if you tie your pet crocodile to a fire hydrant anywhere in the state of Michigan, and in even more trouble in Vermont if you give in to temptation and paint a horse. It's against the law for a donkey to sleep in a bathtub in Brooklyn, New York, while you must not ride an ox in a 'threatening manner' in Jefferson City, Missouri. Missouri is, of course, the state where it's illegal to put a bear in the boot of your car. Happily, you can take your pet goldfish on Seattle buses, provided they are quiet and lie perfectly still. And just in case you're tempted, never carry bees in your hat in Lawrence, Kansas. It's a crime. Birds have a particularly rough time. In Norfolk, Virginia, hens are forbidden to lay eggs before 8 a.m. or after 4 p.m., while in Essex Falls, New Jersey, woe betide the duck that quacks after 10 p.m. Chickens aren't allowed to cross roads in Quitman, Georgia, while in Kentucky, it's illegal to shoot clay pigeons during breeding season. Think about it . . .

Worldwide, animals do seem to throw the law into some confusion. In Malaya, you can be jailed for dancing on the back of a turtle, while in India it's apparently perfectly legal to marry a goat—so long as you're a woman. Strangely, among the Ba-ila people of central Africa it's OK to kill an elephant, so long as you don't laugh at its buttocks afterwards.

We have some equally strange animal laws in Britain. By law, you can't take an elephant through the approach tunnel to Heathrow Airport, and it's illegal for a cabby to carry a rabid dog as a passenger! Cabbies are also still required by law to carry a nose bag and 'adequate foodstuffs for the horse'.

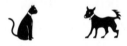

Bats spend over eighty per cent of their life hanging upside down. In many countries, because of vampire legends, they are associated with evil and death, but in China they are regarded as a symbol of health and happiness.

Valerie and John Collins were real animal lovers and fell in love with a stray Chihuahua dog that kept following them in Acapulco where they were on holiday. They smuggled it back to their hotel room, where they fed it, but the next morning it wasn't at all well, foaming at the mouth. Valerie and John took it to a vet, who winced when he saw it. Their 'Chihuahua'

was actually a sewer rat with rabies!

During the 1997 General Election campaign, the Monster Raving Looney Party offered few sensible suggestions on matters of health, defence or taxation. They did, however, have an unusual policy on dogs. If they came to power, they said, all dogs would be required to eat phosphorescent food. What came out of the other end would then glow in the dark and pedestrians would be less likely to tread in something while out walking at night!

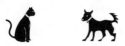

Reedpoint, Montana, thinks it has created a new, gentler and far more humane alternative to the infamous 'running of the bulls' in Spain. Each September, the town hosts the 'running of the sheep', in which brave young men run in front of the sheep as they charge down the main street for six blocks. Injuries are few and far between—and more embarrassing than painful. Other sheep-related events are also staged, including a sheep beauty contest, a competition to find Reedpoint's ugliest sheep, and poetry readings by local shepherds.

Timothy the tortoise is officially the oldest pet in the world. He's known to be at least 147 and could even be much older. Timothy's story starts in the middle of the nineteenth century when he was found on board a Portuguese privateer in the Mediterranean by Captain John Everard. Captain Everard took the animal as booty, and both captain and tortoise served on board HMS *Queen* during the bombardment of Sebastopol in the Crimean War. After that, the pair sailed the world until the captain retired to the family seat in 1892, and Timothy had to adapt to the life of a landlubber. He enjoyed a blissful existence during the twentieth century, disturbed only by a failed love affair in the 1920s, and by the Second World War. Frightened by the vibrations from German bombs, he is described as 'building his own air-raid shelter' and seeing out the war in there. Today, two centuries after he was first found, Timothy still lives in the grounds of Powderham Castle on the River Exe near Dawlish in Devon, and every year he hibernates in a comfy bed of leaves and roots under his favourite giant wisteria and dreams the winter away.

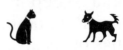

Terrified of being burgled, a man in Schalkhar, Holland, spent over £600 on a police-trained guard dog. Just two days later, his worst fears were realised when burglars broke in during the night. Searching his home to discover what they'd stolen, he quickly realised that the only thing missing was his new guard dog.

Some people love Concorde, citing it as a technological marvel. Some, on the other hand, detest it—and in this group are pigeon-fanciers. Geophysicist Dr Jon Hagstrum conducted a study for the Royal Pigeon Racing Society of Great Britain and uncovered evidence to suggest that pigeons navigate by using sound waves that have bounced off the ground to build up a mental map of the terrain they are flying over. He believes that the sonic boom caused by Concorde has caused birds to become temporarily or permanently deaf—and therefore unable to navigate.

Dr Hagstrum studied four races in which birds were lost, including one from Nantes in France to England in which 20,000 pigeons went missing. In each case he discovered that the birds had crossed the shock wave left by Concorde on its flight path.

With top homing pigeons costing from £45,000 up to £100,000, it's no wonder that pigeon owners are getting into a flap about it. Peter Bryant of the Royal Pigeon Racing Society said that 'if it is proved that sonic booms are disturbing the birds, then we may need to get the timetable of Concorde.'

Did you know . . .
spotted cats are often bullied by
tabby ones.

The reasons are now lost in the mists of time,
but in 1982 England soccer star Jimmy
Greaves thrashed jockey Bob Champion in a
hundred-yard camel race held at a charity
greyhound meeting in Crayford.

The humpback whale has the most complex
repertoire of sounds of any living creature. Not
only do their sounds vary from year to year,
but they also 'talk' with regional dialects.

The American Indians have a legend which
says that at the end of your life you must cross
over a bridge to get into heaven. However,
before you're allowed on to that bridge, you're
judged by every animal you ever met in your
life. If you treated them well, they'll declare
you a suitable person to enter heaven.

Las Vegas is full of weird and wonderful

things, but perhaps nothing is more exotic than '24 Carat Ferret', the ferret rescue headquarters run by C. J. Jones. 24 Carat Ferret—'where ferrets are treated like gold', as their slogan goes—houses up to sixty ferrets at a time and has rescued well over 400 of the intriguing little animals, including one from boxer Mike Tyson's estate. Ferrets aren't everyone's cup of tea, it seems, and exasperated owners often unceremoniously dump their pets when they prove too destructive or too smart to live with. Even CJ has had problems with some of the ferrets she's rescued. One ungrateful specimen by the name of Bam-Bam ate all the numbers off her phone and she still has to make all her calls by guesswork.

It's also now illegal to own ferrets in the neighbouring state of California and they are routinely destroyed as vermin. Pets in danger are smuggled out of the state by a secret organisation called the Ferret Underground Railroad (FUR), and given a new life at 24 Carat Ferret. Many are successfully re-homed with scrupulously vetted new owners in Nevada, and two of the less 'nippy' ones were even taken to local old people's homes where they entertain and cheer up the residents!

In France, when they're not eating snails

they're racing them! At the World Mollusc-Racing Championships in Marseilles, a snail named MacLaren clocked up an astonishing 0.007 mph to romp home five centimetres ahead of his nearest rival over a fifty-one-centimetre course. His record-breaking time was two minutes and forty-five seconds. 'It was a gripping race from start to finish,' reports Gerald Barbe, President of the French Snail Racing Association. 'Happily there were no disputes over the result, unlike last year when one snail was disqualified for drug-taking after we found his owner had slipped him some beer.'

The judges at a big dog show in Sendai, Japan, were amazed at how obedient little Tiko was. She stayed put by her owner's side when called by the judges, and even when tempted by a tasty snack. Her owner, nineteen-year-old Mizi Ozawa, could walk away and Tiko would obediently stay firmly in place. 'The dog was unquestionably the most obedient,' said one of the judges, who unhesitatingly and unanimously awarded Tiko first prize. There was just one little thing the judges had failed to spot. Tiko was stuffed. Fury broke out in the arena as Tiko's owner left with her cup, rosette and £1,000 first prize. 'Of course the dog's obedient—it's dead!' protested runner-up

Yasuo Kimura. Mizi was unrepentant. 'Just because my little Tiko is dead doesn't mean she didn't have the right to win!' she told astonished reporters. The humiliated judges confessed, 'We made a bad mistake—but an honest one. We had less than two minutes to check each pet. What were we to do—check the animal's vital signs?'

Believe it or not, some early Cruft's dog shows in England had special categories for stuffed dogs—a practice that has now thankfully been discontinued.

Did you know . . .
country folk used to believe that if
the sun came out while it was
raining, foxes were holding a secret
marriage ceremony somewhere
nearby.

We all know that cats are priceless, but in 1945 the Welsh king Hywel Dda personally set the price at four pence and described just what made a good cat: 'Her qualities are to see, to hear, to kill mice, to have her claws whole and to nurse and not devour her kittens. If she be deficient in any one of these qualities, one third of her price must be returned.' Four pence was the same price you'd then expect to pay for a 'common house dog' or 'the dog of a foreigner'—and four times the price of a piglet or a lamb—so cats must have been quite highly valued.

You've heard of trains being delayed because of leaves on the line, but snails on the line . . . ?

It happened near the town of Meknes in Morocco, when unusually heavy rainfall caused thousands of snails to congregate at one particular stretch of the Casablanca–Fez railway line.

The slime they left in their trails caused the train wheels to slip and the service was delayed for a considerable time.

CHAPTER TEN

WHO'S A CLEVER BOY THEN?

Kim the four-year-old Border collie puts her sheep-rounding-up skills to good effect—by rounding up stray supermarket trolleys at Sainsbury's store in Swansea.

Her master, Matthew Richards from Gower, is a sheepdog-trial champion and got a job at the supermarket as a car-park attendant. The idea to use Kim came to him soon after he started work. 'I saw how many trolleys were going missing and knew it was a job for Kim. She treats them just like sheep. The customers can't believe it when they see her on her tummy, growing at the trolleys.'

When Kim finds stray trolleys she nudges them into line with her nose, or barks at Matthew to come and give her a hand.

A spokesman for Sainsbury's said, 'We can only put Matthew's success down to dogged determination.'

This tale seems unbelievable but it was reported in the *Sunday Times*. It concerns an English setter named Arli. He belonged to Mrs Elizabeth Mann Borgese, the daughter of Nobel Prize-winning writer Thomas Mann. According to the paper, Arli was quite proficient at typing. That's right. Typing. Apparently he began aged six, using his nose to press the keys. Mrs Borgese spent a great deal of time teaching her dog this incredible trick. The first words he mastered were 'dog' and 'cat' but later he had progressed to phrases like 'bad dog' and 'go to bed'.

This story, about Raggy the nineteen-month-old poodle, really is a tall animal tale. While ordinary dogs are quite content keeping all four paws firmly on the ground, Raggy has decided that he prefers holding his head up high, with the result that he walks around on his hind legs—and can keep this up for ten minutes at a time.

His owner, Ted Mann, from Shurdington near Cheltenham, takes the poodle for walks locally. Previously what would have been a short stroll now lasts for hours, with Raggy teetering around, showing off his new-found skill.

Raggy likes an audience when he performs his party trick, and the attention he gets from passers-by just encourages him to do it even more. Ted says, 'He won't walk past a queue waiting at a bus stop or children playing in the park without standing up.'

Despite nearly drowning in a canal as a puppy, Daisy the boxer now has quite an appetite for swimming, but what makes this unusual is that Daisy swims underwater, having developed a technique of holding her breath for more than thirty seconds.

Daisy's owner, Jennifer Williamson of Derby, introduced Daisy to water at Murrayhill Boarding Kennels' hydrotherapy pool near Melton Mowbray in Leicestershire. The dog suffers from a crippling condition where bits of bone growing in portions of her spine prevent her from being taken on long walks.

After her experience as a puppy she approached the water with caution, but when her favourite toy was thrown in, she leapt into the pool after it and went straight under.

'At first we thought she was drowning, because she just stayed under. But then we realised she was enjoying herself. It was amazing to watch,' said Mrs Williamson.

Soon Daisy was regularly diving and being taught to swim underwater through hoops.

Animal behaviourist Dr Roger Mugford said, 'I think this may be a first. I have been working with dogs for thirty years and certainly have never seen anything like it.'

Daisy's instructor, and owner of the kennels, Peta Hellyer, says that although boxers are a fearless breed, Daisy is exceptional. 'She does things underwater that even I haven't shown her before. I don't know why she does it but she definitely seems to love it.'

Are some pet dogs really psychic? One story that's very hard to explain otherwise concerns Toby the golden Labrador. His master, mechanic Josef Schwarzl, was working alone on a car in a garage in San Jose, California, when he was overcome by carbon monoxide fumes from the car exhaust. At the same time, four miles away, Toby became incredibly

357

agitated, barking and frantically scrabbling at the front door to be let out. When Josef's mother opened the door to see if something was wrong outside, the Labrador squeezed through the gap and ran as fast as he could in the direction of the garage. Mrs Schwarzl jumped in her car to chase the dog and both arrived at the garage to find Josef lying unconscious on the floor. He later recovered in hospital, but no one could explain how Toby had known he was in such terrible danger.

During the Second World War, residents of Exeter were amazed to see dozens and dozens of cats fleeing the city and walking in the countryside in the direction of Tiverton. The reason for their sudden departure became clear that night when the Germans launched a huge air raid on Exeter.

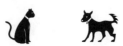

Dolphins can speak whale—it's official. Researchers at Marine World in Vallejo, California, have discovered that dolphins can learn whale language and actually hold a simple conversation with them!

Did you know . . .
mice prefer women to men.

358

Although the intelligence of dolphins and porpoises has been recognised and widely reported, a well-documented incident that happened a few years ago showed a new insight into their behaviour.

At Miami's Seaquarium, several newly captured wild porpoises were put into the holding tank. Next to this was another tank which contained the trained porpoises. Keepers noticed that the two groups called out to each other all through the night.

The next morning the trainer discovered to his shock that the new porpoises already knew how to do the tricks he was about to teach them, presumably after being told what to do by the experienced group via their sophisticated, sonar-based language.

An army sergeant in Kokomo, Indiana, decided to take his large yellow tom cat with him when he was transferred to a new army base in Augusta, Georgia. The cat, however, had other ideas and soon disappeared, only to turn up at the original base in Indiana three weeks later. He'd made the trip of 700 miles with absolutely no knowledge of the route back—his owner had taken him to Augusta by train.

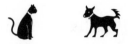

In 1984 John Carter of Long Hilsington discovered a miracle cure for his baldness—albeit one that was more than a little bit ticklish. That was the year that his cow Primrose started to lick his head. Why she did it—or why he allowed her to do it—isn't known, but John claimed that this was the reason why he suddenly grew a head of thick black hair.

Talking birds such as budgerigars don't know how to speak 'budgie' language naturally when they are hatched. They have to learn it by listening to older birds and mimicking them. That's why, when they're raised by people, they naturally mimic the sounds they hear us make.

Georgina the stray tabby was, by all accounts, the Barry Norman of the cat world. She set up home in the Hoylake Cinema on Merseyside and was pampered by the staff there. They said that if she walked out of any film, it'd be a sure-fire flop!

Do cats listen to a word we say? Apparently so. Mrs Gertrud Schonhofen adopted a stray cat she called Minou. Minou ignored her completely when she talked to him in German, but as soon as she mumbled something in French the cat was suddenly all ears. Whether he does what Frau Schonhofen tells him to, though, is another matter entirely.

Herons showed a great level of resourcefulness to overcome the netting that Scottish trout and salmon farmers had put in place over their fish-holding pools. At first it proved a great deterrent, as the herons' feet would get caught in it. Later, though, they started collecting large sticks—just as if they were building a nest—and used these to make a small platform which they laid on the netting. By pushing down on this netting they were able to get at the fish.

At the start of the twentieth century, New York was very different to the huge metropolis it is now. They still grazed sheep in Central Park! A collie called Shep was responsible for keeping the sheep in order and it was, evidently, a job he took very seriously. However, a decision was taken to replace the sheep with new-fangled power mowers, and Shep got the sack. He was bundled into a park truck and sent off into retirement on a farm forty miles away in upstate New York. Almost as soon as he got there, Shep started to worry about his flock—and escaped at the first opportunity. He set off back to New York City, stowed away on a ferry over to Manhattan Island and then from 42nd Street sniffed his way back to Central Park. What was truly extraordinary about Shep's trek was that he had never been outside Manhattan before, but somehow he was able to find it again—and even knew how to make use of the city's ferries!

Savage, a mongrel owned by Lesley Scholes, came to the rescue when her mistress locked herself out of her house, leaving the key in the inside lock. Savage was inside and managed to take the keys out of the keyhole and post them back to a waiting Mrs Scholes through the letter-box.

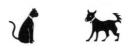

Chimps in America are being taught to use a

special voice synthesiser—just like the one Professor Stephen Hawking uses. One chimp now has a vocabulary of 3,000 human words and can tell scientists exactly what he wants. 'Please buy me a cheeseburger' is apparently his most frequent request.

Nick Carter sounds like the name of a private eye, and the Nick Carter in question did work for the police. In fact Nick Carter was a bloodhound, one of the best sniffer dogs there's ever been. Working with the police force in Lexington, Kentucky, Nick Carter tracked and found over 600 criminals in his distinguished career. On one occasion he successfully tracked down an arsonist whose scent was over four days old.

In the wild, gorillas like to sing. Apparently it sounds pretty awful, but it makes them very happy. They don't usually sing in captivity but do enjoy listening to music. Michael the gorilla, who lives at the California Gorilla Foundation, is apparently a huge fan of Pavarotti and will listen to the maestro for hours on end, often tapping his fingers to the rhythm!

Nini was a large white tom cat who lived at a coffee shop in Venice in the 1890s, where he gained a great reputation as a champion mouser. Word of his skills travelled fast and it wasn't long before he was asked to moonlight at the Venetian State Archive, where he would stop mice nibbling the ancient and important documents stored there. He was also asked to work at the famous Frari church, and so gained a reputation for not just being a skilled mouser, but also being learned and devout. A visitors' book kept in the church contained messages for Nini from various admirers. These included entries from a king and queen of Italy, a pope, a tsar and the composer Verdi.

Did you know . . .
if you wave a red rag at a bull, it's
the movement of the rag which
antagonises it and not the fact that
it's red. Bulls are colour-blind.

In 1978, Donna Jacobs suffered a stroke. She was just twenty-six. From then on she was plagued by seizures and terrible migraine headaches. Her condition deteriorated and she found herself in a wheelchair. Her seizures cost her her job too—and she began to think she had nothing left to live for.

In an attempt to find something special to fill her life, Donna and her husband John adopted a seven-week-old puppy called Patra. The puppy was very sickly at first and needed nursing back to health, but as he grew he started to exhibit some very strange behaviour towards Donna.

Sometimes he would approach her without warning, push her down and bounce on her. He never did this with her husband. At first the couple thought he was just being boisterous, but then they began to worry in case there was some kind of dominance or hostility being shown.

Their vet recommended that they take Patra to see Kathy Cramer, a canine behaviour specialist—and they discovered that their fears were completely unfounded. Quite the opposite. Patra was trying to help Donna. 'Your dog is telling you that something is wrong,' Kathy Cramer concluded.

By sheer luck, Donna had adopted a dog that was able to sense her seizures before they occurred. Patra is now able to provide her with an early warning and has turned Donna's life completely around. Where once she was a virtual recluse, now she is outgoing and has returned to work as a marketing director for a computer company.

In September 1998, Patra received certifications from the Assistance Dogs for Living as a Seizure Alert Service Dog, and was also honoured at the Delta Society's 1998 Beyond Limits National Service and Therapy Animal Awards Gala, sponsored by Purina Pet Foods.

A yellow-fronted Amazon parrot named Basil was voted Britain's Champion Talking Bird at the National Exhibition of Cage and Aviary Birds in Birmingham. Basil, who lives in Nuneaton, demonstrated how he was able to croak like a frog, bark like a dog, ring like a telephone, crow like a cock and recreate the sound of the Charge of the Light Brigade, complete with trumpet calls. Mind you, he was up against some stiff competition. His worthy opponents included Billy Briggs, a cockatiel from Wales, who shouted, 'Show us your knickers', and Pepper, an African grey parrot from Bury St Edmunds who could say, 'Good morning' in Japanese.

Dolphins and whales don't sleep like humans do. They'd probably drown if they did. However, they do like to catnap for a few minutes, resting on the surface of the sea. While doing this, they switch off one half of their brain and rest it while the other half keeps a close eye out for danger.

Marine scientists have identified over twenty different sounds made by dolphins, including greetings, warning cries, expressions of pleasure and anxiety—even call signs individual to each dolphin.

Giraffes suffer from high blood pressure—about three times that of humans. But there's a good reason for it. The pressure is needed to get the blood up their twelve-foot necks. To pump the blood this distance requires a heart two feet long with walls up to three inches thick.

One particularly ingenious black bear at Yosemite National Park worked out a way of stealing food from inside locked Volkswagen cars. Volkswagens are pretty airtight when the doors are closed and the windows wound up. The bear would climb up on to the car's roof and jump up and down on it until the air pressure inside popped all the doors open!

Koalas may be next to impossible to train, but sometimes they can teach themselves some pretty fancy tricks. In 1980, a wild koala nicknamed Cuthbert became fascinated with a motorbike owned by a local farmer. He'd waddle over to look at it, and then one day got up the nerve to hop on the back as the farmer started it up. Once he got the taste for speed, Cuthbert the koala kept coming back for more joyrides, and locals were astonished to see the farmer driving around with Cuthbert on the pillion, clinging on to the human for dear life!

The greatest animal success in the UK pop charts was probably achieved by a Danish all-dog pop group appropriately called The Singing Dogs. In I1955, they stormed up the charts to number 13 with a medley of 'Pat-A-Cake', 'Three Blind Mice', 'Oh Susanna' and 'Jingle Bells'!

A Bulgarian farmer, Mihail Janko, believed that his goat was an excellent judge of human character. Apparently, if shown a picture of a scoundrel it would head-butt the photo. If you showed it a picture of a nice person, it preferred to eat the picture instead. Mihail used the goat to vet his four daughters'

potential boyfriends and to decide the honesty of travelling salesmen.

Some dogs seem to have a sort of psychic link with their owners, knowing when they're about to set off for home, or when they're almost at the door.

Sergeant Bill Johnson was preparing to return from his tour of duty in Vietnam, but didn't tell his family because he wanted to surprise them. Unfortunately his dog back home, Nellie, spoiled the surprise. The day before he was due to get back she ran around the house, picking up lots of Bill's personal items in her mouth and depositing them in the middle of the living room. When she'd finished she sat down at the front door and refused to move until Bill arrived the next day.

A similar bond was reported during the Second World War. A mongrel named Flak was the mascot of a particular bomber. He was very attached to all the air crew and they spoiled him rotten when they were on the base. Flak always knew when they were about to return from a mission and ran out on to the airfield just before their plane appeared.

One day, however, he ran out on to the field and began howling and howling. Flak knew before anyone else on the base that his crew had been shot down over Italy.

Did you know . . .
Isoroku Kimura's Pet Dating
Service in Japan can provide pet
résumés, photos and video previews
at £50 per introduction.

A New York City court heard a case in 1877 where an Irishwoman, Mary O'Shea, was bitten on the finger by Jimmy, an organ grinder's monkey.

After hearing the evidence, the judge dismissed the case. Mary, who had just arrived in America from Ireland shouted out, 'This is a nice country for justice!' as she was escorted out of the courtroom.

As soon as she had left, Jimmy the monkey, who was dressed in a scarlet suit and velvet top hat, shook hands with the judge.

Two maths-whizz monkeys named Rosencrantz and MacDuff have astounded scientists at Columbia University in New York by proving that they can count up to nine without being taught! The monkeys were put in front of touch-sensitive computer screens and asked to rank in ascending numerical order pictures showing different numbers of objects. These included shapes, flowers, apples, trees, penguins and cars. Each time they got it right, they received banana-flavoured snacks for their efforts. Apparently the two monkeys could do the exercise flawlessly from one up to eight, but started to struggle a bit when a group of nine objects was introduced.

'We're not one hundred per cent sure they're counting in the way that humans do,' says Elizabeth Brannan, who worked on the tests. 'However, we do know that these animals can understand the relationship between numbers. For example, they definitely understand that seven is more than six. It shows that the monkeys know things about numbers that we haven't taught them!'

Sign-language experiments in America have shown that not only can apes understand sign language but they can even make up their own names for things all by themselves by combining two of the signs they've been taught. These include 'water bird' (a swan), 'metal hot' (a cigarette lighter), 'listen drink' (Alka-Seltzer) and 'candy drink' (watermelon).

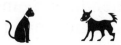

In October 1991, the staff of the casualty department at the Bartlett Memorial Hospital in Juneau, Alaska, received their strangest ever patient—a sickly little black bear cub. The cub, who was exhausted and malnourished, simply pushed open the doors of the casualty department and plonked himself down in the waiting area. Not being equipped to deal with bear emergencies, the hospital called the State Wildlife Service. A biologist from the organisation came out, tranquillised the cub and took him home to feed him back to health on milk and honey. The little bear, who was nicknamed Bartlett, eventually found a home at a special bear safari park called Bear City in South Dakota.

In 1993, Dr Sarah Boysen, a zoologist and primatologist at Ohio State University taught a Vietnamese pot-bellied pig to distinguish between objects including a Frisbee, a ball and a dumb-bell—and to obey the commands 'sit', 'jump' and 'fetch'.

She repeated this experiment four years later and was astonished to see that the pig could distinguish the same objects and remember the commands. 'That tells us that pigs have a tremendous memory for the kind of training and events that they experience,' commented Dr Boysen.

Forget homing pigeons—in nineteenth-century Belgium homing cats were all the rage. Homing-cat owners would take their prized cats to a meet, release them and the first one home was declared the winner. Contests were highly organised, with prizes of a ham or a silver spoon going to the winner. Amazingly, one of the all-time Belgian homing-cat champions was completely blind!

Koko the gorilla, who has been taught to communicate using sign language, has provided researchers with many fascinating insights into how these magnificent creatures think and feel. One day they asked her why gorillas die. She signed 'trouble, old'. Even more boldly, they asked her where gorillas go after they die. She signed 'comfortable hole, goodbye'.

People tend to forget that pigs are actually incredibly intelligent animals. Just how smart they can be was amply demonstrated by a one-year-old Vietnamese pot-bellied pig by the name of LuLu, who undoubtedly saved her mistress's life in August 1998.

Joanne Altsman was enjoying a holiday in a trailer home on Presque Isle, Pennsylvania, when she suddenly started having a heart attack. Her American Eskimo dog, Bear, did nothing except panic and run around the room barking—but LuLu kept a cooler head. 'I was yelling, "Someone help me! Please help me! Call an ambulance!"' Mrs Altsman recalls. 'LuLu looked at my head. She made sounds like she was crying. You know—they cry big fat tears.' Realising that something was seriously wrong, LuLu squeezed out of the trailer's dog-flap, pushed open the gate and trotted out into the middle of the road. Then she lay down on her back with all four trotters in the air, determined to stop the first passing car. Perhaps understandably, the first driver who stopped was too scared to get out of his car, but the second motorist on the scene jumped out and followed the pig back into the trailer, where he found Mrs Altsman semi-conscious on the bed and immediately called an ambulance. When it arrived, LuLu tried to jump on board and escort her mistress to the hospital, but was gently shooed away.

While recovering in hospital, Mrs Altsman learned that she would have died within fifteen minutes if LuLu hadn't taken action. She personally rewarded the pig with a big gooey jam doughnut—and LuLu gained further recognition for her life-saving actions when the RSPCA presented her with their special Trooper Award for Bravery at a gala luncheon in Manhattan on 2 February 1999.

Did you know . . .
in Japan, you can open up a bank
account in your pet's name.

If you don't believe that some animals can possess a sort of sixth sense, then how can you possibly explain what happened to Mrs Rita Kempton and her Jack Russell terrier William in January 1998? Rita was out driving near Huntingdon in Cambridgeshire with William by her side when a lorry forced their car off the road. As the ambulancemen took her away, Rita kept asking for William. No one at the scene could find the dog—and they feared the worst. However, when Rita's ambulance arrived at the hospital, two miles away, there was William—sitting waiting for her! Despite being a hundred miles from home in a place he'd never visited before, William had managed to cross a busy dual carriageway and negotiate a large industrial complex to reach the very hospital his owner was being taken to—before she had even arrived!

'When they opened the doors of the ambulance, there he was,' Rita remembers. 'I couldn't believe it. He had got there before me. He was covered in mud and still a bit shocked, but he went crazy to see me.'

375

Brum was an Alsatian with an apt name—he was the guard dog at the Winstead garage belonging to his owner, Mr Randall. But when he wasn't guarding, he developed a new skill—fetching tools for the mechanics. If one of them asked for a hammer or screwdriver, for instance, he'd trot off, have a good poke about in the toolbox and then fetch the appropriate implement.

During the Second World War, a small cat named Bomber was able to tell the difference between approaching German and Allied aircraft by the sound and tone of their engines. He also instinctively knew that the sound of the German aircraft meant danger. Before the official air-raid siren went, he'd rush for the air-raid shelter, acting as an early-warning system of an enemy attack.

Similarly, another cat, called Sally, who lived near London's docks, could detect enemy aircraft approaching, and would leap up at the gas masks hanging in the hallway of her home. When the door was opened she'd run to the air-raid shelter and scratch at the door. When her owner was safely inside she'd then run next door, alert the neighbours, and dash back to the safety of the shelter.

The winner of the 1965 award for the Best Talking Parrot was an African parrot named Prudle—and he held this honour for the next eleven years. Prudle had a vocabulary of 800 words and unlike most parrots, who mimic what they've already heard, he could make up his own, understandable sentences. Who's a clever boy then?

We know dogs have a remarkable sense of smell, but Boo the whippet found his way into the award books—and the pages of *The Lancet*—when he successfully sniffed out a cancerous mole on the leg of his owner, Mrs Bonita Whitfield.

Boo used to paw continually and sniff at a small mole at the back of his owner's leg. To Mrs Whitfield, this behaviour was annoying, but she couldn't get her dog to stop. In fact, so insistent was Boo at drawing attention to the mole that Mrs Whitfield finally went to see her doctor. She thought it would be a complete waste of time—his and hers—but was shocked when her GP referred her to King's College Hospital in London. There, tissue from the mole was analysed and found to be cancerous. The mole was removed safely and Mrs

Whitfield was all right.

Her specialist, Dr Williams, put forward the theory that these type of skin cancers (called melanomas) might give out a distinctive smell which dogs can detect. Whatever the reason, Boo saved the life of his owner and was awarded a medal for life-saving by the charity PRO Dogs in 1989.

The same uncanny ability was demonstrated by George, a six-year-old schnauzer, who was trained to sniff out explosives but progressed to tracking down skin cancer. The change in career happened because of the frustrations of Dr Armand Cognetta, an American dermatologist. He had seen one of his patients die because of an inaccurate diagnosis by a doctor, who had told him there was nothing unusual about his mole.

His inspiration to train George came from reading about Boo in *The Lancet*, and he persuaded George's owner, retired police-dog handler Duane Pickel, to help him out with his trials. Duane had trained dogs for work in Vietnam, and from his experiences there, he knew that dogs could sniff out illnesses before they became apparent—in his case, tropical diseases caught in the Vietnam jungles.

Under the dermatologist's supervision, Duane began to get George used to the smell of melanoma samples in test tubes, and then trained him to locate them. Eventually George could retrieve the samples with an accuracy of ninety-nine per cent. George then moved on to actual cancer patients who'd volunteered for the research—in these cases he would sniff all round them, and on the command 'Show me' would place his paw on the suspected skin cancer—again, with incredible accuracy.

But one day in the trials Dr Cognetta doubted what George was telling him. The moles of one of the cancer patients, James Garafolo, had all been tested as being free from cancer, but George began to sniff one area obsessively. This particular mole was then retested and was still negative. But still George went crazy about this one particular spot—so much so that Mr Garafolo decided to have it removed—and was glad he did, saying, 'When it was tested after surgery they found a potentially deadly set of cancer cells. I owe my life to George.'

Dr Cognetta is cautious about George's success, claiming, 'It's amazing what George has done but we shouldn't jump to conclusions until further scientific testing is done. I don't want people to have false hopes or expect they can train their dogs at home to do this.'

George has also taken part in a feasibility study to see if dogs can achieve early detection of TB, lung cancer and prostate disease by smelling breath and urine. Handler Duane Pickel is optimistic about George's—and other dogs'—continued success in the medical field, saying, 'In my experience, dogs are smarter than eighty per cent of the people I've worked with and a hundred per cent of the people I've worked for. There is very little on this earth more dependable than a dog's nose.'

Undeterred by a lack of traditional twigs and leaves with which to build a nest, an enterprising pigeon living in a hangar at Oxford airport has built hers out of bits of old aircraft. The nest, which the pigeon put together from nuts and bolts and scraps of discarded steel, weighs well over 2 pounds and measures a foot across. Baffled RSPB inspectors have called the nest 'one in a million'.

Did you know . . .
experiments at the University of
Cambridge have shown that a sheep
can recognise a photograph of a
ram she likes!

Mrs J. Davis of Midvale, Utah, was in her living room one day when she heard someone say, 'I want my mummy!' Worried in case a lost child had wandered into her house, she got up, but the only other living thing in the house was Mr Lucky, her young Boston terrier.

Thinking she must have been imagining things, Mrs Davis settled back down; then the voice started again, but this time it sounded nearer. Confused, Mrs Davis got up again—she couldn't believe her eyes, or her ears.

The voice was coming from Mr Lucky! It was an odd sort of sound, slightly mechanical, but she could still understand the words. Over the next few days Mrs Davis heard her dog say twenty words and a few phrases, including 'I will' and 'I want some'.

How or when Mr Lucky got his strange powers, no one knew. The *Utah Desert News* investigated the phenomenon and was so impressed with Mr Lucky's vocal abilities that Associated Press issued the story worldwide in April 1953.

If an ape has a dirty mark on its face and is placed in front of a mirror, it will immediately start rubbing its own face, rather than its mirror image. Science historian Adrian Desmond claims that this proves that apes are the only creatures apart from man who have an awareness of their own image.

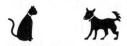

Over the years, Dalmatians have garnered a reputation for being absolute dimwits. This is cruel slander. Unhappily, because of bad breeding, many of the Dalmatians we keep as pets are stone deaf and can't hear what we're telling them. Dalmatians are actually pretty smart fellas.

Juliette, the Dalmatian belonging to the Eisenman family of Washington State, is profoundly deaf—and yet she's one of the best-trained dogs you'll ever meet, despite not being able to hear commands. The Eisenmans have trained her exclusively using sign language. In three years they have taught her over thirty different signs—things like 'good girl', 'no', 'sit', 'food', 'lie down', 'walkies' and 'play ball'.

The Eisenmans' perseverance and Juliette's willingness to learn mean that now she responds to and interacts with the family and their children like any other dog. When they started out, no one believed a dog could be trained this way, but the Eisenmans were determined to succeed. You could say that all this criticism fell on deaf ears!

Scientists at Duke University in Durham, North Carolina, have been conducting fascinating experiments into cat ESP. They've tested whether cats could identify cat food hidden in identical sealed containers without the aid of sight or smell. Time after time the cat 'guinea pigs' chose the right containers, leading the researchers to conclude, 'The experiment yielded significant results under conditions that make clairvoyance in cats the most likely explanation.'

Although the various clicks, whistles and grating noises made by dolphins are regarded by scientists as a distinctive language, a psychologist at the University of Hawaii claims that a pair of dolphins he observed in captivity can actually comprehend English grammar.

He taught them thirty words and they were able to understand instructions that used these words in hundreds of different combinations.

In one experiment, one of the dolphins was said by the psychologist to have understood a new way of using the word 'in' which proved a rudimentary knowledge of grammatical rules.

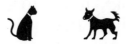

All dog owners know that their pets love trees. What they do there is their own business. But a Welsh setter called Jim went one further—he could identify them. One day he was out in woods with his owner, Sam Arsdale, near their home in Missouri. For a joke, Sam asked his dog to find an elm tree. To his astonishment, Jim did just that. He did the same with a birch, a sycamore and a beech. It was uncanny.

Jim's skills were investigated by scientists at

the University of Missouri, who confirmed that not only did Jim have this ability, but he could also perform the same feat if given commands in German and French.

The researchers were baffled. They refused to accept that Jim, a three-year-old dog, understood not just one language, but three. The only explanation they could offer was that he was somehow communicating with his owner via ESP.

Lord Thompson was one of Britain's first air ministers and travelled everywhere accompanied by his pet terrier. One day in October 1929, however, his dog started to act nervously. He wouldn't eat and spent the whole time whimpering. Nevertheless, Lord Thompson took him to Cardington in Bedfordshire, where they were going to board the new R101 airship on a voyage to India. En route, though, the dog ran away and Lord Thompson took off without him.

Somehow the terrier must have sensed the impending disaster. Just a few hours after take-off, the R101 crashed in flames on a hillside in Beauvais, France, killing nearly everyone on board.

Margaret Baldwin was asleep in her home in Missouri when her blue-point Siamese, Mao, who shared her bed, woke up and immediately started pawing her hair. Mao usually slept soundly, but this time something had startled her. Margaret tried to settle the cat and go back to sleep herself but Mao kept pawing her and licking her face.

The cat was extremely nervous and Margaret's first thought was that she'd heard a burglar in the house. She made a thorough check of the house—there were no intruders—then went back to bed. By now, however, Mao was in a frenzy, howling and trying to signal to Margaret that something was wrong. Then Margaret heard the sound that everyone in Middle America fears—the unmistakable wail of a tornado-warning siren. She took refuge in her basement shelter as the house shook violently in the storm. It turned out that the tornado had struck just two blocks away, completely devastating the area. Somehow Mao had detected the tornado before the weather bureau did. After that Margaret always watched her cat closely during storms—Mao was her own personal tornado early-warning system.

Did you know . . .
just as humans are either right- or
left-handed, elephants are either
left- or right-tusked!

A chimp named Washoe was the first to be taught Ameslan, the American Sign Language for the deaf. This took place at the University of Nevada, where researchers were convinced that chimpanzees had the mental ability to learn sign language even though they didn't have the right vocal cords to communicate by talking.

The experiments were led by Allen and Beatrice Gardner, husband and wife psychologists, in 1966, and started when Washoe was eight months old. At first they showed her objects, then manipulated her fingers and hands to make the appropriate signs. Training lasted from twelve to sixteen hours a day and Washoe soon learned to mimic her teachers' actions. By 1967 she was putting together simple sentences; for example, if she was thirsty she would make the symbol for 'give me', and then the sign for 'drink'. Two years later Washoe had mastered about 140 signs and 240 combinations of three or more signs, such as 'you tickle me' or 'hug me good'.

In 1971 the research moved to the Institute for Primate Studies in Oklahoma. It was here that Washoe met other chimps for the first time in her life. The first time she saw them she signed 'black bugs'. In 1979 Washoe 'adopted' an eleven-month-old male chimp called Loulis, and she taught the sign language to him. Occasionally he would throw a tantrum and Washoe would ignore him. In these instances Loulis would keep signing 'hug' until he got one.

The experiments continued with great success. Washoe was comfortable and well cared for, but there was one phrase that she kept signing, much to the sadness of her keepers: 'let me out'.

Koko the gorilla has also learned human sign language. At the age of three, while still really a baby, Koko used sign language mostly to ask for food and drink and cuddles. She has also created her own swear words. If she wants to insult someone, she'll call them a 'rotten bird' or a 'bad gorilla nut'. When one of the researchers working with her told her off, she swore back at them, saying, 'Penny dirty toilet devil!'—the meaning of which is pretty clear! She also uses words to lie. On one occasion she had pulled a sink away from its fittings, then tried to put the blame on Dr Patterson's assistant by signing, 'Kate bad there'. Another time Dr Patterson noticed she was chewing a red crayon; she signed to Koko, 'You're not chewing that, are you?' Koko made the sign for a lip and began rubbing the crayon over her own lips, pretending she was just putting lipstick on. By all accounts, Koko uses language to make jokes, shows an understanding of death and even helped Michael, another gorilla, to learn sign language.

Koko has learned to use a camera and loves the telephone. She dials numbers at random just to hear a human voice at the end of the line. She once dialled the operator, who immediately put a trace on the call, worried that she was talking to a dying man—either that, or a heavy breather.

Koko even took an intelligence test and this rated her IQ at 95, just slightly less than an average human child of the same age.

Despite all this, Koko never thinks of herself as human. When Dr Patterson asked her, 'Are you an animal or a person?' Koko proudly signed, 'Fine animal gorilla!'

Today, the star pupil at the American Language Research Center is a chimpanzee. A pygmy chimp, in fact, called Kanzi. The Center has several chimps who can communicate by using a keyboard to punch out different geometrical shapes, each of which represents a different word. What makes Kanzi different, though, is his ability to understand English without the researchers relying on gestures to explain what they're saying.

Although he can't make whole sentences, he can use the keyboard to create two- or three-word phrases. One of his chums at the Center was another chimp called Austin and the two often played together before settling down for the night. After Austin was transferred to another research centre, Kanzi became very despondent. One day he went to the keyboard and typed the symbols for 'Austin' and 'TV'. Kanzi's researcher knew what he wanted—a video of Austin that she'd taken several weeks before. She gave Kanzi the video, and just watching it made him a lot happier.

A study carried out in Germany on the influence of pet dogs surveyed nearly 500 children aged between fourteen and eighteen. Results indicated that children with dogs were more content, more goal-orientated and had better relationships with their parents. Children without dogs were more likely to drink, smoke and be estranged from their parents.

The Australian lyre bird is a brilliant impressionist. Not only can it imitate any other bird which it hears, but it can also do pretty decent impersonations of almost any other sound. Lyre birds have been known to impersonate barking dogs, chain saws and even speeding railway trains!

No one is sure why they do it, but elephants in captivity have been known to twist and braid hay and straw and make themselves garlands which they then wear around their necks.

Mandy, a Jack Russell belonging to Ray Roche, liked to get about—but couldn't be bothered with running alongside Ray as he rode his bike. Instead she'd leap up a ladder and then on to his shoulders. Mandy soon developed a perfect sense of balance, and the sight of her standing on Ray's back as he cycled along soon became a familiar one in their village of Quedgeley in Gloucestershire.

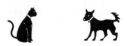

In 1998, users of the Internet got to hold one of the strangest on-line conversations of all time. Eight thousand people logged on to 'talk' to Koko, the famous gorilla whom scientists have taught to communicate in sign language. Her trainer, Dr Francine Patterson, keyed in Koko's signed answers. Among the messages that came in was a marriage proposal—Koko wisely ignored this—and a question about what she would like for her birthday, to which

Koko replied, 'Food and smokes'. She wasn't asking for cigarettes, though—gorillas are intelligent creatures after all—sadly she was asking for her pet kitten Smokey, who had died in an accident some time before.

Did you know . . .
under Section 23 of the Royal and
Other Parks and Gardens
regulations, it is illegal to touch a
pelican unless prior written
permission has been obtained.

The terrifying earthquakes that struck Turkey in 1999 were completely unpredicted—but animals seemed to know they were coming. A resident of Ismet, one of the worst-hit areas, reported that she was woken up by all the dogs howling together like wolves the weekend before the earthquake hit. They continued to howl on and off for four days until the earthquake began. Cats were also reported to be acting nervously, digging their claws into the ground. Even bird behaviour was affected, with birds becoming strangely silent and hopping continuously from tree to tree on the day before the earthquake, which destroyed over 100,000 buildings.

The same phenomenon has been reported around the world before other terrible earthquakes. In 1997, just before the Italian town of Assisi was hit by an earthquake, dogs were reported to have become wildly agitated and started barking, while the cats began to hide. Experts say that if they can only discover how the animals know an earthquake is coming, thousands of lives could be saved. The Chinese already take animal warnings very seriously. In 1995, many lives were saved when the authorities decided to evacuate the city of Haicheng after pets became agitated. A quake hit the city later the same day.

Primo was a four-year-old black, tan and cream Alsatian who belonged to Leslie Dennis of Hull. One Easter, Les and Primo were on holiday in Scotland and Les decided that the two of them should climb Ben Nevis. They set off in the early morning; there were a few snow flurries, but apart from that, the first part of their climb was uneventful. They reached the 4,406-feet summit by mid-afternoon, but on the way down the snow returned, covering the path. By the time night had fallen, Les and Primo were trapped on the mountain in heavy snow. They were in danger of freezing to death if they stayed on the exposed peak, and there was only one hope open to them.

Holding firmly on to Primo's leash, Les let his dog take the lead, guiding him back down as he sniffed out their tracks. By now they were in the middle of a ferocious blizzard, but

Primo kept on, leading his owner downwards by his keen sense of smell alone. Hours later, the dog led his owner right back to the safety of the hotel they had originally set out from.

Pikki was a small fox terrier who belonged to a Russian animal trainer at the turn of the century. She could carry out the usual tricks that circus dogs do, but what was remarkable was her 'proven' telepathic ability.

During tests carried out under strict laboratory conditions by the neurologist Professor Vladimir Bechterev, Pikki was said to be able to pick up mental commands sent by her master with an almost hundred per cent success rate.

The tests included pointing to certain pictures with her paw or pulling an object out of a drawer or from a table top. The tests also demonstrated that Pikki did not rely on her owner alone to detect telepathic messages. The professor himself sent mental messages which she picked up, including those sent from a completely different room!

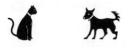

One of the strangest animal mysteries of all time concerns a German horse called Clever Hans. A retired schoolteacher named Wilhelm von Osten trained Hans—and other horses in his care—to 'think about problems they were set' and then answer by tapping their hoofs on the floor.

Clever Hans quickly learned numbers, and the letters of the alphabet—but then went on to do things he had not been trained to do! When Osten wrote '35 + 15' on a blackboard, Clever Hans clopped out '50' with his hoofs. The horse could add up!

The Kaiser got to hear about this and demanded an explanation. A whole procession of royal vets, animal trainers and zoologists duly trooped down to Hans's home in Elberfeld to watch him in action. They said it had to be a trick; Hans was somehow getting signals from Wilhelm—but they couldn't tell how he was doing it.

Meanwhile, Clever Hans's accomplishments went from strength to strength. He could tap out the day and the date, solve complex equations and even read music!

The whole world denounced Wilhelm as a fraud, but no one could work out how the fraud—if fraud it was—was being perpetrated.

Before he died, Wilhelm took on a new partner, a wealthy jeweller called Karl Krowl, and taught him how to train horses. He left Clever Hans to Karl's care, and Karl then took on two more horses, Muhamed and Zarif, who apparently were geniuses too and could soon do division and subtraction on command.

Once again, learned men flocked to see the Elberfeld horses and were baffled. The leading Swiss psychologist Clarparede completely discounted any hint of a fraud.

Karl decided to go further. He wanted to teach his horses to talk. First of all he taught them a code of syllables so that they could effectively tap out the German language with their hoofs, then he tried to get them physically to speak. Muhamed tried but could not, and in his frustration he began to tap out a message on the floor—'Ig hb Kein gud sdim'—'I do not have a good voice'!

To this day, no one has satisfactorily explained the mystery of the amazing Elberfeld horses.

Snakes can supposedly hypnotise their victims into a state of paralysis before striking, but one cobra in India was out-stared by a humble cat.

It happened in 1922 when a British Army officer was walking along the veranda back to his room. He turned a corner and was immediately confronted by a terrifying sight just feet away from him—a deadly cobra raised up from its coils, a position adopted by the snakes just before they strike.

The officer knew that any sudden move might trigger the cobra into biting him. He also knew that the snake might strike without warning. Frozen to the spot, he contemplated his fate. Then he noticed something odd—the snake was now looking past him and seemed transfixed, swaying gently from side to side.

Cautiously, the officer turned around to see the source of the cobra's diversion. It was his own cat, who was staring so intently into the eyes of the snake that it held it in a trance.

Seeing that he was temporarily out of danger, the officer drew his pistol and killed the cobra. A harmless house cat had saved him from one of the deadliest creatures known.

Did you know . . .
if it wants to, an ostrich can roar
just like a lion.

A performing horse named Morocco was the talk of Elizabethan England, and was mentioned by name in the writings of Shakespeare, Ben Jonson and Sir Walter Raleigh. He was famous for his silver horseshoes and could count the spots on two dice (banging his hoofs on the ground to indicate the correct number), recognise colours and dance. He was also said to be able to return a glove to its rightful owner after being told the owner's name, and to select certain playing cards that had all been placed face down on a stage. In 1600 he performed his greatest feat, climbing the steps all the way to the top of the old St Paul's Cathedral.

Morocco was owned by John Banks, who exhibited him all round the country and also in France. At one particular fair in Orléans, local monks accused Banks of being a witch and Morocco of being the devil, and imprisoned them both. At their trial, Banks stressed their innocence, and to prove it, he told Morocco to choose someone in the court who wore a crucifix. Morocco found one adorning a hat; he went up to the hat, knelt and kissed the crucifix. The magistrates immediately released both of them, believing that a witch or the devil himself could not show such respect for the cross.

After Morocco's death, Banks became a successful wine merchant and his trademark was a picture of his famous performing horse.

Chris the beagle—or 'The Mathematical Mongrel', as his master called him—baffled the world of science in the 1950s with his uncanny ability to do sums. Whether his master asked him a simple subtraction or a complex square root, somehow Chris always got the answer right, tapping the number out with his paw on his master's arm. Despite the close scrutiny of top scientists under laboratory conditions, no one was able to work out just how Chris did it.

A bulldog named Princess Jacqueline could talk. She belonged to Mabel Robinson of Waterville in Maine and could apparently mimic twenty words and short phrases—and understand what they meant—like 'hello', 'I will' and 'goodbye'. It sounds really far-fetched, but in the 1930s Jacqueline was examined by Dr Dunlap of Johns Hopkins University who discovered that as well as the usual canine voice box, Jacqueline possessed vocal cords very similar to those of humans.

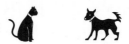

The intriguingly named Peri-Nympsie, a Siamese cat owned by a Miss Norris in Worcestershire in the 1920s, was by all accounts an incredibly talented pet. According to contemporary reports, Peri-Nympsie could understand a hundred different commands, and would hold a duster in her front paws and follow her owner round the house when she was doing the housecleaning, imitating her actions. It was also claimed that she would assist Miss Norris when it came to making dinner. Miss Norris would get out all the ingredients needed to prepare a meal and Peri-Nympsie would push the jars and containers to her when requested.

Peri-Nympsie sadly died in 1932, and *Fur and Feather* magazine carried her obituary, describing her as 'human-like in intelligence and fierce in her loyalty'.

Everyone thought it had to be a hoax. A horse that passed on psychic messages with the aid of a large typewriter, working the giant rubber keys with its muzzle. Preposterous! The horse, with the rather grand name of Lady Wonder, was a sensation in America in the 1930s. Everyone thought the idea of a psychic horse was a lot of fun—but it was obviously a trick perpetrated by its trainer. Determined to expose the 'wonder horse', a journalist called Katherine Warren went to conduct the most unusual interview of her life. Far from exposing Lady Wonder as a scam, she came away shocked. The horse had successfully told her her own middle name and correctly identified two numbers she had written on a piece of paper in her pocket—things her trainer couldn't possibly have known.

As you might expect, Lady Wonder was particularly good at predicting the outcome of horse races—but her finest hour came when she was asked to help find a missing four-year-old boy. Little Danny Matson had vanished from his home in Quincy, Massachusetts, and despite a massive police search, no one had found any sign of him. Lady Wonder typed that he was in the vicinity of 'Pitts Field'. The police raced to Pittsfield, Massachusetts—but found no sign of the boy. Then one of them remembered that a local quarry was called 'Field and Wilde's Pit'. The search switched to the quarry—and they found the little boy almost immediately, cold and scared but otherwise unharmed . . .

Tom and Sticky were brother and sister cats that lived on a farm near Okehampton in Devon. When the farmer died, his widow Alice moved to a new house in the town of Newton Abbott. Unfortunately, the new house was too small for two cats so she kept Tom and gave Sticky to her sister Joyce, who lived in Plymouth.

About eight months after moving in, Tom started acting strangely, pacing the room with his ears flattened, looking very agitated. Suddenly he leapt up at the front door to be let out. Alice tried everything but couldn't calm him down. In desperation she called Joyce for advice, but she too had problems—Sticky had disappeared.

Alice wanted to leave Tom at home and help her sister look for Sticky, but Tom wouldn't have any of it. In the end she took him with her to Plymouth, but when they arrived at Joyce's house, he leapt out of the car and bolted down the street, then stopped at a corner and turned to stare at Alice. Both women decided to follow him and were led through a warren of backstreets until they ended up at a piece of waste land containing an old wartime air-raid shelter. Tom ran straight to it and began clawing at a sack that had been tied with rope.

To Alice and Joyce's amazement, the sack moved. They quickly loosened the rope and there inside was poor Sticky, terrified and close to death.

Once Sticky had been nursed back to health, Alice and Joyce decided that brother and sister should never again be parted.

Did you know . . .
dogs living in Uruguay are issued
with their own ID cards containing
their name, address, photograph—
and nose print.

What's the best way to track down a missing dog? The answer's another dog, and in particular a very special dog named Sadie Sue. Sadie is a bloodhound owned by Bill Bailey in New Mexico who specialises in finding missing pets.

To locate a missing dog, Sadie Sue is given something that carries its distinct scent— bedding, a collar or even stray dog hairs. She's tracked missing dogs to ditches, construction sites, locked buildings—you name it, anywhere a pooch can wander off to and get into trouble.

On one occasion the distraught owners called Bill to find their dog who'd disappeared from their house. They'd spent a day looking all round the neighbourhood for him, asking local people if they'd seen him running away or being abducted, but no one had noticed anything.

Bill took Sadie Sue to see the owners and let her sniff one of the dog's toys. She immediately scampered off into another room and scratched away at a closet—their dog had been locked inside all the time.

Slick, a German shepherd, is a resident counsellor at the Hospital Hospitality House in Kalamazoo, Michigan—somewhere for families with terminally ill relatives to go. That might seem a strange job for a dog, but sometimes pouring your heart out to a sympathetic stranger—even a dog—can really help in the grieving process.

Slick actually belongs to the owner of the Hospitality House, Kay Darst, who has numerous examples of how the dog has helped residents suffering from severe emotional trauma. Men apparently respond well to Slick because generally they don't like talking openly about their feelings.

On one occasion a man was distraught, having to decide whether he should take his terminally ill mother off a life-support system. He was too emotional to talk about it with anyone. However, he confided in Slick all his fears and worries. The two of them went for a long walk in the hospital grounds, and on his return he had a clear picture of what he must do—he let his mother pass on naturally.

In another instance, Slick bounded upstairs to one of the rooms. Inside a mother whose child was dying had been sobbing her heart out. Slick snuggled up to her and stayed with her that evening. The woman later admitted that having Slick there helped her tremendously in facing up to her plight.

Whether it's being a shoulder to cry on, a warm paw to hold or just the fact that she's there, Slick has proved invaluable in helping people come to terms with their grief.

It's not an exaggeration to say that the cat has actually saved human civilisation. Only its ability to catch and kill rats ended the Great Plague in the fourteenth century. As it was, three out of every four people in Europe died from the disease—a total of twenty-five million people.

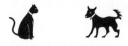

He may be the toughest silverback gorilla in the Metropolitan Toronto Zoo, but Charles is also the most sensitive. When he's not laying down the law to the other gorillas, he loves to paint. Charles first discovered his love of art as an infant when his keepers gave him some paints to play with, and now, at the age of twenty-three, Charles has just enjoyed his first gallery exhibition.

His patron, Catherine Hathorn of the Framing and Art Centre, swears that Charles really is making art. 'When you see him hold up one of the paintings and turn it to make the paint flow in a certain direction, then turn it again to make it stop, you realise he is really thinking about what he is doing,' she says, referring to Charles's art style as 'abstract expressionism'. Others agree. In just one month, Charles sold $34,000 worth of paintings—with all the money going to provide much-needed funds for the zoo's gorilla habitat.

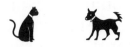

Just what is it about the Russian city of Minsk that makes the local creatures so talkative? In 1980 the Soviet Tass news agency gave details of Karlusha, a talking raven who inhabited the river banks near the city. He was said to have a vocabulary of about sixty words and could recognise the different fish caught in the river—entertaining anglers by announcing their catch each time they landed a fish.

In 1986 Tass reported that a Russian parrot had learned Shakespeare's eighth sonnet in English. According to the report, it could also recite a poem by Pushkin, preferring the English translation. The parrot belonged to Boris Kozyrev, who lived in Minsk, and was said to be an avid follower of English-language lessons on Soviet TV.

Sally the chimp was one of London Zoo's biggest attractions in the 1880s. She had learned to count up to twenty, and her party trick was to give visitors exactly the number of pieces of straw they asked for.

Many people take great comfort in stroking their pet cat. It gives them reassurance and sometimes consolation. However, some people claim that one cat in particular possessed miraculous healing powers!

This was Rogan, a stray marmalade cat who was found a new home by the Cats Protection League. Rogan went to live with his new owner, Mrs Bailey, and his 'powers' were discovered after someone stroked him for about thirty minutes to find that she'd completely recovered from a recent nervous breakdown. Word spread, and soon Rogan was visited by people with such diverse problems as back pain, deafness and fading eyesight. After touching Rogan they all seemed miraculously cured of their ailments.

But Rogan didn't have to be physically present to help heal people. He could also sit on the pile of letters he received and go into a trance, somehow transmitting his healing powers to the people who'd written.

Rogan even helped cure a fellow feline, a cat called Smudgie who lived a distance away. Smudgie was suffering from Key-Gaskell syndrome, a sort of cat anorexia. Rogan's owner took some combings from his coat and sent them to Smudgie, who took one sniff and rushed to his food bowl for his first good meal in a long time.

This encouraged Mrs Bailey to send combings of Rogan's fur all over the world, with amazing results. Rogan's fame grew and he went on a tour across the United States and was the subject of a Japanese documentary.

Sadly, Rogan died in 1986, and although Mrs Bailey didn't really want another cat—after all, who could replace Rogan?—she claims she heard his voice telling her to visit the local Cat Rescue Centre. She says she was drawn to one particular cat, who put his front paws on her face, curing her of a minor ailment. At this point Mrs Bailey understood what Rogan had wanted. This new cat, which she called Gus, was going to be the medium through which Rogan would continue his healing . . .

Did you know . . .
the albatross can glide on wind currents for up to six days without needing to beat its wings.

At the height of the London Blitz, Rex the mongrel took it upon himself to protect his family and friends during air raids. Whenever the warning siren sounded, Rex would run to fetch his owner's gas mask and then insist that everyone follow him to the shelter. Anyone lagging behind would be rounded up like a sheep and barged in the legs to keep them moving. Once everyone was safely inside, Rex would stand guard at the entrance, growling at the sky and the enemy bombers above. Only when he heard the all-clear signal would he let his charges out of the shelter.

One of the Second World War's most celebrated rescue dogs was a beautiful German shepherd called Irma, who helped to find people trapped in bombed-out buildings in London. Irma always seemed to know if the victims were alive or dead. If she detected someone alive under the rubble, she would bark furiously. If they were dead, however, she remained sombrely silent and would just wag her tail to indicate what she had found. The job obviously upset her. When a victim was pulled dead from the ruins, Irma would alternate between licking their faces and looking up at her handler, as if begging him to do something.

On at least two occasions, Irma continued to search ruins when the human rescuers had given up hope—and was proved right both times. She steadfastly refused to leave one ruined building and repeatedly ignored her handler's instructions to come away. Eventually her human companions joined her—and two little girls were plucked safely from deep under the rubble. Another time, she located a woman who had been trapped between two floors of a collapsed building for nine hours. Rescuers had had no idea she was there.

After the war, Irma took part in the victory celebration march and was even introduced to the Queen.

The highlight of Ben the pit pony's day was

lunch time. His driver would stop work deep down in the mine, open his big lunch box and produce a pile of thick doorstop sandwiches which miner and pony would then share between them. One day, however, Ben refused to come over for his daily feast. His driver waved a tasty sandwich at him, but Ben didn't want to know. He kept pawing at the ground and tossing his head about, obviously alarmed by something. The driver trusted Ben's instincts and got up to follow the pony as it moved quickly away down the shaft. Moments later, the roof caved in, burying the now abandoned sandwich box under hundreds of tons of rubble.

In the winter of 1996, a cat named Skipper won $3,720,000 on the lottery in Galveston, Texas. His family used a device called a lottery shaker to decide their numbers, and one day found the cat playing with it and batting it around the floor. By accident he had chosen six numbers—8, 11, 16, 25, 26 and 42. On a hunch, his owners decided to play Skipper's numbers and all six came up!

When Silvana Burnett saved the life of Freddie, the Maltese/poodle cross, she had no idea that just six weeks later he would save her life in return. Freddie's original owners were moving from their home in Edmonton in Canada, and rather than taking the dog with them, they had decided to have him put to sleep. Silvana, who had always liked Freddie, was horrified when she heard and offered her neighbours $50 for him. They took it and Freddie moved in with Silvana.

Six weeks later, Silvana was having a bath when she suffered a sudden asthma attack, blacking out and sliding under the water. When she came to, Freddie was standing on top of her in the now empty bathtub, jumping up and down on her chest as if trying to revive her. In his mouth was the plug. He'd wrenched it free and drained away the bath water before Silvana could drown.

When disastrous floods hit southern California in 1993, all the rescue services were quickly overwhelmed and civilian volunteers were called upon to help save people and property. One volunteer was Lori Watkins of Imperial Beach. She decided to take her pet pit bull terrier Weela with her, and despite the fact that Weela had had absolutely no rescue training, she quickly proved herself a true heroine. During the terrible days and nights following the floods, she successfully guided a rescue team through an area of quicksand, dragged human rescue workers free when they became stuck in treacherous mud and led other dogs safely to higher ground. Her greatest achievement, though, was in saving thirty lives. A group of people whose homes had been washed away were all set to try to cross a river on foot. Weela blocked them and refused to let them cross. She was right. The usually shallow river had been swollen and there was now a deadly undertow just beneath the surface which would have swept them away. By the time the emergency had subsided, Weela had been credited with saving thirty people, twenty-nine dogs, thirteen horses and a cat. No wonder she won the Ken-L-Ration Dog Hero of the Year Award!

Dakota the golden retriever was a sickly puppy. Rather than pay for expensive operations, his owners abandoned him and he ended up being cared for by the Golden Retriever Rescue Club in Houston, Texas. Eventually, he found a new home with Mike Lingenfelter. Mike had recently suffered from some major heart problems and it was felt that having a loving pet would be good therapy for him. Soon after moving in with Mike, however, Dakota demonstrated a strange ability. He could predict when his owner was about to have an attack of angina. Mike now completely trusts his pet's judgement and takes his medication whenever Dakota tells him to. He believes that Dakota has saved his life on at least three separate occasions by providing an 'early warning'. Most extraordinary of all, though, one day Mike was being visited by a friend when Dakota went up to the friend and started warning *him*. Thankfully, the friend took the warning seriously too and went straight to the nearest hospital casualty. He had literally just arrived inside the hospital when he was struck down by a major heart attack. Of course, doctors were on hand in a matter of seconds and saved his life, but he would almost certainly have died without Dakota's warning—just one most reason why the Delta Society named the golden retriever Service Animal of the Year in the Beyond Limits Awards for 1999–2000.

Did you know . . .
relatively speaking, cat fleas take
off with greater acceleration than
the space shuttle.

One of the most inspirational dogs I have ever heard about has to be Rolf (no relation), an Alsatian who lived with a railway-crossing guard in Germany in the 1930s. Rolf was devoted to his master's children and possessed a good deal more sense about the dangers of playing near the railway than they did. One day he saw them playing on the line and just managed to herd them away before an express train thundered by. The children were saved but Rolf was struck and severely injured. The heroic dog had lost both hind legs and few expected him to survive. However not only did Rolf pull through, but he refused to let his new disabilities ruin his life. He carried on playing with the children he adored, and learned to run again—and to swim and jump ditches—with just two legs. His incredible recovery attracted the interest of the German army's dog trainers, who tested him on assault courses so tough that even fit and able dogs had difficulties with them. Rolf conquered them all, learning to climb stairs, scramble up a ladder and negotiate a narrow gangplank.

Dogs and cats are known to have incredible homing instincts, finding their way back home over hundreds of miles, but as for hamsters . . .

The Cummins family of Edmonton, Alberta, in Canada, couldn't believe their eyes when their pet hamster suddenly reappeared years after they'd lost it—especially as they'd moved house twice in the meantime.

However, on closer examination the explanation was far less mysterious than they had first thought. When it had first disappeared the hamster had never actually left the house. It had burrowed into their sofa, using it as a comfortable nest, and had survived on foraging the scraps of food from the family's other pets, and drinking from the cat's water bowl. It did this at night—so nobody had ever seen it!

Did you know . . .
there are around 40,000 muscles in
an elephant's trunk, and it is so
sensitive it can be used to pick up
a pin.

Geologist Jim Berkland of Santa Clara in California has a very unusual way of predicting when an earthquake is about to strike. He studies his local paper for the number of 'Lost Cat' advertisements. Berkland claims that cats know when an earthquake is due, and tend to go missing from their homes just before a major tremor hits the region.

Dieter Rothschild lives in Switzerland with his pet goat, Bleatie. Dieter's a keen cyclist and Bleatie follows him everywhere—but if she picks up speed and runs ahead of the bike, it means she's had enough and wants to go home!